Management Accounting

Second Edition

To achieve success in business it is vital to be aware of how central management accounting is to the efficient running of organizations. *Management Accounting* is an introductory text, tailor-made for students learning about the practical application of accounting within organizations. Leslie Chadwick shows how management accounting can vary according to the type of firm, and gives examples of the various roles it can play within each kind of organization. The principal techniques are explained in a user friendly manner and include: absorption costing, marginal costing, activity based costing, budgetary control, standard costing and capital investment appraisal. Throughout, the text focuses on the key importance of accounting as a management tool with the power to increase the success of any firm.

This volume, the second edition, is written in a stimulating, accessible style. A key feature is Leslie Chadwick's 'teaching by objectives' approach, which clearly sets out what the reader should know and be able to do. He also offers step-by-step examples, question and answer sections, multiple choice questions, lists of key words and self-asessment exercises.

A welcome addition to a dynamic new series for the MBA and undergraduate student, this book will also be ideal for managers on short-term executive programmes, one-semester courses and distance-learning courses.

Leslie Chadwick MBA, FCCA CertEd is Head: Industrial Placements at the University of Bradford Management Centre. He is a leading expert on financial and management acounting and has written widely on the subject, his most recent books being *The Essence of Management Accounting* (2nd Ed 1997), *The Essence of Financial Accounting* (2nd Ed 1996) (both Prentice Hall) and *The Collins Dictionary of Business* (co-authored, 2nd Ed 1993). He has also during the course of his career been a regular contributor to many of the UK's leading professional journals, and has lectured/presented papers in many countries throughout the world.

Elements of Business Series
Series editor: David Weir
University of Northumbria

This important new series is designed to cover the core topics taught at MBA level with an approach suited to the modular teaching and shorter time frames that apply in the MBA sector. Based on current courses and teaching experience, these texts are tailor-made to the needs of today's MBA student, and also many other courses at the postgraduate and undergraduate levels.

Other titles in the series:

Business and Society
Edmund Marshall

Managing Human Resources
Christopher Molander and Jonathan Winterton

Business and Microeconomics
Christopher Pass and Bryan Lowes

Business and Macroeconomics
Christopher Pass, Bryan Lowes and Andrew Robinson

Managerial Leadership
Peter Wright

Financial Management
Leslie Chadwick and Donald Kirby

Business Economics: Concepts and Cases
Malcolm Greenwood and Martin Carter

Management Accounting

Second edition

Leslie Chadwick

Management Accounting

I(T)P® A division of International Thomson Publishing Inc.
The ITP logo is a trademark under licence

British Library Cataloguing-in-Publication Data
A Catalogue record for this book is available from the British Library

First published by Routledge in 1993
This edition published by International Thomson Business Press 1998

Typeset by J&L Composition Ltd, Filey, North Yorkshire
Printed by Clays Ltd, St Ives plc

ISBN 1–86152–260–6

International Thomson Business Press
Berkshire House
168–173 High Holborn
London WC1V 7AA
UK

http://www.itbp.com

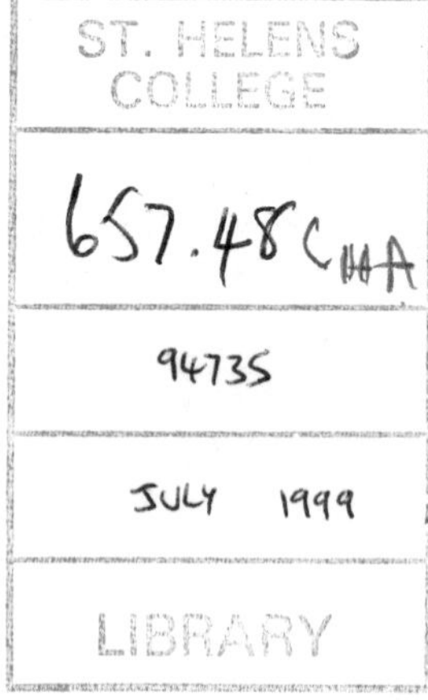

Contents

Figures

Tables

Preface

The main objective of this book is to provide you with a readable, understandable, enjoyable, clear and concise review of the principles of management accounting.

The book aims to meet the needs of managers, executives and students on:

- modular and one semester courses;
- short courses;
- distance-learning courses;

and all those individuals who would like to acquire an insight into the subject without getting involved in a professional-type accounting text which is too wide and too deep.

This book should be of particular interest to students on MBA foundation courses; those on Year 1 undergraduate courses in business studies or Years 1–3 of undergraduate courses for non-business students and non-accounting students, and also students taking combined degrees plus BEC HNC/HND courses in business and in non-business areas, for instance computing. The book is also intended for use on distance-learning programmes such as those offered by the Open College, the Open University and the various private sector tutors.

This book is written in a user-friendly style, using the principle of 'teaching by objectives' and adopting an open learning approach. Each chapter, with the exception of Chapter 1, includes a good selection of self-assessment questions, suggested answers for which are provided in a separate appendix at the back of the book.

Each chapter utilizes a variety of approaches to help convey its message, e.g. the question-and-answer technique, step-by-step illustrations, a keyword approach, and multiple-choice objective questions, etc. There is a summary at the end of each chapter, as well as suggestions for further reading.

A final appendix provides advice for those managers or students who have to submit projects/dissertations.

Acknowledgement

Thanks are due to Iain Ward-Campbell for his contribution towards the chapter on capital investment appraisal, and also to Norman Scholes for supplying some of the self-assessment questions.

Leslie Chadwick, MBA, FCCA, Cert. Ed.

1

An Introduction to Management Accounting

LEARNING OBJECTIVES

When you have read this chapter, you should be able to:

- understand the role played by management accounting in an organization;
- appreciate the need for predetermined management accounting systems;
- know what is meant by costs classified according to type, location and behaviour.

The role of management accounting

The aim of management accounting is to provide management with information which will help them to:

- achieve their objectives/goals;
- formulate policy;
- monitor and assess performance;
- appreciate the financial implications of changes in the internal and external environment in which the organization operates;
- plan for the future;
- make comparisons between alternative scenarios;
- manage more efficiently the scarce resources which are at their disposal;
- control the day-to-day operations;
- focus their attention on specific issues which really need their consideration;

- solve a variety of problems, e.g. investment decisions;
- take account of behavioural factors.

Thus, the role of management accounting is to provide relevant information which will assist management with decision-making, planning economic performance, controlling costs and improving profitability. However, note that the information generated by the management accounting function is just one component part of the decision-making process. It is not the 'be all and end all'; it must be used in conjunction with other data.

Which cost?

There are many different types of cost. During your studies you will encounter:

- absorption, or full costs;
- marginal, or variable costs;
- fixed costs;
- historic costs;
- predetermined costs, e.g. budgets and standard costs;
- relevant, or incremental costs.

There are other costs, too, e.g. replacement costs, opportunity costs, sunk costs, etc.

Historic costing

This is the ascertainment of costs after they have been incurred. The cost of a job or process is ascertained after the job has been completed by adding to the value of materials used the cost of direct labour employed, the costs of production overheads incurred, and also a charge for administration overheads.

The main value of this type of costing lies in the comparison with costs of a previous period, or costs of another factory under the same management, and as a basis for price fixing and estimates.

The main disadvantages of historical costing are that:

- No objective standard is available against which to measure performance.
- The results relate to the past and, therefore, management cannot take early corrective action. Action can only be taken after the job or process has been completed, and this could be too late.
- Past performance as a measure of control is not always reliable, because one bad performance may be compared with another bad performance!

Predetermined costing

In order for management to control costs, budgets and standards must be set for each element of cost, i.e. materials, labour and overheads.

Standard costing and budgetary control are modern techniques which measure actual costs against predetermined standards or budgets and which, by analysis of the variances between the actual and the standard or budget, provide management with a means of continuous comparison and control.

The three phases of cost control are:

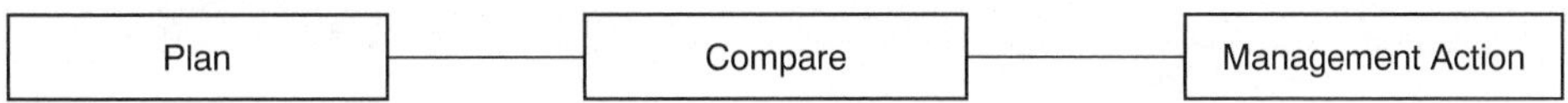

The main advantages of standard costing/budgetary control are:

- efficiency is compared against objective standards/budgets;
- continuous control of operations;
- forward planning is used;
- management can save time by using the principle of management by exception (see Chapter 7).

The main disadvantages are the extensive pre-planning needed to install such systems, and the operating costs involved.

The classification of costs

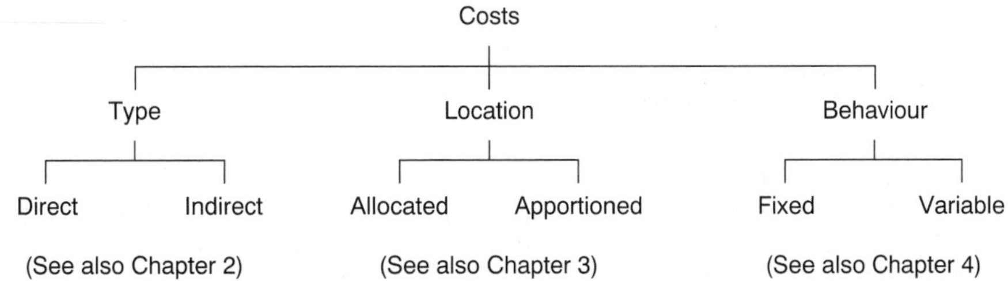

Costs may be classified in a number of ways.

By type

Direct costs are those which form part of the product, e.g. direct labour, direct materials and direct expense. The indirect costs, frequently called the overheads, are those costs which do not form part of the product, e.g. a cleaner's wages, maintenance materials, office rent, etc.

By location

Costs shared between departments or cost centres.* In absorption costing, overhead costs are either allocated or apportioned to the various departments/cost centres.

By behaviour

The marginal costing system depends upon being able to divide costs between variable costs (i.e. marginal costs) and fixed costs.

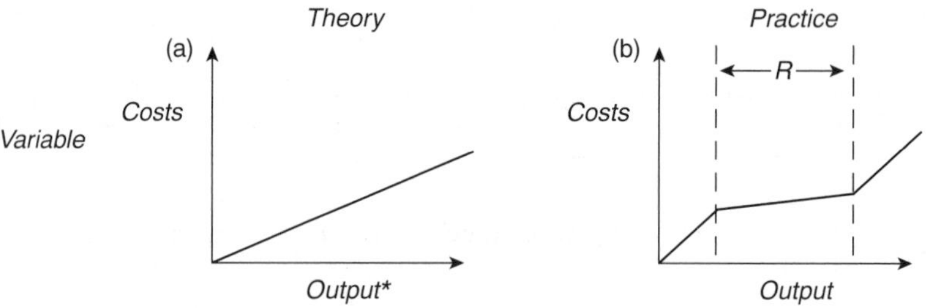

Figure 1.1 **Variable costs**
* *Output may also be described as the level of activity*

Variable costs Vary with the level of output (e.g. direct materials and direct labour) within a relevant range (*R*), and in the short term.

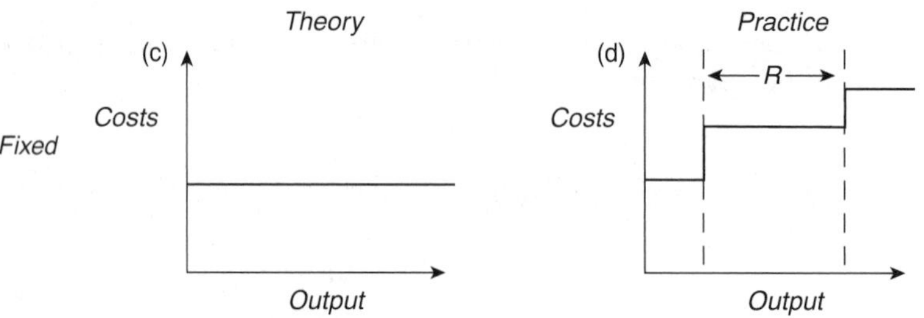

Figure 1.2 **Fixed costs**

Fixed costs Those which remain unchanged irrespective of the level of output (e.g. rates, rent, salaries) within a relevant range (*R*), and in the short term. There are also semi-variable costs (also called semi-fixed costs) which are a combination of both fixed and variable costs.

By product

Costs could also be divided according to products or product lines.
Relevant and sunk costs will be dealt with in Chapter 9.

* A cost centre is just a name given to a department, location, or machine group, etc.

The role of management accounting is to provide management with relevant information to assist them to:

- achieve objectives;
- formulate policy;
- monitor and assess performance;
- assess environmental change;
- plan;
- evaluate alternatives;
- improve efficiency;
- control operations;
- focus their attention;
- solve problems;
- appreciate behavioural factors.

FURTHER READING

Atrill P & McLaney E (1994) *Management Accounting, An Active Learning Approach,* Oxford: Blackwell

Chadwick L (1997) *The Essence of Management Accounting* (2nd Edition), London: Prentice-Hall

Drury C (1994) *Costing: An Introduction* (3rd edition), London: Chapman and Hall

The Elements of Cost

LEARNING OBJECTIVES

When you have read this chapter, you should be able to:

- know what is meant by the 'elements of cost';
- understand what inventory control is concerned with;
- know the costs which should be included in an organization's stock-holding costs, and how such costs can be reduced;
- appreciate how materials are valued using FIFO, LIFO and AVE CO methods of valuation;
- understand why the time-recording system and payroll analysis are important to the management accountant;
- appreciate how incentive or productivity schemes work, and why management favour productivity deals;
- know how the rate of labour turnover is calculated, and the inputs which have to be considered in arriving at the cost of labour turnover;
- distinguish between direct and indirect expenses.

The self-assessments and additional questions which are included relating to methods of stock valuation have been included to help you understand how they affect product costs and stock valuations. You will find the suggested answers to these self-assessments, and to all which follow in subsequent chapters, in Appendix 2. You should attempt each of the self-assessments without looking at the suggested answers, as this should assist you to identify any problem areas and weaknesses in your knowledge.

The elements of cost

The cost of a product or service may comprise all or some of the following elements:

Direct material plus Direct labour plus Direct expense	i.e. the prime cost

and

Overheads e.g. indirect materials and indirect labour.

Materials

Direct materials are those materials which form part of the product; indirect materials do not, but are required for other production purposes.

Materials management and inventory control

Materials management and inventory control is concerned with:

- ensuring that material is available when it is required, but at the same time keeping stock levels to an acceptable minimum;
- the system of internal control governing the recording, ordering, purchasing, storage and issuing of stock;
- the planning of future material requirements;
- keeping to a minimum the amount of capital tied up in stocks, and the associated stock holding costs;
- the prevention and detecton of errors and fraud.

The costs of holding stocks

When asked the question, 'How do people set a value on the cost of holding stocks?', one eminent purchasing executive replied: 'This is a question to which I have never really found a satisfactory answer. I have posed the question to numerous accountants and the net result was one that could only be described as useless from the point of view of practical application' (Lockyer, Muhlemann and Oakland, 1992).

It is rather surprising that many accountants are not particularly interested in this very important area, especially when one considers the substantial amount of working capital tied up in stocks of materials, fuels, work-in-progress and finished goods.

In most industries the cost of material forms a significant part of the final selling price of the product. Management must strive not only to increase the productivity of labour, but also to increase the efficiency of material requirements planning (MRP), thereby improving the productivity of capital. Thus, other than increasing the selling price, which may be sensitive to competition and external factors, materials management may, by direct inventory reduction and increased efficiency, play its part in increasing the productivity of capital employed.

The principal aim of materials management is to keep stocks at an acceptable level, consistent with the risks involved. Stock-outs can cost firms dearly in terms of lost production, idle time and lost orders; the setting of stock levels and levels of service must therefore involve a trade-off, hence the need for up-to-date information, continuous monitoring and frequent reviews.

Holding costs

What is the cost of holding stocks in your company or industry? A rule of thumb puts the cost of holding stock for one year in the region of 25p for every £1 of stock held (Ray, 1980). This indicates that holding costs comprise a significant portion of business expenditure. However, it must be remembered that there will most certainly be quite wide variations between the holding costs of different companies and industries.

Which figures need to be included in the calculation of holding costs? It can be observed (Fig. 2.1) that the holding costs of stocks include the costs of acquisition, storage, controlling, handling and rehandling, administration and other costs such as insurance and financial charges; all these costs are in addition to the cost of the actual stocks themselves.

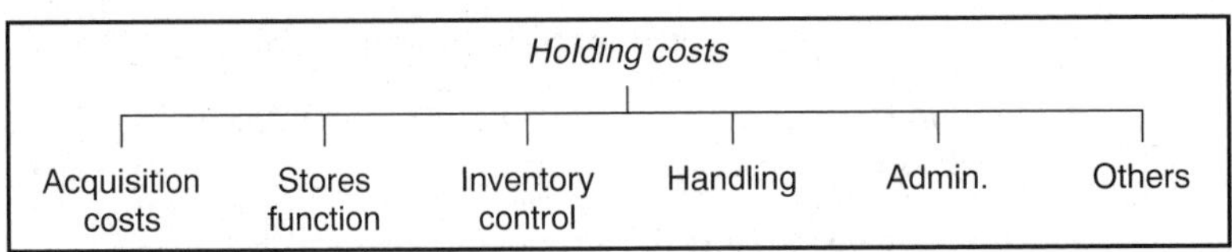

Figure 2.1 **The costs involved in holding stocks**

Acquisition costs

The principal cost in the procurement of bought-out stock items is the cost of the purchasing function, which is made up of staff wages and salaries, office accommodation and equipment and overheads, e.g. light and heat, fax and telephone, stationery etc. All the costs of ordering, finding suitable suppliers and negotiating terms should be included.

Receiving department costs of personnel and resources used for receiving and the inspection of goods inwards may also be classed as acquisition costs.

The stores or warehouse function

The stocks of raw materials, work-in-progress and finished goods all take up factory space, which is valuable in terms of expense and scarcity. Factory and office space is an extremely expensive commodity and it must be utilized efficiently. The overheads associated with the space used for storage are many, including rent and rates, insurance of buildings and equipment, light and heat, fire prevention, cleaning and maintenance. To this must be added the wages and salaries of stores and warehouse personnel. There is also a substantial investment in the stores themselves – warehouse equipment, e.g. bins and racks.

In addition there may also be losses attributable to shrinkage, deterioration, obsolescence and pilferage.

Inventory control

A lot of time and effort should be devoted to this area, in order to keep stock levels to an acceptable minimum and thus bring about savings in holding costs.

The costs applicable to this area involve material requirements planning, monitoring and review, the chief element being manpower. Expenditure upon internal audit related to stock control should also be included under this heading. The cost-benefit of the system of inventory control should not be overlooked.

Handling

There could well be quite a hefty investment in handling equipment, e.g. overhead cranes, etc. In addition to the capital outlay for such equipment, further expenditure has to be incurred to cover running costs, maintenance and servicing: e.g. drivers' wages, power, fuel and lubricants.

Administration

It may be more appropriate to include certain items of expenditure which could quite rightly appear under this heading, under some other heading, e.g. management of purchasing and material requirements planning. However, the costs of the financial and cost accounting recording systems for stocks acquired/issued and payments to suppliers must be accounted for.

Others

Insurance Insurance premiums paid out to cover stock losses cannot be ignored. Insurance premiums are almost certain to rise when a firm increases the value of the stock it holds during the year. As pointed out already, insurance must also be taken out to cover buildings, equipment and other risks, e.g. employer's liability and public liability.

Set-up costs Where a company manufactures some of its own components this involves a number of other costs in addition to the direct materials and labour, e.g. setting costs, machinery, patterns, etc. and an appropriate share of overheads.

Imported materials Various fees, duties, freight and foreign exchange charges relating to the importation of stock comprise yet another element in the calculation of holding costs.

Stock-out costs The cost of being out of stock can be very high in terms of losses of production, sales, future orders and profit.

The cost of capital Stock represents capital tied up in goods, and capital has to be paid for, either through interest charges or dividends. After all, it should be noted that capital does have an opportunity cost.

The calculation of a company's holding costs is not an impossibility. Holding costs can be identified and classified under a number of headings (Fig. 2.1). However, even without actually calculating a company's holding cost, it is almost certain that a vast sum of money is expended in this area, and that because there are numerous variables the holding cost will be unique for each individual company.

Companies do keep an analysis of their payroll and materials used and should therefore be in a position to calculate with accuracy some of their holding costs. Overheads can be allocated and apportioned to departments/cost centres according to established cost accounting practices.

It must be remembered that as stocks increase in volume, value and variety, the complexity of management planning and control also increases. Thus holding costs escalate.

What can be done to reduce stock-holding costs?

Vast sums of money are paid out each year in the UK so that enterprises may hold stocks of materials, fuel, work-in-progress and finished goods. The aggregate holding costs of UK manufacturing, suffice it to say, is an amount of great magnitude, running into billions of pounds. There is a tendency on the part of materials management to over-stock, the avoidance of running out of stock being their priority. This means that in addition to carrying stocks which may not be required for some time to come, the firms concerned also have to cover certain holding costs unnecessarily. Increased stock levels, in addition to increasing holding costs, will also increase risk (Fig. 2.2).

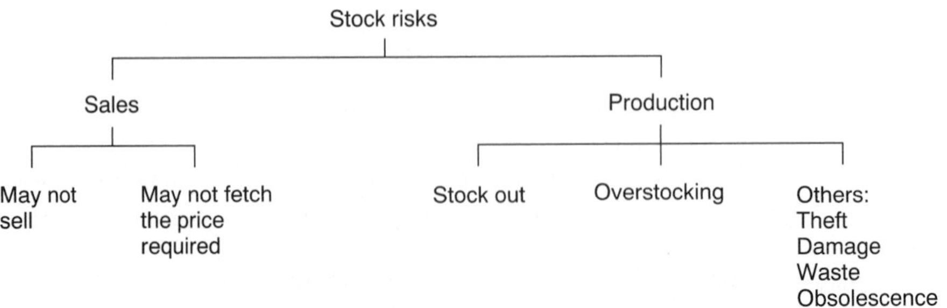

Figure 2.2 **The risks associated with stocks**

Thus, if the investment in stocks is reduced and the rate of turnover increased, losses due to theft, deterioration, damage and obsolescence should fall. Effective inventory control can bring about a reduction in holding costs and therefore improve profitability. It must, however, be recognized that a significant portion of stocks held represents a fixed investment, which should be financed from long-term sources.

How can the value and volume of stocks held be reduced?

There are several courses of action open to management. However, it is appropriate at this point to stress the potential dangers and other considerations associated with reducing stock levels. The first danger is that if this resulted in a stock-out, the firm could be penalized for late delivery, and lose future orders. Second, in times of high inflation the value of stocks held may appreciate at a rate which exceeds the holding costs! Thirdly, if materials are ordered in smaller quantities, bulk discounts may have to be sacrificed.

The regular delivery system/JIT (just in time)

It may be possible (e.g. where a company is engaged in batch or flow-line production) to employ a system in which suppliers deliver certain components on a daily or weekly basis. Within a short space of time these components are used up in production. The finished goods are also, if possible, held for as short a time as is practicable and are dispatched to customers at frequent intervals.

This system depends upon very careful planning, co-ordination and co-operation between production, marketing and finance. Its advantages are that it can reduce dramatically the amount of capital tied up in stocks, the storage space required and associated overheads, handling and rehandling, and losses due to deterioration, pilferage and obsolescence.

In the event of a strike or sudden drop in orders it may be necessary to arrange for suppliers to suspend deliveries, although this could well involve penalty payments.

Bought-out finished stock/the use of subcontractors

Rather than manufacture certain products or components, it may be worthwhile to use subcontractors. The implications for the reduction of holding costs by employing the services of a subcontractor are as follows:

- reduction of various items of stock needed to manufacture the product or component;
- less storage space needed;
- overheads are reduced, e.g. rent, lighting, administration;
- handling and rehandling reduced;
- receiving department's volume of work is cut;

- savings on equipment needed for handling and storage;
- purchasing effort simplified.

There are additional savings to be gained, because the production facilities are all provided by the subcontractor. This means that the company concerned does not have to invest heavily in the machinery and factory capacity necessary to produce the particular product or component concerned.

The employment of subcontractors can be described as a **hedge against the obsolescence** of machinery. The risk involved of machinery becoming obsolete or needing replacement rests firmly with the subcontractor.

The decision to use a subcontractor is not necessarily a simple one, as management must take into account price, production capacity, employees, quality control, delivery promises and competitors. One thing that is certain is that organizational problems will be diminished in the areas of material requirements planning and production management.

Thus, where competent subcontractors are available to produce a particular product or component, careful consideration should be given to employing them.

Pareto analysis

It may well be the case that 20 per cent of stock accounts for 80 per cent of the value. If this is so, and management exercises more effective control over the relevant 20 per cent, they are in fact controlling a vast proportion of the value of stock held.

Pareto analysis can also be applied to retailing; for instance, 20 per cent of the product lines could account for 80 per cent of profits. So management should identify those profitable, fast-moving lines.

Stock may be graded as 'A' items, 'B' items, 'C' items, and so on, 'A' items being those which are controlled most carefully – for instance those which would cause immediate production hold-ups, fast-moving profitable lines, those with long lead times, and so on.

Coding and classification systems

Firms have been known to place orders with outside suppliers for components which were lying idle in their own stores, because of deficiencies in their coding and classification system!

Standardization

It is possible to produce a variety of products using, where practicable, standard parts. The use of standard parts can achieve a substantial reduction in the number of lines stocked, and thus bring about a reduction in holding costs.

Example A bus manufacturer had five different types of automatic doors. As a result it had to stock five different types of automatic door gears, each with its own maximum, minimum and reorder stock levels. The stock-holding on this one item could have been reduced by a significant amount had the bus company standardized the type of automatic door to be fitted to their buses.

Surplus assets

A strategy of surplus asset recognition and disposal allows stocks which may never ever be used to be sold, which would improve the cash flow. The same goes for capital equipment which is surplus to requirements.

Matching

Various computer packages are available and have made it easier to match stock-holding with production requirements. Obviously this is one of the main aims of materials management; what was once a dream is now a reality for certain types of business enterprise. Stocking only what you are going to use and sell calls for close co-operation between materials management, production and marketing. It is no use having a warehouse full of products for which there is no demand!

Variety reduction

Variety is expensive. Variety of the number of products produced or components stocked increases complexity, e.g. the automatic door gears mentioned earlier.

Review of maximum, minimum and reorder levels

Stock levels referred to should be reviewed at frequent intervals in order to take account of seasonal fluctuations. In the real world, the level of activity in production departments is likely to vary from week to week and month to month. Therefore the stock levels should also vary, to match materials requirements to production requirements. Some firms set maximum, minimum and reorder levels but then leave them in operation for periods in excess of one year!

Sub-stores

Where sub-stores are in existence this usually means that the particular company is likely to hold more stock than a company with only one central store would. The simple truth of the matter is that all stores will have their own maximum, minimum and reorder levels, as highlighted by Fig. 2.3.

The old argument of centralized versus decentralized stores is well-known. However, the effects on holding costs of having decentralized stores should not be underestimated. The additional holding costs – space, handling and rehandling, administration, cost of capital, etc., of decentralization may far outweigh the advantages gained from having the stores in closer proximity to the production departments.

Component 391	*Factory X*	
	Max.	*Min.*
	units	*units*
Main stores	50	10
Sub-store A	8	3
Sub-store B	10	4
Sub-store D	5	2
	73	19
	Factory Y	
	Max.	*Min.*
	units	*units*
Central stores	60	15

Figure 2.3 Inventory levels – centralized v. decentralized stores

Design

More careful cosideration at the design stage could improve materials utilization. Management must answer important questions relating to materials, such as:

- Which type of material should be used?
- What else could be used in its place?
- Should the operative working with the material be unskilled, semi-skilled or skilled?
- Which item of plant and machinery is most suited to the manufacture of the product?
- Is it necessary to work to very fine tolerances?

The type of material used certainly affects costs, but costs can also be affected by design factors, the method of manufacture and the skills possessed by the operatives. Good design should ensure that the product can fulfil its function without unnecessarily using expensive materials, and should keep scrap and waste to a minimum. Why use a bar made of brass when one made from cheap plastic would do exactly the same job without impairing the performance of the product? Design can reduce the materials used in value and volume and thus bring about a corresponding reduction in holding costs.

Monitoring and organization

In addition to investing in physical assets such as plant and machinery, firms also need to invest in organization. Control systems, aided where necessary by computers, can help to reduce losses caused by inefficient or unco-ordinated systems, purchasing errors, deterioration, pilferage and obsolescence.

If inventories are going to be managed efficiently and holding costs reduced, it is imperative that all business functions co-operate, co-ordinate and communicate effectively.

In today's complex business world it is essential to monitor the internal and external environment in which the firm operates. Internally, management must ensure that regular reviews are carried out in relation to systems of internal control, stock levels, design, production methods and forecasting techniques.

Monitoring the external environment can assist the firm to identify threats and opportunities and enable them to respond to change more quickly. This area further highlights the need for co-operation between functions; for instance, information provided by marketing could prevent purchasing from wastefully ordering a component which is to become obsolete within a short space of time.

Operational research and statistical techniques

If forecasting and control procedures are to be improved, management must become more familiar with OR and statistical techniques. As pointed out earlier, relevant computer packages are available, and management need to find out what such packages can do for them. This field provides great scope for improving materials management and reducing expensive holding costs, e.g. for matching stocks and production; fixing levels of service and the risk of a stock-out.

Behavioural aspects

The attitude that 'thou shalt not run out of stock' needs changing to 'thou shalt ensure that stocks are kept to an acceptable minimum.' Materials managers must really begin to appreciate that they are operating in a constantly changing environment which calls for frequent reviews of stock levels to be carried out.

The role of audit

Internal and external auditors can help to detect and prevent errors and fraud; their contribution towards satisfactory control of materials should not be ignored.

Conclusion

Management must endeavour to improve the productivity of the capital employed. Stocks held as raw materials, work-in-progress and finished goods represent tied up capital. Why finance the purchase and holding of stocks which may not be required for several months?

If the value and volume of stock held can be reduced, savings should be possible as follows:

- Interest charges – less capital tied up, less finance required for holding stocks.
- Storage space – less required. Substantial savings in rent, rates, insurance, light, heat and personnel.
- Insurance – lower premiums to cover a lower value held in stock.

- Capital equipment requirement and associated revenue expenditure reduced, e.g. running costs, interest charges.
- Handling – better utilization of capital equipment, e.g. more frequent deliveries. However, this area should be looked at very carefully, as handling charges could increase.

The rewards from improved materials management should not be under-estimated. At the same time, the effect of inflation on stocks, and the risk of a stock-out, should not be ignored. Decision-making in the real and imperfect world requires management who can see both sides of the argument and who can base their decisions on the relevant facts, appreciating that trade-offs are inevitable.

Self-assessment 2.1: Stock-holding costs

Provide a brief answer (three to five lines in length) for each of the following questions, and then compare your answers with those which appear in appendix 2.

1 Why do we describe stocks of materials, fuels, work-in-progress and finished goods as capital tied up?

2 What are stock-holding costs?

3 Which costs could be included as stock-holding costs?

4 What can management do to reduce stock-holding costs?

5 What are the advantages of keeping stock levels to acceptable minimums?

6 In addition to receiving cash from the sale of surplus stocks, how else could the business benefit?

7 Why can the employment of a subcontractor provide financial benefits?

8 Why is variety related to materials expensive?

The valuation of materials

There are a number of methods which can be used to value material which is issued to production/services or which remains in stock. We will look at three of the methods:

- FIFO – first in, first out;
- LIFO – last in, first out;
- Ave Co – average cost.

The following data will be used to illustrate each of the methods:

	Casting		Part No ZYP 416780	
19X3		**Units**	**Price per unit**	**Total value**
August 1	Stock on hand	100	£5	£500
September 3	Received GR 1869X*	200	£6	£1 200
September 5	Issued IN5317**	150		
September 30	Received GR1911X	100	£7	£700
October 4	Issued IN5921	180		

*GR = Goods received note
**IN = Issue note

FIFO

Issues are priced in the order in which they arrive, i.e. in chronological order. This means that in times of rapid inflation, prices charged to products will be lower than the prices being paid for new supplies and the stock valuation will be priced at current prices.

Simplified stores ledger		**Part No. ZYP 416780**		
Material: Casting 120mm				
Date 19X3	**Details**	**Quantity**	**Price/Calc**	**Value**
		units	£	£
FIFO				
Aug. 1	Balance b/f	100	5	500
Sept. 3	Received per GR1869X	200	6	1 200
	Balance	300	–	1 700
Sept. 5	Issued per IN 5317	150	100 × £5 + 50 × £6	800
	Balance	150	6	900
Sept. 30	Received per GR1911X	100	7	700
	Balance	250	–	1 600
Oct. 4	Issued per IN 5921	180	150 × £6 + 30 × £7	1 110
	Balance c/f	70	7	490

Under this method the material charged to a similar job or product will tend to vary; an identical job commenced on the same day could be charged with materials at entirely different prices. However, the method does price or value the issues in the same order as that in which the stock should be physically issued. Note, also that FIFO is the method which is professionally advocated for external reporting purposes by SSAP 9 (in Statements of Standard Accounting Practice 9). Before we take a look at the remaining two pricing methods, please note that they are just methods of pricing for the valuation of material issued to production and that which remains in stock. They are *not* methods for the physical issuing of stock. Whatever the method of pricing adopted, it is recommended that stock is issued in the order in which it arrived, i.e. FIFO, to avoid losses caused by deterioration, evaporation and obsolescence etc.

LIFO

Simplified stores ledger		**Part No. ZYP 416780**		
Material: Casting 120mm				
Date 19X3	**Details**	**Quantity**	**Price/Calc**	**Value**
		units	£	£
LIFO				
Aug. 1	Balance b/f	100	5	500
Sept. 3	GR1869X	200	6	1200
	Balance	300	–	1700
Sept. 5	Issued per IN 5317	150	150 @ £6	900
	Balance	150	100 @ £5 + 50 @ £6	800
Sept. 30	Received per GR1911X	100	7	700
	Balance	250	–	1500
Oct. 4	Issued per IN 5921	180	100 @ £7 + 50 @ £6 30 @ £5	1150
	Balance c/f	70	£5	350

With LIFO, the issues are priced using the last price of the materials which came into stock, as illustrated. In periods of rising prices this method tends to charge the most current prices to jobs and/or products, and to value the closing stock at the earlier prices. As with FIFO, identical jobs or products begun within a day of each other could be charged different amounts for the same material. You should note that, according to SSAP 9, LIFO is *not* an acceptable method for external reporting purposes, nor is it an acceptable valuation method for UK taxation purposes.

AVE CO

Simplified stores ledger		Part No. ZYP 416780		
Material: Casting 120mm				
Date 19X3	**Details**	**Quantity**	**Price/Calc**	**Value**
		units	£	£
AVE CO				
Aug. 1	Balance b/f	100	5	500
Sept. 3	GR 1869X	200	6	1 200
	Balance	300	Ave. 5.67*	1 700
* £1 700 Value / 300 = *£5.67*				
Sept. 5	Issued per IN 5317	150	5.67	850
	Balance	150	5.67	850
Sept. 30	Received per GR 1911X	100	7	700
	Balance	250	Ave. 6.20**	1 550
Oct. 4	Issued per IN 5921	180	6.20	1 116
	Balance	70	6.20	434
** £1 550 / 250 = *£6.20*				

There are a number of different ways of using average prices for pricing issues and the valuation of stock. The one which we have used is the weighted average cost method. You will observe that when a new consignment of materials is received, we recalculate the average price. For a period of time all issues made are priced at the same average price. It is recommended for use for stocks where there are wide fluctuations in price. The average cost method is also acceptable for external reporting purposes.

In conclusion, please appreciate that there are several methods, e.g. replacement price, standard price, etc. Although you are not expected to become a genius with the calculations, now see if you can understand the methods by coming to terms with the numbers involved in the self-assessment which follows.

Self-assessment 2.2: Pricing methods

Turbo wheels, part number SS193, have over the past six months been purchased and issued as follows:

	Purchases units	per unit £		Issues units
March	100	15	April	160
May	200	16	June	180
July	100	20	August	120

There was an opening stock of 100 units valued at £12 each at the start of the period.

Show your calculations of issues and stock valuations, using:

1 FIFO (first in, first out);

2 LIFO (last in, first out);

3 AVE CO (average cost, using the weighted average method).

Materials – cost information

A materials analysis, which is a summary of all the issue notes, will provide a wealth of information for cost and management accounting purposes. The analysis can be divided into direct and indirect materials, and then further subdivided, as required between, for example:

- products;
- production departments;
- machine groups;
- services, etc.

Labour

Direct labour is the labour which is used for the immediate task of producing goods and services; indirect labour is the labour which is used for other purposes, e.g. canteen staff, cleaners, etc. Nowadays, direct labour can be recorded as either a fixed or a variable cost. For example, an amount which is paid for each unit produced would be a variable cost, whilst a fixed amount which is paid whether or not anything is produced would be recorded as a fixed cost. Do not assume that all direct labour costs are variable.

Time recording

A key supply of data for the costing of labour is the time-recording system. Time can be recorded on time sheets, on time cards and via computer keyboards, etc., all of which can be used to record the time spent by direct and indirect workers, as illustrated in Fig. 2.4.

Direct Labour	*Indirect Labour*
Attendance time	Attendance time
Productive time	
Idle time	
Overtime	Overtime
Analysed by	*Analysed by*
Department	Department
Machine Group	Machine Group
Operation	Activity
Activity	
Product	

Figure 2.4 Time recording data

The payroll analysis, which is the summary prepared from an analysis of time sheets, time cards and/or information keyed in to the computer, provides the management accounting function with an abundance of useful information. This information can be used in the absorption of overheads, for product costing, and for the preparation of budgets and standards. From your review of Fig. 2.4 you should appreciate that in addition to producing an analysis of direct labour, it is also possible to produce an analysis of indirect labour. For example, the time spent by a cleaner (indirect labour) per department/cost centre can be recorded.

Methods of remuneration

The following methods of remuneration are quite widely used:

- time rate, where the employee receives a rate per hour, i.e. an amount per hour for each hour worked;
- guaranteed minimum earnings, in which the employee's earnings are made up to a specified amount;
- a fixed wage or salary, where the wage or salary paid is the same every week or month. It may be based on a specific salary scale and/or subject to a periodic review, e.g. yearly;
- productivity deals, where the pay is based on and linked to productivity – the idea being that pay increases are self-financing, i.e. paid for by increased productivity;
- incentives/bonus schemes, based on time saved, sales targets, etc., leading to the payment of a bonus;
- profit-sharing and employees' share schemes, designed to promote more interest amongst employees in the business and its products/services;
- perks, in the form of cars, meal vouchers, holidays, medical and pension schemes, nursery provision and training courses;
- various combinations of the above.

Recent developments in the labour markets, some of which are still taking place, include:

- more businesses and organizations using flexi-time, where employees may work their own hours, within certain parameters;

- because of rapid advances in technology the trend towards certain types of work being done from home, e.g. in publishing, design, treasury management, etc;
- better deals for women with young children.

Cost and management accountancy must therefore keep in touch with developments in the labour market, and must be able to provide figures relating to alternative courses of action. The following example is typical of the type of scenario which might require evaluation.

Example: current scheme v. an incentive scheme Thirsk Antics Ltd employ twelve production workers who work a basic thirty-nine-hour week at £10 per hour. Their guaranteed weekly wage is £390 each. The maximum number of overtime hours which may be worked in a week is twelve hours per worker, paid for at time and a half.

It takes one operator one hour to produce one unit of product. The demand for the product varies from a minimum of 348 units per week upwards.

Following detailed studies, an incentive scheme is proposed, in which the time allowed to produce one unit would be 45 minutes and pay would be based on a guaranteed weekly minimum of £400, units being paid for at £8 per unit. Overtime would be paid at a premium of £5 per hour.

Using the information which has been supplied, the following table sets out some of the possible outcomes.

Per employee	Current scheme	Proposed incentive scheme
Minimum output		
29 units (i.e. $\frac{348}{12}$)	(29 units × £10 = £290)	(29 units × £8 = £232)
Guaranteed minimum	*£390*	*£400*
For 39 hours:		
	(39 units × £10)	(39 hours ÷ .75) = 52 units × £8
	£390	*£416*

(For minimum output and the 39 hours the cost per unit for the current scheme is £10, and £8 for the proposed scheme)

	Current scheme £		Proposed incentive scheme £
For 51 hours (maximum hours):			
(51 units × £10)	510	(51 hours ÷ .75) = 68 units × £8	544
Plus overtime premium 12 hours × £5	60		60
	£570		£604

Maximum output with existing labour force	(12 × 51 units)	(12 × 68 units)
	= *612 units*	= *816 units*
Cost per unit at 51 hours:	*£570*	*£604*
	51 units	68 units
	£*11.18* per unit	*£8.88*

It can be observed that although each employee's pay would go up under the incentive scheme, the cost per unit would be lower than under the current scheme, but this is provided that the employees can in fact produce units in the 45 minutes allowed under the proposed scheme. An employee who would produce the units in less time than the time allowed would earn even more.

The cost of labour turnover

One of the costs which management tend to ignore is the cost of labour turnover. They ignore it because it is very difficult to calculate and involves the exercise of subjective judgement.

How is the rate of turnover calculated?

The rate of labour turnover is calculated by dividing the number of persons leaving in the period under review by the average number of persons on the payroll during the period, and is expressed as a percentage.

Which costs should be included?

The costs which are associated with the employment of labour are:

- administrative, e.g. advertising, recruitment, selection, engagement and the personnel function;
- training, e.g. induction training, training courses, the cost of running training establishments;
- production, e.g. losses caused by new employees such as defective production;
- damage to morale and motivation.

What can be done to reduce labour turnover?

Management needs to find out why employees leave, and should take appropriate corrective action. The personnel department could interview all leavers and report their findings to management.

Self-assessment 2.3: Labour

Prepare brief (three or four-line) answers to the following questions:

1 What kind of information can be produced from an analysis of time sheets, time cards and labour times recorded via computer terminals?

2 How can the payroll analysis help management to plan for the future?

3 Why are productivity deals popular with employers?

4 In our example, Thirsk Antics Ltd, why did the cost per unit produced come down under the incentive scheme?

5 In Thirsk Antics Ltd, how much would employees earn if they produced seventy-five units in 51 hours (i.e. 39 basic hours plus 12 overtime hours) under the proposed incentive scheme?

6 How is the rate of labour turnover calculated?

7 What costs should be included in the cost of labour turnover?

8 How can management reduce the cost of labour turnover?

Expenses

A direct expense is an expense which can be traced to a particular department, service, product or process. Indirect expenses cannot be traced to a particular service, product or process, e.g. overheads such as the insurance of buildings, factory rent, etc.

Self-assessment 2.4: Direct and indirect expenses

See if you can sort out which of the items listed below are direct or indirect expenses:

1 Payments to a window-cleaning company for cleaning the canteen windows and paintwork.

2 The cost of cleaning fluid used to clean the machines in the robotic machine department.

3 Electricity charges for lighting all of the organization's premises, inside and out.

4 An amount paid to a security firm for the security of all the company's premises.

5 Plant hired for the packing department.

Overheads such as indirect material, labour and expenses can be dealt with using an absorption costing approach or a marginal costing approach. These two approaches will be considered further on in this text.

The elements of cost

The elements of cost may be divided up as follows:

Prime costs	**Overheads**
Direct materials	Indirect materials
Direct labour	Indirect labour
Direct expense	Indirect expense

Materials

From a management accounting view point you should note that:
A materials analysis for both direct and indirect materials may be prepared from stores issue notes or requisitions, detailing:

- when the material was used;
- where it was used;
- what is was used for;
- how much of it was used, etc.

This should provide a lot of very useful data for budget preparation purposes. Also note that records can be kept for the usage of indirect materials.

Efficient and effective materials management and inventory control is very important. It is concerned with the availability, internal control, planning and holding costs of stocks of raw materials, fuels, work-in-progress and finished goods, and with the prevention of errors and fraud.

Stocks can be described as capital tied up in goods, i.e. money which for the time being is lying idle and not earning a return. Thus, stocks should be kept to an acceptable minimum. However, there is a trade-off. If stocks are too low and a stock shortage occurs, i.e. a 'stock-out', orders or customers may be lost because of broken delivery promises.

In addition to capital tied up in stocks there are also holding costs. The cost of holding stocks can be significant. In addition to buying the stock, and the interest on the capital used, there are also costs associated with the stores function, inventory control, handling and administration.

Holding costs may be reduced by management action, which could involve:

- the regular delivery system JIT (just in time) delivery;

- bought-out finished goods and the use of subcontractors;
- Pareto analysis;
- improved coding and classification systems;
- standardization;
- the sale of surplus assets;
- matching;
- variety reduction;
- regular reviews of stock levels;
- a reappraisal of sub-stores;
- improved design;
- monitoring and organizational activities;
- operational research and statistical techniques;
- taking notice of behavioural factors;
- internal and external auditors.

Benefits of this approach include lower interest payments, the freeing of space, a reduction in overheads, less capital equipment needed, etc.

Material issued to jobs or products can be valued using a number of different methods, including:

- FIFO (first in, first out) – values the material in the order in which it has arrived;
- LIFO (last in, first out) – values material using the latest price first;
- AVE CO (average cost) – uses a simple or weighted average price to value issues to production;
- standard cost (see Chapter 8);
- replacement price.

The method selected can affect the value of material charged to jobs/products and the value of raw material stocks. The questions which you need to answer are:

- Do you want job/products priced as near as possible to current prices?
- Do you want your raw material stock valuations to be valued as near as possible to current prices?

Finally, you should not lose sight of the fact that they are just methods of valuation. Material should always where possible be issued using a FIFO approach, to avoid losses caused by evaporation, deterioration and obsolescence.

Labour

Cost and management accounting will extract information from:

- the time-recording system, which may use time sheets, time cards and/or computer terminals;
- the payroll analysis;
- the idle time analysis;
- machine utilization analysis.

The information should help with the costing of jobs services and products, and to evaluate incentive schemes and prepare budgets and standards.

Types of labour	Direct and indirect.
Methods of remuneration	Time rate, guaranteed minimum earnings, fixed wage/salary, productivity deals, incentives, profit sharing, employee share schemes, perks. Various remuneration packages involving combinations of the above plus others can be found in practice.
The cost of labour turnover	This cannot and should not be ignored. It is made up of administrative costs, training costs, and production losses, etc. Labour turnover can also affect morale and motivation.
Expenses	To classify expenses as direct or indirect is not always such an easy task. Indirect materials, labour and expenses are termed overheads.

FURTHER READING

Dyson J R (1994) *Accounting for Non-accounting Students*, London: Pitman

Weetman P (1996) *Management Accounting, An Introduction*, London: Pitman

The elements of cost: additional self-assessments
Self-assessment 2.5: Quick questions

Define the following terms using your own words:

1 Direct materials.

2 Materials management.

3 Acquisition costs (*re* stock-holding costs).

4 JIT (Just in Time).

5 Pareto analysis.

6 FIFO (first in, first out).

7 Direct labour.

8 Idle time.

9 The payroll analysis.

10 The rate of labour turnover.

Self-assessment 2.6: Methods of stock valuation

Schwartman & Co have purchased product XY934 as follows:

	Units	Per unit £	Total £
21 May	50	60	3000
14 June	80	76	6080
30 June	40	72	2880
17 July	30	64	1920
28 July	20	65	1300
	220		£15180

On 30 July, 140 units were sold for £11,760

You are required to compute the profit and closing stock valuation using the following methods:

1 FIFO;

2 LIFO;

3 AVE CO.

Self-assessment 2.7: FIFO LIFO AVE CO

McRae Ltd bought and issued its stock of raw material XL5007 as follows:

Bought	**Units**	**Per unit**
1 January	1000	£5
20 February	800	£6
4 March	700	£8
Issues		
5 January	500	
25 February	1000	
16 March	500	

You are required to write up the stores ledger, using FIFO, LIFO and AVE CO for the period.

3

An Introduction to Overheads and Total Absorption Costing

LEARNING OBJECTIVES

When you have read this chapter, you should be able to:

- select, use and briefly comment on methods of overhead apportionment;
- use the direct labour hour method and the machine hour method of overhead absorption/recovery;
- prepare, in good form, overhead distribution tabulations;
- briefly discuss the limitations of absorption costing.

As you work through this study please look carefully at the critical comments which are made from time to time, and particularly at the limitations which are noted. It is hoped that this approach will help you to develop your comprehensional skills.

Direct materials
Direct labour
Direct expense
Overheads (indirect materials, labour and expense)

Figure 3.1 The elements of cost

The direct elements of cost, i.e. direct materials, direct labour and direct expense, are those expenses which can be traced and identified to the particular product or service which is being produced. The fourth and final element of cost overheads, i.e. the indirect materials, indirect labour and indirect expense, cannot be traced or identified with the goods or service being produced.

At the very outset, you should appreciate that it is necessary to decide whether to adopt an absorption (total) costing approach or a marginal costing approach. This chapter deals with the treatment of overheads within an absorption costing environment. Marginal costing will be dealt with in a later chapter.

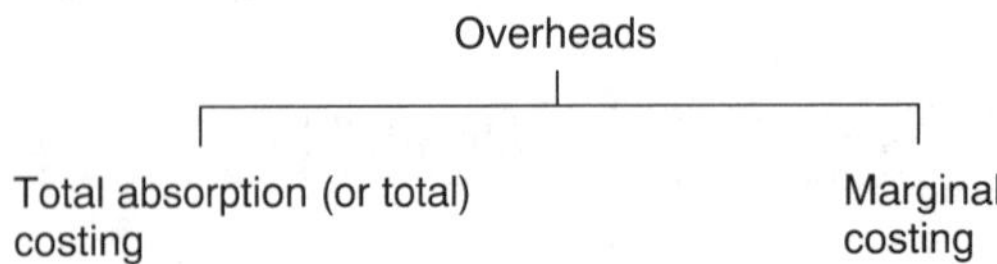

Figure 3.2 **The treatment of overheads**

Total absorption costing charges all or most of the overheads (in particular, the production overheads), to cost objectives, cost centres and products. Marginal costing, on the other hand, charges only the variable overheads. The fixed overheads in a marginal costing system are treated as period costs, i.e. they are written off in the period in which they are incurred.

What are overheads?

Overheads consist of the indirect expenditure of an organization, the indirect materials, indirect labour and indirect expense. However, you must remember that the distinction between direct and indirect expenditure is not always clear cut. To illustrate the uncertainty which may arise, here are some examples which should help you to appreciate the problem:

	Direct expenditure	**Indirect expenditure**
Advertising	for a specific product, e.g. soap powder	for promoting the company 'image'
Cleaning	a product before it is packed e.g. giving components a wash in paraffin	of the production department floors and walls e.g. cleaning fluid
Wages	of operatives involved in the production process	idle time e.g. waiting time, time spent on training new operatives

From a product-costing point of view, materials which form part of the product are direct. Those materials which do not form part of the product are indirect. The labour which is used to transform the raw materials into finished goods is direct. However, where employees are paid a certain guaranteed amount whether or not they produce anything, such an amount is a fixed cost. Expenses which are incurred solely on behalf of a particular product are direct, those which cannot be traced to a particular product are indirect.

Self-assessment 3.1: Direct and indirect expenditure

See if you can distinguish between the direct and indirect elements of expenditure in the following list, placing a tick under the appropriate heading:

Expenditure	**Direct**	**Indirect**
1 Wool used in the manufacture of carpet yarns.		
2 Liquid soap which is used in the wash room.		
3 The electrical cable used to rewire a machine which is used for cutting wood shapes.		
4 The silicone which has to be put into motor vehicle components called silicone fan drives.		
5 The 30ml bottles into which correcting fluid will be put.		
6 The oil which has to be added to the mix during a process for manufacturing a special plastic.		
7 Wages paid to the canteen staff of a factory.		
8 The salary paid to a departmental manager who oversees the production process.		
9 The wages of someone employed to operate a milling machine which performs certain operations on the components being produced.		
10 The salary of the supervisor of a machine department.		

Why is it important to account for overheads?

The UK Statement of Standard Accounting Practice (SSAP 9) relating to stocks and work in progress, requires that jobs should include all manufacturing overheads for stock valuation and profit measurement purposes; the way in which overheads are treated will affect stock valuations and the reported profits or losses. You can see from this that SSAP 9 advocates the use of absorption costing for stock valuation purposes.

It is also essential that we account for overheads in order to assess properly the cost of products, processes and services, as well as defining cost objectives and cost centres. The costs which are produced may be used to assist in the setting of prices and the making of quotations. It is therefore necessary to have pre-determined overheads, to know how much will have to be recovered in the next accounting period. The predetermination of costs is a prerequisite for being able to prepare quotations for jobs etc.

Overheads must also be controlled, e.g. by making frequent comparisons of the actual overheads with the planned overheads. The perception that indirect costs are uncontrollable should be resisted. Overheads can and must be controlled, so as to ensure efficient management of the scarce resources which they represent.

Accounting for overheads provides a lot of information for decision-making purposes.

Total absorption costing

Total absorption costing, which is also known as Total, Full or Absorption costing, seeks to ensure that each product, process, cost objective, cost centre, etc. bears a fair share of the overheads. The principle aim of total absorption costing is to ensure that all costs are covered – hence the term overhead recovery, which means exactly the same as overhead absorption.

Absorption costing does not and cannot provide accurate and realistic costs. When you have completed this chapter it is hoped that you will be able to appreciate why this is so.

Why predetermination of overheads?

The absorption method for dealing with overheads depends upon the predetermination of overheads. Thus, well before the start of the next accounting period the relevant overheads have to be carefully estimated. The reason for this is that costs have to be absorbed and accumulated hour-by-hour and day-by-day as products or jobs are being worked on. To be in a position to charge overheads to products or jobs as the work progresses means that we have to compute predetermined overhead absorption/ recovery rates for each department cost centre through which the products or jobs are to pass. Once again, note the term 'overhead recovery'. The overheads are being recovered i.e. absorbed by production.

Total absorption costing – a step-by-step example/ commentary

Figure 3.3 provides you with an overview of the total absorption costing method. This is now followed by a step-by-step example and an explanation of how the system works.

STEP 1: The predetermination of overheads

The indirect materials, labour and expenses will have to be estimated well before the commencement of the next accounting period. The process of forecasting the forthcoming period's overheads will take into account numerous factors, such as:

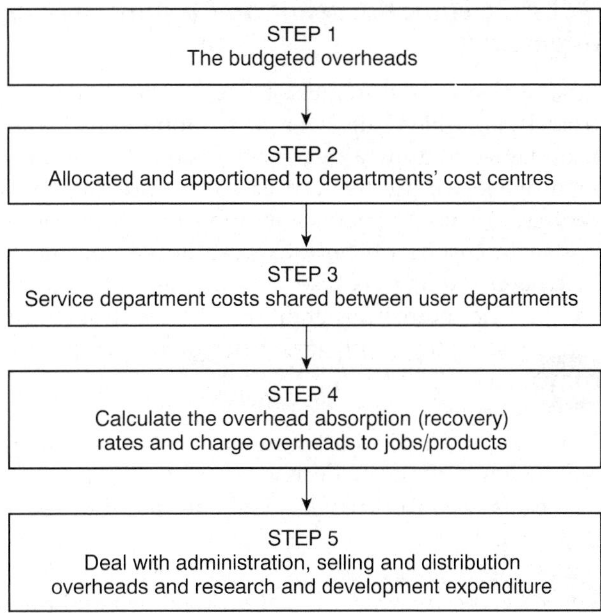

Figure 3.3 The absorption of overheads

- the actual figures for the current period to date and for earlier periods;
- the payroll analysis, *re* indirect labour for the current and earlier periods;
- the departmental analysis of indirect materials for the current and earlier periods;
- budgets for the next accounting period, *re* the levels of output activity in terms of production, sales, capital expenditure, personnel etc.;
- the anticipated rate of inflation and price movements;
- environmental influences – social, political, technological and economic, as well as changes in factor and product markets;
- information provided by managers, subordinates etc.

For example, the depreciation of plant and machinery can be estimated using the current balances held by each department and taking into account the anticipated disposals and acquisitions. This would take into account many of the items listed above, e.g. capital expenditure budgets, the level of activity, technological changes, etc.

You should note that companies and other organizations do keep records about overheads e.g. the payroll analysis for indirect labour and the materials analysis for indirect materials department by department, cost centre by cost centre. Although the historic data is no real guide as to what will happen in the future, it can be a great help and a starting point in the process of estimating the overheads for a future period, particularly when looked at in conjunction with other more relevant information.

STEP 2: The allocation and apportionment of overheads to departments

First, we need to distinguish those overheads which can be allocated to departments from those which will have to be apportioned. Just what does this mean? In this text, we try to draw a clear distinction between the words allocation and apportionment when we use them in the context of sharing out the overheads between cost centres. We use the term allocation for those overheads which can be traced to a particular cost centre. Such expenditure can be allocated to the cost centre concerned i.e. charged direct because it is traceable. It can be said, therefore, that allocation charges the indirect expenditure (the overheads) on the basis that the expenditure can be identified with and belongs to the particular department or cost centre concerned.

Examples of overhead expenditure which can be allocated would include the costs of employing a cleaner who is employed to clean a specific department, or of special lubricants used for keeping plant and machinery in good working order in a certain department.

Those overheads which cannot be identified and traced to a particular department or cost centre have to be apportioned between cost centres using some arbitrary basis. Such overheads will have been incurred on behalf of the company as a whole, or on behalf of many cost centres. Such overheads have to be apportioned using whichever basis appears to be the most equitable and appropriate. In practice, and indeed in examination questions, you will have to select the method of apportionment you consider to be the most suitable for each item. Your over-riding consideration should be fairness i.e. the selection of the most equitable basis of apportionment.

Here are some examples of bases of apportionment which are sometimes used:

Overheads which cannot be identified with a particular cost centre	**Basis of apportionment**
Rent of buildings	Floor area or cubic capacity i.e. the space occupied
Personnel costs	Number of employees
Lighting and heating (electrical)	Kilowatt hours, cubic capacity, or floor area
Insurance of plant and machinery	Estimated replacement values
Insurance of buildings	Floor area or cubic capacity
Power	Technical estimates
General factory overheads	Machine hours or direct labour hours

The questions which you should be asking yourself when attempting to select the most equitable method of apportionment are whether or not it is an expense which varies with:

- the space occupied;
- the number of employees;

- consumption;
- value;
- or time.

Where metered consumption figures are not available, technical estimates will have to be obtained. However, with the technological advances that have been made in recent years it is becoming more feasible to obtain metered consumption figures at an economic cost.

From an examination point of view you have to make your selection on the basis of the limited amount of information provided, e.g. having to apportion depreciation on the basis of the value of the machinery and equipment held by each cost centre. Such text book methods of apportionment will not always be used in the real world, where more commonsense methods tend to exist.

Self-assessment 3.2: Methods of apportionment

Having studied the guidelines applicable to the selection of suitable methods of apportionment, now select the correct answers to the following multiple choice problems:

1 The rent of business premises should be shared out between cost centres according to:

A floor area or cubic capacity

B the number of employees

C the replacement value of machinery and equipment

D the number of kilowatt hours

2 The insurance of buildings is best apportioned to cost centres using:

A floor area or cubic capacity

B the number of employees

C the replacement value of machinery and equipment

D the number of kilowatt hours

3 The canteen expenses should be apportioned to cost centres by:

A floor area or cubic capacity

B the number of employees

C the replacement value of machinery and equipment

D the number of kilowatt hours

4 In the absence of more realistic information, supervision should be split up according to:

A floor area or cubic capacity

B the number of employees

C the replacement value of machinery and equipment

D the number of kilowatt hours

5 Which of the following bases of apportionment is most suited to sharing up the lighting costs between departments and cost centres?

A floor area or cubic capacity

B the number of employees

C the replacement value of machinery and equipment

D the number of kilowatt hours

We will now make a start on our illustration, which has been designed to provide you with a comprehensive practical review of the mechanics of absorption costing. We will also provide you with a number of relevant comments as we progress.

Wik Engineering Co. Ltd, a small jobbing engineering firm, employs a total absorption costing system. Step 1 of the total absorption costing process, the predetermining of overheads, has now been completed and the following figures have been produced relating to the next accounting period:

Cost centre	**Depreciation of machinery and equipment**	**Indirect labour**	**Indirect materials**
	£'000	*£'000*	*£'000*
Machine department	11 600	2 574	1 450
Paint department	360	246	82
Assembly department	140	336	156
Services:			
Stores	80	646	110
Power	890	712	50
Administration, selling and distribution	380	1 886	230
	£13 450	£6 400	£2 078

These figures were arrived at by reviewing past records and taking account of changing circumstances and various other factors.

Other expenditure which was estimated and identified with particular cost centres was as follows:

	£'000	£'000
Storekeeping expenses	40	
Power expenses	700	
Administration, selling and distribution	496	1 236

The expenditure which could not be identified and traced to cost centres was estimated and the basis of apportionment agreed as follows:

	£'000	Basis of apportionment
Rent of buildings	3 000	Cubic capacity occupied
Depreciation and insurance of buildings	600	
Light and heat	1 400	
Supervision	8 400	No. of employees
Welfare/personnel costs	600	
Repairs and maintenance	2 480	Technical estimates

The information relating to the bases selected was as follows:

	Machine	Paint	Assembly	Stores	Power	Admin./ selling and dist.	Total
Cubic capacity (% of space)	48	34	8	2	2	6	100
No. of employees	6	4	3	1	1	3	18
Technical estimate *re* repairs and maintenance (as a %)	70	5	5	5	10	5	100

We now have sufficient information for completing Step 2, and can prepare the overhead distribution tabulation (Table 3.1) up to the point at which we deal with the apportionment (sometimes referred to by other writers as the reallocation) of the service departments' costs.

STEP 3: The apportionment of service department costs

Having completed the allocation and apportionment to cost centres of all of the overheads we now know the total overhead cost of providing each service. This information may prove useful for the purpose of making internal and external comparisons e.g. in cases where such services are available from external suppliers.

This third step also recognizes that the service departments' services are used by the other cost centres, and that their costs need to be shared out between all of the users.

Table 3.1 *Overhead distribution tabulation, Wik Engineering Co, Ltd*

		Total	Machine dept	Paint dept	Assy. dept	Stores	Power	Admin. and selling and dist.
		£'000	*£'000*	*£'000*	*£'000*	*£'000*	*£'000*	*£'000*
Allocated overheads:								
Indirect labour		6400	2574	246	336	646	712	1886
Indirect materials		2078	1450	82	156	110	50	230
Depreciation of machinery/equipment		13450	11600	360	140	80	890	380
Indirect expenses		1236				40	700	496
		23164	15624	688	632	876	2352	2992
Apportioned overheads:								
(Cubic capacity)	*£'000*							
Rent and Rates	3000							
Depreciation and Ins Bdgs	600							
Light and heat	1400	5000	2400	1700	400	100	100	300
(No. of employees)								
Supervision	8400							
Welfare/personnel	600	9000	3000	2000	1500	500	500	1500
(Technical estimate)								
Repairs and maintenance		2480	1736	124	124	124	248	124
Carried forward to Step 3		39644	22760	4512	2656	1600	3200	4916

There are various methods which may be used to apportion the service departments' costs between the user departments. For the purposes of our Wik Engineering Co. Ltd. example we will assume that both services are apportioned via technical estimates and that these are as follows:

	Machine dept	Paint dept	Assembly dept
Stores cost divisible (%)	50	25	25
Power cost divisible (%)	62.5	25	12.5

The above-mentioned service departments did not provide any service to the administration and sales/distribution function. Had this been the case, some of their costs would have also had to be apportioned to administration and sales:

Layout and presentation is important. Note that we have tried to produce a good clear tabulation, giving the information which is illustrated a reasonable amount of space. The bases of apportionment were indicated in the brackets. You should also observe that items which are apportioned using the same basis have been grouped together, totalled, then apportioned, e.g. the £5,000,000 which is shared up according to cubic capacity.

Knowing this, we can now find out the total overhead cost of each production department (Table 3.2).

***Table 3.2** Sharing out the service department costs*

	Total	Machine dept.	Paint dept.	Assy. dept.	Stores	Power	Admin. and selling and dist.
	£'000	£'000	£'000	£'000	£'000	£'000	£'000
Brought forward from Step 2	39644	22760	4512	2656	1600	3200	4916
Stores shared		800	400	400	−1600		
Power shared		2000	800	400		−3200	
	39644	25560	5712	3456			4916

Stores and power were apportioned using technical estimates.

STEP 4: The selection and calculation of overhead absorption rates

Now that we have accumulated the overhead cost for each production department and administration and sales, it is necessary to decide upon which of the overhead absorption rates should be used to recover each production department's share of the overheads. These so-called absorption (recovery) rates are the means by which the overheads find their way into the job or product costs. The selector has the task of choosing the most appropriate method for each production department. As a lot of overheads tend to vary more with time than output, it would appear that preference should be given to a time-based method, such as direct labour hours or machine hours.

For the purposes of our Wik Engineering illustration, we will restrict ourselves to machine hours for the machine department and direct labour hours for the paint department and the assembly department. We will use a machine hour rate to recover the overheads of the machine department against production because for that department machine time is more important than direct labour time, the department being quite highly mechanized. The remaining two production departments are not very highly mechanized and therefore a direct labour hour rate is considered to be more appropriate.

To be able to make these calculations you must appreciate the fact that both the machine hours and direct labour hours have to be predetermined. These figures will have to be estimated from information obtained from a number of sources e.g. historic data, forecast levels of activity, productivity, etc.

For Wik Engineering we will assume that this task has been completed and that the predetermined (budgeted) figures are as follows:

	Machine dept	Paint dept	Assembly dept
	'000	*'000*	*'000*
Machine hours	18000	900	none
Direct labour hours	8250	6800	5400

Calculation of the absorption rates

$$\frac{\text{Overheads of the department}}{\text{Hours}} = \textbf{the rate per hour}$$

We compute the absorption rates for Wik Engineering as follows:

Machine dept.

$$\frac{\text{Machine dept overheads}}{\text{Machine hours for the machine dept}} \quad \frac{£25\,560\,000}{18\,000\,000} \text{ hours}$$

= **£1.42 per machine hour (*Machine hour rate*)**

For every machine hour spent producing a job or product in the machine department, £1.42 will be charged (i.e. added) to the cost of the particular job or product concerned.

Paint dept.

$$\frac{\text{Paint dept overheads}}{\text{Direct labour hours for the paint dept}} \quad \frac{£5\,712\,000}{6\,800\,000} \text{ hours}$$

= **84p per direct labour hour (*Direct labour hour rate*)**

Assembly dept.

$$\frac{\text{Assembly dept overheads}}{\text{Direct labour hours for the assembly dept}} \quad \frac{£3\,456\,000}{5\,400\,000} \text{ hours}$$

= **64p per direct labour hour (*Direct labour hour rate*)**

STEP 5: The treatment of administration, selling and distribution overheads, and R&D expenditure

We have included this step in order to give you a complete picture. Decisions will have to be taken on whether to include all or some of these overheads in job or product costs or simply to write them off to the profit and loss account. For the purposes of our Wik Engineering example, it has been assumed that all of the administration and selling and distribution figure of £4,916,000 was charged as an expense to the profit and loss account.

To complete our Wik Engineering example, we will now use the information to work out the cost of a job.

Job YWX336 has just been completed and we have received the following information to assist us in preparing our job cost:

	£
Materials:	662
Labour: machine dept	8 hours at £7.00 per hour
paint dept	3 hours at £6.00 per hour
assembly dept	2 hours at £5.50 per hour

The job took 28 machine hours to complete in the machine department.

Wik Engineering job cost: Job No. YWX336

		£	£
Materials			662.00
Labour:			
Machine dept	(8 × £7)	56.00	
Paint dept	(3 × £6)	18.00	
Assy. dept	(2 × £5.50)	11.00	85.00
			747.00
Overheads			
Machine dept	(28 machine hrs at £1.42)	39.76	
Paint dept	(3 direct lab. hrs at 84p)	2.52	
Assy. dept	(2 direct lab. hrs at 64p)	1.28	43.56
	Cost of job:		£790.56

If, as time progresses, it is found that changes have taken place which affect the basic assumptions upon which a lot of the estimating was dependent, it will be necessary to revise the rates.

Self-assessment 3.3: Calculating the absorption (recovery) rates

The predetermined overheads, including service department overheads allocated and apportioned to departments, were as follows:

	Machine Group I	Machine Group II	Assembly	Total
	£	£	£	£
Period 3	**26 880**	**27 000**	**18 120**	**72 000**
Direct labour hours	6 000	8 000	10 000	
Machine hours	19 200	21 600	Nil	

You are required to:

1 Calculate machine hour absorption rates for the two machine departments and a direct hour rate for the assembly department.

2 Calculate the direct labour hour rate for the whole factory.

Self-assessment 3.4: Costing a job

The following data relate to job no. XYP 008165:

	Machine Group I	Machine Group II	Assembly
Direct labour hours	6	8	5
Employee wage rate per hour	£8	£9	£7
Machine hours	20	21	Nil
Overhead absorption rate	£1.40 per machine hour	£1.25 per machine hour	£1.812 per direct labour hour

The materials used for the job amounted to £67. Now see if you can calculate the cost of this job.

Self-assessment 3.5: Total absorption costing

You have been provided with the following budgeted overheads which relate to the forthcoming period for Cut Gate plc:

	£
Rent and rates	36 000
Light and heat	26 000
Welfare and canteen	21 000
Insurance of buildings	12 000
Insurance of machinery	6 400
Works manager's salary	19 000

Department	Indirect labour	Depreciation of machinery and equipment	Other overheads allocated
	£	£	£
X	12 000	24 500	3 460
N	7 700	5 500	2 240
Q	8 300	4 000	1 140
Maintenance	18 000	2 580	1 300
Stores	23 000	1 500	2 380
	£69 000	£38 080	£10 520

You are also provided with the following additional information:

	X	N	Q	Maintenance	Stores
Number of employees	4	16	16	2	2
Floor area (square metres)	360	240	240	120	240
Replacement value of machinery and equipment (£'000)	180	45	45	15	15
Use of stores (%)	20	40	30	10	–
Use of maintenance (%)	70	20	10	–	–
Machine hours	65 000	12 000	–		
Direct labour hours	7 500	32 000	20 000		

You are required to:

1 Prepare a departmental overhead distribution tabulation.

2 Calculate the overhead absorption rates using a machine hour rate for department X and a direct labour hour rate for departments N and Q.

3 Using the following data, prepare a quotation for Job 16783 RBP:

Direct material: £2 941

Direct labour:

Department X 17 hours @ £9
Department N 10 hours @ £11
Department Q 5 hours @ £8

Department X 30 machine hours

Mark-up: 40 per cent on cost

The limitations of total absorption costing

Figure 3.3 and the illustrations which followed earlier in this chapter can also help you to pinpoint and appreciate the limitations of the system. Each of the steps described has drawbacks, dealt with below.

Step 1, the budgeted overheads From the word go, you must remember that the figures which are being used are only estimates. It is, in fact, most unlikely that the budget and actual figures will ever agree – predicting the future is not easy. The bases on which the budgets were based may change. Thus, the system should have sufficient flexibility to enable budgets to be reviewed and revised as and when necessary. However, this is not always the case.

Step 2, allocation and apportionment of overheads The allocations of materials and labour etc. by departments depend upon estimates e.g. the time spent by cleaners in each department. Those overheads which cannot be traced to specific departments will have to be apportioned on an arbitrary basis e.g. by floor area or number of employees etc. The selection of bases depends upon the subjective judgement of the selector e.g. the management accountant.

Step 3, apportionment of service department costs The way in which service cost centres are shared out between users has also to be determined. Technical estimates may be used but are still only estimates. Other methods which may be used will be at the whim of the selector. For example, the stores cost may be split up between user departments according to the number of issue notes (requisitions). If this method is used, no account is taken of size, weight or value!

Step 4, selection and calculation of overhead absorption rates The departmental overheads which are used have been arrived at subject to all the drawbacks highlighted for steps 1 to 3. Another problem which arises is the selection of the method of overhead absorption (recovery) which is to be used. Again, the selection depends upon the views and preferences of the selector. A further problem which emerges is that the denominator has also to be estimated, for example the number of direct labour hours, machine hours, units to be produced, etc.

Step 5, the treatment of administration, selling and distribution overheads, and R&D expenditure This is another issue which has to be faced up to. Should it be included in the product cost, or excluded from the product cost and written off in the profit and loss account? The answer to these questions rests with the selector.

Other problems which result from the use of total absorption costing are:

- the problem of having to deal with the under- or over-absorption of overheads.
- using the system for decision making, which is quite a dangerous thing to do. The aim of absorption costing is to ensure that all costs are covered; it is simply not possible, with total absorption costing, to produce realistic and accurate job or product costs.

Other methods of overhead absorption/recovery

Earlier in this chapter we looked at the direct labour hour rate of overhead absorption/recovery and the machine hour rate of overhead absorption/recovery. You may recall that these methods were recommended, because a lot of the overheads which have to be shared out between cost centres vary more with time than with output. Both of those methods take time into account. However, there are other methods which you may come across, some of which will include the following.

- The rate per unit. This has limited application, in that it is perfect for a single product environment. Having said that, it isn't much use elsewhere.
- Percentage of wages.
- Percentage of material cost.
- Percentage of prime cost*
- A blanket rate – an overall rate which covers all of the departments in a factory; i.e. the same rate e.g. a rate per direct labour hour, is applied to every department. It does not take account of departmental variations in terms of overhead costs.

* For example, if overheads are £500,000 and prime cost (i.e. direct material + direct labour + direct expense) are £2,000,000, a rate of 25 per cent, i.e. $\frac{£500,000}{£2,000,000} \times 100$, will be added to the prime cost of the job or product in order to help recover the overheads.

Total absorption costing:

- attempts to ensure that all costs are covered;
- does *not* aim at producing fair and accurate job, product or inventory costs.

How it works

As outlined in Figure 3.3, absorption costing has five main steps:

Step 1 The predetermination of the overheads. The payroll analysis and the indirect materials analysis should prove to be most helpful for the budget preparation process.

Step 2 The allocation and apportionment of those overheads to user cost centres. Bases of apportionment may be floor area, number of employees, etc.

Step 3 The apportionment of service department costs to user cost centres.

Step 4 The calculation of the overhead absorption rate (recovery rate) for each department and the application of those rates to enable overheads to be charged to products, jobs, etc. Time-based overhead absorption rates such as direct labour hours and machine hours are preferable, because a lot of the overheads involved vary more with time than output.

Step 5 Dealing with administration, selling and distribution expenses, and R&D.

What are the limitations of total absorption costing?

Some of the limitations of total absorption costing are caused by having to estimate and budget the overheads and the number of direct labour hours and/or machine hours, for the forthcoming period.

Other limitations result from the subjective judgement of the selector e.g. the management accountant, *re*:

- the selection of the bases of overhead apportionment;
- the choice of overhead absorption/recovery rates;
- service department costs;
- administration costs;
- selling and distribution costs;
- R&D expenditure.

Absorption costing also involves the problem of under- or over-absorption of overheads, which we shall look at in greater depth in Chapter 5.

FURTHER READING

Drury C (1994) *Costing: An Introduction* (3rd Edition), London: Chapman & Hall

Weetman P (1996) *Management Accounting, An Introduction*, London: Pitman

Williamson D (1996) *Cost and Management Accounting*, London: Prentice Hall

Overheads and absorption costing: additional self-assessments

Self-assessment 3.6: Absorption costing multiple-choice test

Select the answers which you consider to be correct to the following multiple-choice problems:

1 Indirect costs can also be described as:

A overhead costs

B prime costs

C variable costs

D total costs

2 Indirect costs which cannot be identified with a particular cost centre are shared out between cost centres using:

A a recovery rate

B an absorption rate

C a method of apportionment

D a method of allocation

3 Which of the following is *not* an indirect cost?

A material which forms part of the product

B wages of a production department cleaner

C materials used for machine maintenance in the production department

D materials used to clean the production department floor

4 Which of the following methods of apportionment is most suitable for allocating the rent of buildings between cost centres?

A number of employees

B machine hours

C kilowatt hours

D floor area

5 You are provided with the following information relating to Job 224488X: Materials £240, Labour £96.

Absorption rate	Machine department *£3.50 per machine hour*	Assembly department *£2.25 per direct labour hour*
Direct labour hours for the job	12	8
Machine hours for the job	20	4

The cost of the job is:

	£
A	387
B	396
C	415
D	424

Self-assessment 3.7: Absorption costing quick questions

1 From the following data, calculate a machine hour absorption rate for the 'T' section and a direct labour absorption rate for the 'Q' section:

Period 3	'T' Section	'Q' Section	Total
Machine hours	56 000	12 000	68 000
Direct labour hours	16 000	32 000	48 000
Overheads	£134 400	£57 600	£192 000

2 Using the above data, calculate a 'blanket' overhead absorption rate for both sections using direct labour hours.

3 Describe briefly four of the limitations of absorption costing.

4 Describe briefly how absorption costing works.

5 Why is it difficult to distinguish between direct and indirect expenditure?

Self-assessment 3.8: Mason Van Chad Construction Ltd

One of your clients, Mason Van Chad Construction Ltd, owns a small engineering firm which up to now has based its quotations on the cost of materials and labour, plus a percentage to cover overheads and profit. They have now accepted your advice to relate costs to departments (A, B and C) through which the work passes and to charge overhead to jobs on the basis of departmental direct labour hours.

With your assistance they have produced the following data for the forthcoming period:

Expense	£	Proposed basis of departmental apportionment
Rent, rates and insurance	31 000	Floor area
Indirect labour	19 500	Direct labour hours
Depreciation	11 000	Replacement valuations
Repairs and maintenance	6 000	Technical estimate, as follows: A £2 700; B £1 890; C £1 410
Consumable stores	4 500	Direct labour hours
Canteen	10 000	Number of employees
Works manager's salary	13 000	Allocation as follows: A £3 500; B £5 500; C £4 000
National Insurance	2 000	Number of employees
General administration	30 000	Ratio of quotations, based on past experience, as follows: A 5/12; B 4/12; C 3/12

Jack Mason estimates that Department A will work 6,000 direct labour hours in the period, Department B 4,000 and Department C 2,000. Hourly wage rates are Department A £5, Department B £4.50 and Department C £4. The number of employees in each department is Department A forty, Department B twenty-five, Department C fifteen. Departmental floor areas (in square metres) are: Department A 15,000, Department B 18,000 and Department C 17,000. The replacement value of the plant and machinery used in each department is Department A £20,000, Department B £18,000 and Department C £6,000.

You are required to:

1 Prepare a departmental overhead distribution tabulation/summary.

2 Calculate the direct labour hour overhead absorption rates to be charged for the work which passes through each department.

3 Prepare a quotation for a job, to which the following data relate:

Direct material	£856.00
Direct labour:	
Department A	twenty-four hours
Department B	ten hours
Department C	six hours
Profit (mark-up)	20 per cent on cost price

Note: This firm does not have any service departments.

Self-assessment 3.9: Techtex plc

Techtex plc is a manufacturing company which has two production departments, Machining and Assembly, and two service departments, Maintenance and Handling.

The estimated factory expenses for the quarter ending 31 December 19X3 are as follows:

	£
Indirect labour:	
Machining	20 000
Assembly	8 800
Maintenance	39 700
Handling	12 000
Supervision	6 000
Canteen	7 200
Rent and rates	25 000
Fuel and light	7 500
Other costs:	
Machining	4 230
Assembly	420
Maintenance	300
Handling	320
Plant insurance	1 880
Plant depreciation	23 250

The following additional information is available and is to be used, where appropriate, in apportioning the expenses to departments:

	Machining	**Assembly**	**Maintenance**	**Handling**
Floor area (sq.m)	12 000	9 000	3 000	1 000
Number of employees	40	60	15	5
Cost of plant	£300 000	£100 000	£50 000	£20 000
Plant annual (on cost) depreciation rates	20%	25%	10%	15%
Direct labour hours	3 880	15 120		
Machine hours	6 750	1 100		

Of the total maintenance cost, 10 per cent is to be charged to Handling, and the remainder to the production departments on the basis of 30 per cent to Machining and 70 per cent to Assembly.

The cost of the Handling department is to be charged via technical estimates, 40 per cent to Machining department and 60 per cent to Assembly department.

You are required to:

1 Prepare a departmental overhead distribution summary.

2 Calculate the machine hour rate for the Machining department, and a direct labour hour rate for the Assembly department.

3 Prepare a quotation for a job to which the following data relate:

Direct material: £1 186
Direct labour:
Machining five hours @ £6 per hour
Assembly eight hours @ £5 per hour
Machine hours: seven (in Machining department)
Profit: 30 per cent on cost

Marginal Costing and Break-even Analysis

LEARNING OBJECTIVES

When you have read this chapter, you should be able to:

- understand and use the marginal cost equations to solve problems involving:
  - alternative strategies
  - changes in selling prices, variable costs and/or output
  - profit targets
  - break-even calculations
  - limiting factors (key factors);
- suggest the type of action which management could take to reduce the effect of a limiting factor or eliminate it outright;
- construct elementary break-even charts;
- appreciate the limitations of marginal costing and break-even analysis.

Fixed and variable costs, a recapitulation

Before we look at marginal costing it may be worth reminding ourselves of what we mean by:

- fixed costs;
- variable cost;
- semi-variable costs.

In Chapter 1 we looked at cost behaviour theory and practice. Our practice definitions ended up as:

Fixed costs Those costs which remain unchanged irrespective of the level of output (activity) in the short-term, within a relevant range.

Variable costs Those costs which vary directly with the level of output (activity) in the short term, within a relevant range.

Semi-variable costs Those costs which include both a fixed and a variable element. For instance, a production worker may be paid a fixed salary (the fixed element) and a bonus based upon output (the variable element).

Note that output is frequently referred to as the 'level of activity', and may be measured in percentage terms.

How marginal costing works

S − VC = C
C − FC = P or L
C = FC + P or C = FC − L
C + VC = S

Figure 4.1 Marginal cost equations

Looking at Fig. 4.1, your reaction may be 'what does it all mean?'

The short answer is that it is simply marginal costing arithmetic, i.e. marginal cost equations in an abbreviated form. Believe it or not, marginal costing arithmetic is simple to follow and reasonably easy to understand.

We will now look in turn at each of the calculations in Fig. 4.1, illustrating and explaining how marginal costing actually works.

S − VC = C (Sales less Variable Cost = Contribution) This marginal cost equation, using the figures assumed below, means:

	Per unit	% of sales	Total 1000 units
	£		£
Sales (S)	50	100	50 000
Less Variable cost (VC)	30	60	30 000
= Contribution (C)	20	40	£20 000

Marginal costing is all about the relationship which exists between sales, variable costs and the contribution. In computing the contribution, only those costs which are variable, i.e. those which vary directly with the level of activity within a relevant range, are used. These variable costs, also called marginal costs, can be identified with and traced to the product concerned. However, it is not always as easy as one would imagine to distinguish costs as either fixed costs or variable costs, as we will see when we take a look at the limitations.

A vast proportion of the variable costs can be direct materials, i.e. the material which forms part of the product, and direct labour, i.e. the labour used to transform the raw material into a finished product. Thus, in addition to being called variable costing, marginal costing is sometimes referred to as direct costing.

The contribution is rather like a gross profit. It is the name which is given to the profit which arises before the fixed costs are deducted.

C − FC = P or L (Contribution less Fixed Cost = Profit or Loss) The second of our abbreviated calculations does, in fact, help us to answer the question 'what does the contribution contribute towards?' It contributes towards the recovery of the fixed costs (FC) and profit (P).

		Total
		£
	Contribution (as above)	20 000
Less	Fixed costs (assumed figure)	16 000
	Profit	£4 000

Notice that we did not express the fixed costs as a cost per unit. This is because in marginal costing the fixed costs are treated as **period costs** i.e. they are simply written off during the period in which they are incurred; they are not included in the product costs. Marginal costs, because they only include the variable costs in product costs, are more accurate than products costed using total absorption costing. Marginal costing is therefore preferable when it comes to decision making. It is, in fact, both folly and dangerous to cost products according to total absorption costing for decision-making purposes. Total absorption costing simply cannot deliver sufficiently accurate and reliable costs for decision-making purposes.

If the fixed costs had been greater than the contribution of £20,000, the result would have been a loss. For example, if the fixed costs had been £27,000 the position would then have been:

Contribution		Fixed costs		Loss
£20 000	less	£27 000	=	(£7 000)

C = FC + P *or* **C = FC − L** (Contribution = Fixed Cost plus Profit, or less Loss) Our third set of equations shows that we can work out the contribution by adding the fixed costs to the profit (or subtracting the loss).

This brings us to a very important technique which can be used when management set a profit target. The profit target problem can be resolved by adding the profit target which has been set to the fixed costs which have to be covered. The resulting figure is the contribution which needs to be generated, i.e:

Profit target + Fixed costs = Contribution needed

If, for the next period, the selling price and variable costs remain the same, but fixed costs are expected to go up to £22,000 and management set a target profit of £8,000, we need to generate a contribution of:

Profit target		Fixed costs		
£		£		
8 000	plus	22 000	=	£30 000

With the contribution remaining at £20 per unit, we will need to sell:

$$\frac{\text{Contribution needed}}{\text{Contribution per unit}} \quad \frac{£30\,000}{£20} = 1\,500 \text{ units}$$

This, in terms of sales value, is:

Units which must be sold		Selling price per unit		
1 500	×	£50	=	£75 000

C + VC = S (Contribution + Variable Cost = Sales) This final equation reinforces the point made at the outset, i.e. marginal costing is about the relationship between the contribution, the variable cost and sales. If you know two of the three, then because of the relationship which exists, you can also work out the other figure.

	Contribution	+	Variable costs	=	Sales
Per unit	£20	+	£30	=	£50
Total	£20 000	+	£30 000	=	£50 000
As a percentage of sales	40%	+	60%	=	100%

The contribution expressed as a percentage of sales, i.e. 40 per cent in the above example, is called the *profit volume ratio* (or PV ratio).

What can marginal costing be used for?

Having introduced you to the arithmetic of marginal costing, we will now have a look at some illustrations. Each of the illustrations is followed by a self-assessment, so that you can check your progress by receiving instant feedback. This approach, it is hoped, will help you to consolidate your knowledge and understanding of the techniques involved.

Marginal costing can be used:

- to assess alternative courses of action, or the effects of changes in selling prices, variable costs and the volume of output. This is why some authors refer to marginal costing as 'cost volume profit';
- to help solve profit target problems;
- to calculate the break-even point or to carry out some break-even analysis;

- for limiting (or key) factor problems;
- to assist management with decision making, e.g. make-or-buy decisions, or special contract evaluations.

An illustration of changes in selling prices, variable costs and output and profit targets

The current position for a company's product, a small boat, is as follows:

	Per unit £'000	Total (25 units) £'000
Selling price	36	900
Less Variable costs	20	500
Contribution	16	400 (or 25 × £16 000)
Less Fixed costs		320
Profit		£80

The directors estimate that production of the twenty-five units only took up 60 per cent of the production capacity. To achieve a higher utilization they resolve to consider two schemes for the forthcoming period, which they hope will increase sales by another ten units:

Scheme 1 Reduce selling price by £4,000 per unit.

Scheme 2 Increase variable costs by £4,000 per unit.

Fixed costs, it is envisaged, will be £328,000 for either scheme.

You are required to:

1 Calculate the outcome if either scheme was used and achieved sales of thirty-five units.

2 Calculate the outcome if things went wrong and only twenty-five units were sold.

3 Calculate the number of units which would have to be sold to produce a profit equal to the current profit of £80,000.

1 The effect on the contributions would be:

	Scheme 1 Per unit £'000	Scheme 2 Per unit £'000
Selling price	32	36
Less Variable cost	20	24
Contribution	**12**	**12**

Commentary The schemes are different, the contributions are the same; if the selling price goes down by £4,000, the contribution goes down by £4,000, i.e. existing contribution £16,000 less reduction in selling price £4,000 = £12,000. Equally, if the variable costs go up by £4,000, the contribution will go down by £4,000, i.e. again £16,000 − £4,000 = £12,000.

Now back to the answer:

	Scheme 1 or Scheme 2	
The sale of 35 units will generate a contribution of: 35 units × £12 000 =	*35 units* *£'000* 420	
Less Fixed costs	328	
Profit	**£92**	(i.e. an increase of £12,000 in profits)

	Scheme 1 or 2
2 If only 25 units were sold the contribution would amount to: 25 units × £12 000	*25 units* *£'000* 300
Less Fixed costs	328
Loss	**£28**

3 This problem requires us to display our knowledge of the marginal costing technique for dealing with profit targets.

We need to calculate the contribution required as follows:

	£'000
Fixed costs	328
Plus Profit target	80
Contribution required	**£408**

We then divide the contribution required by the contribution per unit, to see how many units must be sold:

$$\frac{\text{Contribution required}}{\text{Contribution per unit}} = \frac{£408\,000}{12\,000} = 34 \text{ units}$$

Commentary Management should be informed of the likely outcome if things go wrong. The financial information is just one piece of the decision-making jigsaw; it cannot and should not be used in isolation from other available information, e.g. non-financial factors.

Self-assessment 4.1: Giessen plc I

You have been provided with the following information for period one:

	Per unit £	**20 000 units £'000**
Selling price	25	500
Less Variable cost	20	400
Contribution	5	100
Less Fixed costs		80
Profit		20

The directors propose to increase sales in period two by adopting one of the following strategies:

1 Increase quality at a cost of £3 per unit.

2 Reduce the selling price by £1 per unit.

3 Spend £15,000 on advertising (a fixed cost).

Fixed costs in period two are expected to be £90,000 (excluding advertising). The directors all agree that they should aim at earning a profit of £36,000 in period two. *You are required to*:

1 Calculate in terms of units and value the sales volume needed for each of the strategies which will achieve the profit target.

Self-assessment 4.2: Giessen plc II

Using the information for period one in Giessen plc I, and assuming sales of 20,000 units, fixed costs of £90,000 and the profit target £36,000, you are required to calculate how much the company can afford to pay in period two for a new semi-automatic machine which will cut variable costs by £2.50 per unit.

Step variable costs – an example

The following information relates to a microcomputer for period 3:

Output in units	Selling price per unit £	Variable cost per unit £
0 to 5 000	400	260
5 001 upwards	400	250

The fixed costs are expected to be £600,000 and the budgeted (i.e. target) profit is £160,000.

If we wish to know how many units we will have to sell to meet the target, we must first calculate the contribution per unit for the two positions:

	Up to 5 000 units per unit £	Over 5 000 units per unit £
Selling price	400	400
Less variable cost	260	250
Contribution	£140	£150

Next, we work out the total contribution which is needed:

	£'000
Fixed costs to cover	600
Plus Profit target	160
Contribution required	£760

	units	Contribution per unit £	total £'000
We then multiply the contribution per unit for outputs up to 5,000 units by 5,000, to see if it will generate the £760,000 needed. You will observe that we are (£760,000 – £700,000) £60,000 short of our required contribution. If we divide this shortfall by our second-level contribution of £150 per unit, it will tell us the number of units in excess of 5,000 which we must sell:	5 000	140	700
$\frac{£60\,000}{150}$ = 400 units i.e.	400	150	60
	5 400		£760

We must therefore sell 5,400 units.

Self-assessment 4.3: Montpele Ltd

Montpele Ltd manufacture a single product. You are provided with the following data relating to the forthcoming period:

	£'000
Budgeted fixed costs	258
Budgeted profit	100

The product has a selling price of £250 per unit up to 6,000 units, and £240 per unit for all sales in excess of 6,000 units.

Variable costs are expected to be £210 for outputs up to 4,000 units, £190 for 4,001 to 6,000 units, and £175 per unit for outputs in excess of 6,000 units.

You are required to:

1 Calculate how many units must be sold to achieve the target profit.

Break-even point calculations

We can use marginal costing information to calculate the break-even point, the point at which sales revenue and costs are equal. We can compute it, in terms of value and quantity, provided that we have all the appropriate information.

In terms of value:

Break-even point = fixed costs ÷ profit volume ratio (FC ÷ PV ratio) *or*

$$\text{Break-even point} = \frac{\text{fixed costs} \times \text{sales}}{\text{sales} - \text{variable costs}}$$

This formula can be used where unit costs are not available.

In terms of units:

$$\text{Break-even point} = \frac{\text{fixed costs}}{\text{contribution per unit}}$$

We will look at break-even charts later on in this chapter.

Break-even calculations illustrated

We will now use the following data to illustrate how we calculate the break-even point in terms of value and units:

	per unit £	6000 units £'000
Sales	200	1200
Less Variable costs	160	960
Contribution	40	240
Less Fixed costs		220
Profit:		£20

$$\text{The profit volume ratio} = \frac{\text{contribution (per unit or total)}}{\text{sales (per unit or total)}} \times 100$$

$$= \frac{£40}{£200} \times 100 = 20\%$$

The break-even point in value = fixed costs ÷ profit volume ratio

$$= £220\,000 \times \frac{100}{20} = \mathit{£1\,100\,000}$$

Using the alternative formula:

$$\frac{\text{Fixed costs} \times \text{sales}}{\text{Sales} - \text{variable costs}} = \frac{£220\,000 \times £200\,000}{£200\,000 - £160\,000} = \mathit{£1\,100\,000}$$

The break-even point in terms of output units is:

$$\frac{\text{fixed costs}}{\text{contribution per unit}} \quad \frac{£220\,000}{£40} = \mathit{5\,500\ units}$$

The units needed to break even can be converted to the break-even point in value by multiplying the 5,500 units by the selling price per unit of £200 = *£1,100,000*.

Self-assessment 4.4: Break-even calculations

The following budgeted information applies to Eve Break Ltd. Product GSL sells at £500 per unit and has a variable cost of £375 per unit. Fixed costs for the forthcoming period are expected to amount to £80,000.

You are required to:

1 Calculate the profit volume ratio:

2 Calculate the break-even point, using the profit volume ratio.

3 Calculate the break-even point in units, using the contribution per unit.

Limiting factors

A limiting factor constrains what an organization can and cannot do, hence its other names – governing factor, key factor, and principal budget factor. If a particular factor is so important that it influences everything else, it must be taken into account first when attempting to maximize profits or produce realistic budgets. It is, in fact, the starting point of the budgeting process.

Some examples of key factors are:

- supply – raw materials, finished goods;
- demand – sales demand;
- labour supply;
- production capacity;
- warehouse capacity;
- finance availability;
- government measures – restrictions etc.

Which is the limiting factor?

	Material supply	Production capacity	Estimated sales demand
Gold ear-rings (pairs)	10000	200000	180000
Shirt (units)	500000	300000	170000
Tops (units)	800000	200000	21000
Sunbeds (units)	48000	25000	35000

The simple answer is, that which places the most immediate constraint over the activities described. With the ear-rings, it does not matter about being able to produce 200,000 units or sell 180,000 units, because you only have sufficient material available for the period to make 10,000 pairs. Thus, material supply is the limiting factor in this case.

For the other items listed, the key factors are: sales demand of 170,000 units for shirts; 21,000 units sales demand for tops and 25,000 units production capacity for sunbeds.

Limiting factors are never static and management can, by their actions, reduce their effect or eliminate them altogether. For example, management can increase the material supply or reduce the need to use certain materials by:

- using substitutes;
- searching for new suppliers at home and abroad;
- improving product design and manufacturing methods to reduce waste and achieve better material utilization.

If the limiting factor is sales demand, management can embark upon a variety of actions, such as:

- reducing their prices;
- increasing quality;
- advertising;
- special promotions;
- targeting specific markets or market segments;
- improving marketing management.

Self assessment 4.5: Limiting (key) factors – management action

Now see if you can list five courses of action which could be introduced to reduce the effect or eliminate the following limiting factors:

- labour supply;
- production capacity;
- warehouse capacity;
- finance.

The action which management can take where government restrictions or legislation are the limiting factor is largely limited to the following types:

- writing or sending petitions to MPs or their local council;
- protesting via their trade association or chamber of commerce;
- seeking the support of pressure groups, e.g. trade unions.

Limiting factor arithmetic

Limiting factor arithmetic is relatively simple. Instead of using the contribution per unit, we use a technique which can be described as the contribution per unit of the limiting factor. For example, the contribution may be expressed as:

- a contribution per lb or kilo;
- a contribution per gallon or litre;
- a contribution per hour or minute.

The aim is to maximize the contribution per unit of the key factor. The following example should give you a good insight into how we deal with limiting factor arithmetic.

The supply of materials to a company are limited to 4,000 kilos per period, and the company must make a choice between producing product A or product B. Details are as follows:

	Product A £	Product B £
Selling price per unit	800	250
Variable cost per unit	600	120
Contribution	£200	£130
Material required for one unit	4 kilos	2 kilos
The contribution per kilo	$\frac{£200}{4}$ = £50 per kilo	$\frac{£130}{2}$ = £65 per kilo
Maximum contribution (4 000 kilos × contribution per kilo)	= *£200 000*	= *£260 000*

Thus, by using all of the material for producing product B, the total contribution is £60,000 greater than that which would be earned by using all of the material for product A.

Self-assessment 4.6: Time is money

The productive time is limited for the next month to 8,000 hours. The company may use the time to produce one of three products, details of which are as follows:

Product	**F** £	**T** £	**I** £
Selling price (per unit)	75	61	72
Less Variable cost	55	50	60
Contribution	£20	£11	£12
Time taken to produce one unit	4 hours	2 hours	3 hours

Which product should the company produce?

Break-even analysis

We have already looked at how to calculate the break-even point. We will now show you how to construct and use break-even charts.

Break-even charts

Marginal costing and break-even analysis looks at costs according to how they behave. A break-even chart is made up of three lines:

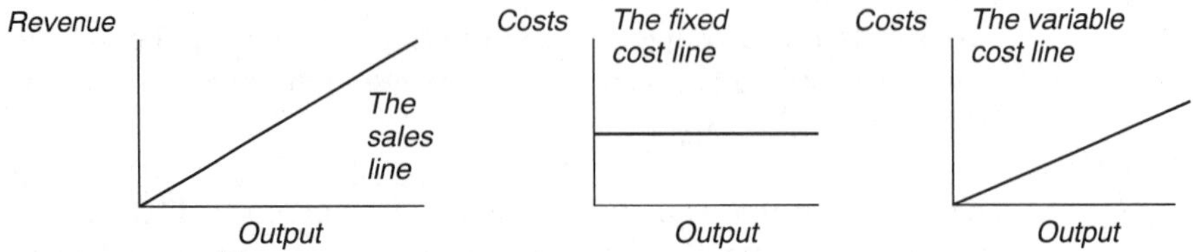

The relationship between sales, costs and profit can be displayed diagrammatically by using a break-even chart; see Fig. 4.2.

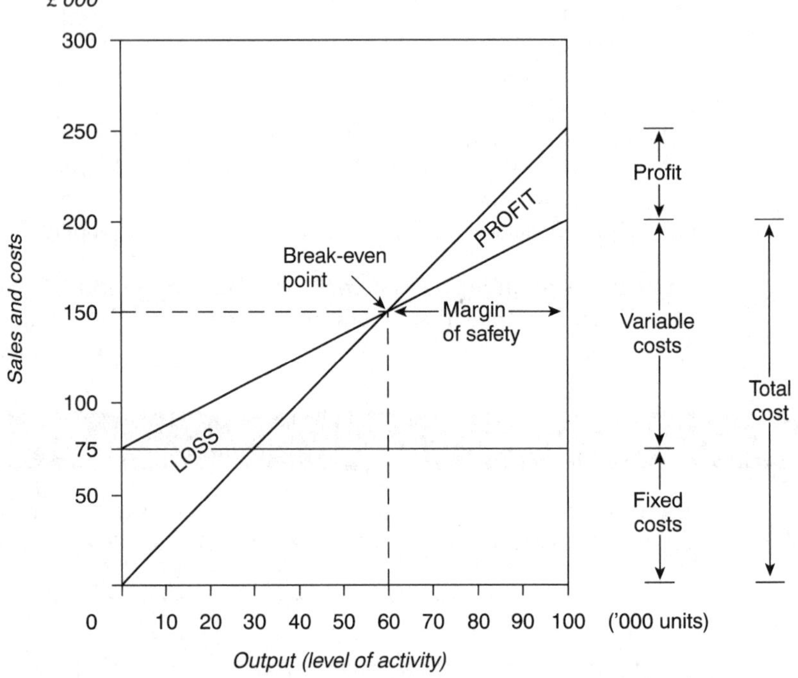

Figure 4.2 **Break-even chart**

Note that the variable costs are added to the fixed costs and that the variable cost line becomes the *total cost line.*

The distance between the break-even point and the expected level of output is called the *margin of safety.* It indicates the degree to which sales must fall before a loss-making situation is reached.

The following alternative method (Fig. 4.3) uses a contribution approach. In this chart the fixed costs are plotted parallel to the variable costs. Thus, the fixed cost line becomes the total cost line.

Data:

	£
Fixed costs	75 000
Variable costs	125 000
Total cost	200 000
Sales	£250 000

The advantage claimed for this break-even chart is that it will always show the contribution being generated by a given level of sales – the contribution being represented above the break-even point by fixed cost plus profit, and below the break-even point by fixed costs less the loss.

The vertical line (*A*) in Fig. 4.3 drawn at 80 per cent output shows how we can project a line at any level of activity and then read off the position in terms of sales, costs and profits (or losses). Thus, a break-even chart can be used to answer questions relating to what would happen at different levels of activity.

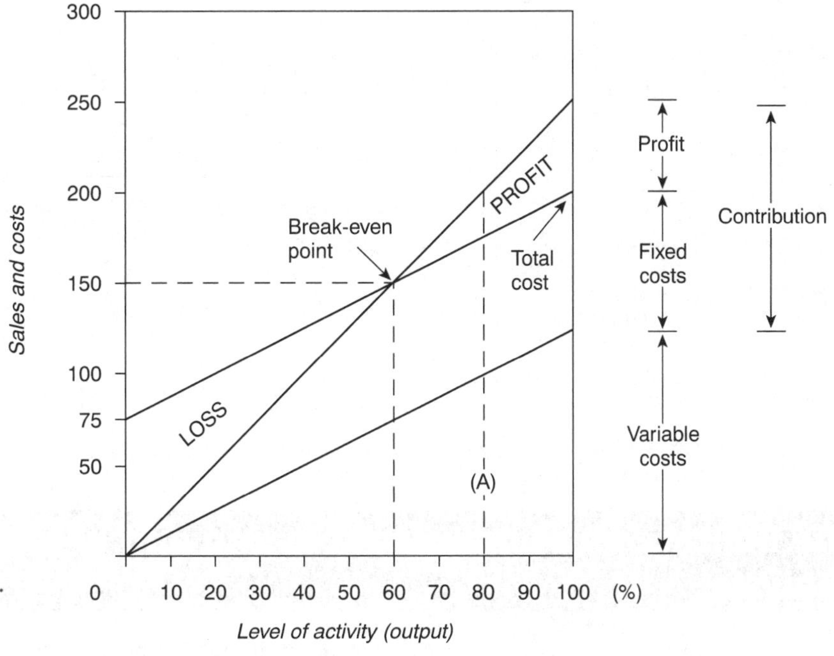

Figure 4.3 A contribution break-even chart

Self-assessment 4.7: Break-even charts

Using the data provided, see if you can construct the two types of break-even charts which were described above.

Data:	Sales	£60 000 (50 000 units) 100% Activity
	Variable cost	£30 000
	Fixed costs	£15 000

The profit graph/profit volume diagram

This is just another type of break-even chart; using the same data as we used in self assessment 4.7, we can produce the profit graph shown in Fig. 4.4.

You can see from Fig. 4.4 that when the fixed costs have been covered, the break-even point is reached; above the break-even point we make a profit.

The sales line on the graph could have been substituted by the output or level of activity line.

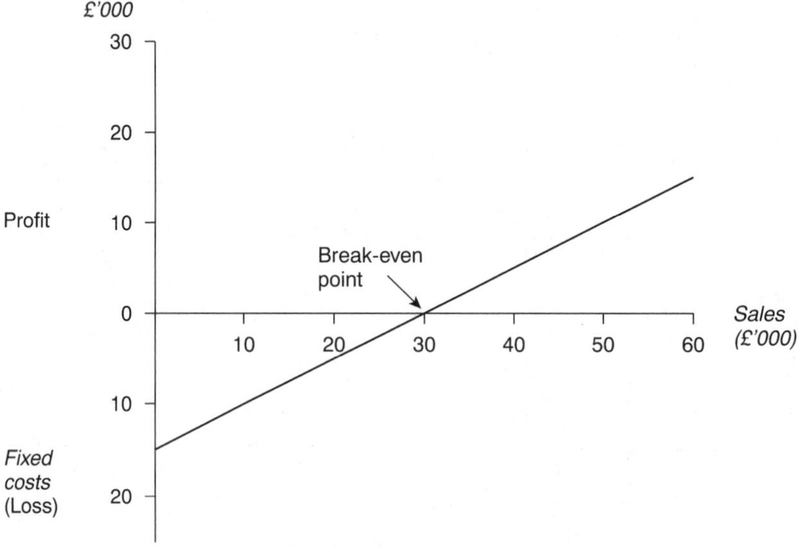

Figure 4.4 **Profit graph (profit volume diagram)**

The limitations of marginal costing and break-even analysis

Marginal costing and break-even analysis may appear relatively simple to apply. Beware, there are certain difficulties and drawbacks:

- First, the separation of costs into fixed costs and variable costs is not as straightforward as you may think. For instance:
  - Production workers who are paid a fixed wage, and are involved in transforming raw materials into finished goods may be described as direct labour, but they are paid a fixed amount whether or not they produce anything!

- The rent of a machine or equipment at a fixed amount per month would be treated as a fixed cost; if the rental was based on output, however, it would be treated as a variable cost!
- The wages paid to cleaners who spend some of their time cleaning finished products before they are packaged, and the remainder of their time cleaning the factory.

- Second, the fact that in the long term all costs are variable. Thus, break-even analysis and marginal costing is better suited to the short term.
- There is also the danger of using the figures and charts in isolation, independent from other quantitative and qualitative data. As mentioned before, such financial information is not the only aspect to be considered in decision making. Rather, it is just one of several inputs.
- Several of the assumptions tend not to apply to the real world:

Assumption	*The real world*
Variable costs vary directly with output	Yes, but only within a relevant range
Fixed costs will remain the same irrespective of the level of output	No. They will be fixed within a relevant range. They tend to go up in steps
Sales = production	In practice, stocks are held of work-in-progress and finished goods. When production is increasing, sales may in fact be going down!
A constant product mix	Even in the short-term the product mix may not be constant. The product mix has to respond to market forces
A constant selling price	Sales of the same product can be made at different prices to customers/markets/market segments
Efficiency is constant	No it isn't! Productivity levels may vary from day to day, week to week

- Managerial decisions can affect selling prices and costs; e.g. a decision to sub-let part of the factory could reduce certain costs such as business rates, light and heat, cleaning etc.
- Its use could lead to the growth of sales for growth's sake. The belief that increased sales will bring about an increase in profits is not always true. An increase in the volume of sales could involve an increase in fixed costs.
- Finally, there is a danger that marginal costing could lead a company into a situation in which not all costs are covered, e.g. by fixing a selling price which yields an inadequate contribution.

Marginal costing and break-even analysis treat costs according to their behaviour. The marginal cost of a product is simply another description for the variable cost of the product. Marginal costing excludes fixed costs from product costs. The fixed costs are treated as period costs, i.e. they are written off in computing the profit (or loss) of the period to which they relate.

The contribution

The sales less the variable cost is called the contribution, which contributes towards the recovery of the fixed overheads and profit. The contribution approach can be used to solve a variety of problems. In appropriate circumstances and if at all possible, you will find that it is useful to draw up a contribution table. Figure 4.5 shows the contribution per unit for each of the alternative courses of action under review. In addition, if required it could also show the profit volume ratio for each alternative. Note that it is easier to work in terms of the contribution per unit if this is possible.

	Proposals		
	A	B	C
	£	£	£
Selling price per unit	32	40	60
Less Variable cost per unit	24	30	48
Contribution per unit	8	10	12
Profit volume ratio	25%	25%	20%

Figure 4.5 Contribution table

Uses

Marginal costing can be used to:

- compute the effects of changes in selling prices, variable costs and the volume of output, and also the effects of alternative courses of action;
- provide data which will be helpful in solving profit target problems;
- calculate the break-even point;
- solve limiting factor problems;
- provide management with information to assist them with their decision making

Some useful calculations

1 Contribution per unit × units sold = total contribution.

2 Fixed cost plus profit target = total contribution needed.

3 Contribution needed divided by contribution per unit = number of units which must be sold.

4 $\frac{\text{contribution}}{\text{sales}} \times 100$ = profit volume ratio.

5 Fixed costs ÷ profit volume ratio = break-even point.

6 Contribution ÷ limiting factor = contribution per unit of the limiting factor.

Limiting factors

Limiting factors are also called key factors, governing factors or principal budget factors. A limiting factor may be defined as: when a factor is of such importance that it influences all the other budgets and must always be taken into account first before all the functional budgets are prepared.

Limiting factors dictate what firms can and cannot do, because they place a constraint on their activities. Limiting factors may be the supply of raw materials; sales demand; labour supply; production capacity; warehouse capacity; finance availability; or government restrictions.

You should note that management can, by their actions, reduce the effect of the limiting factor or even eliminate it altogether.

Break-even analysis

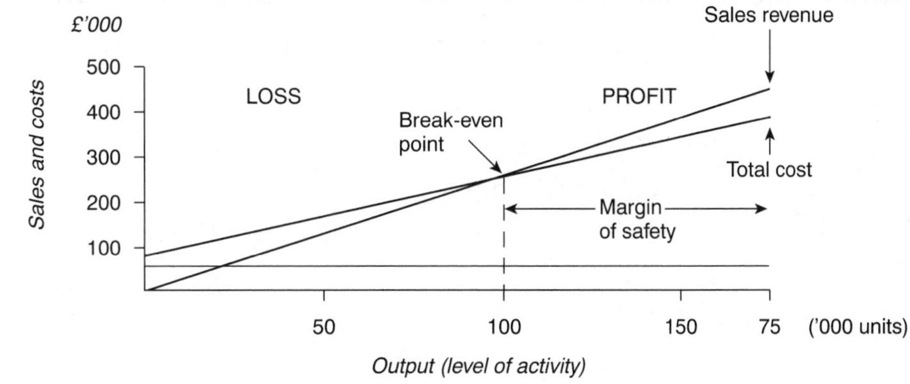

Figure 4.6 **Break-even chart**

There are a number of alternative ways of drawing a break-even chart. The chart should only be used in conjunction with other data. Decisions cannot and should not be made based solely on the chart.

The break-even point is the point at which sales and costs are equal. Above it, we make a profit, below it, we make a loss. The margin of safety represents the difference between the break-even point and the normal expected level of output.

Limitations

Marginal costing and break-even analysis do have limitations, for example:

- the problem of deciding whether costs are fixed or variable;
- in the long term, all costs are variable;
- the danger of using the information independently of other data;
- the assumptions used may not hold true or may change significantly
- decisions made by management can affect the figures, even in the short term;
- its use could lead to sales growth for growth's sake, and/or a failure to cover all costs.

FURTHER READING

Atrill P and McLaney E (1994) *Management Accounting, An Active Learning Approach*, Oxford: Blackwell

Chadwick L (1997) *The Essence of Management Accounting* (2nd Edition), London: Prentice-Hall

Weetman P (1996) *Management Accounting, An Introduction*, London: Pitman

Marginal costing and break-even analysis: additional self-assessments

Self-assessment 4.8: Marginal costing test

1 Define in your own words and give an example of each of the following terms:

(a) fixed costs;

(b) variable costs;

(c) semi-variable costs.

2 Which type of cost does the line on this graph illustrate?

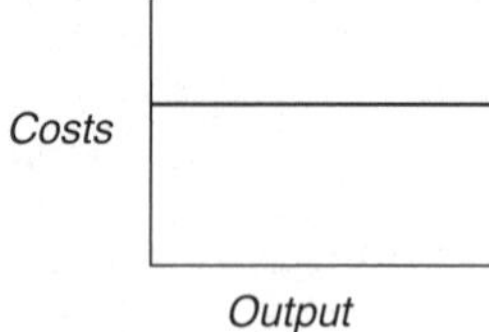

3 By what other name is marginal costing known?

4 How is the 'contribution' calculated, and what is meant by the term?

5 In order to illustrate the equation C = S − VC, fill in the following table:

Sales	Variable cost	Contribution
£	£	£
5000	2000	____
____	11000	2500
16400	____	5300

6 Complete the table set out below to show C = FC + P *or* P = C − FC etc.

Contribution	Fixed cost	Profit
£	£	£
11000	5000	____
____	12100	7000
7100	____	2100

7 Now fill in the missing figures in the following table:

Sales	Variable cost	Contribution	Fixed cost	Profit
£	£	£	£	£
24300	4100	____	6000	____
____	3000	8000	2500	____
7500	____	____	3300	1700

8 What is a limiting factor (also called governing factor, key factor, etc.)?

9 Which two items are used to calculate the profit volume ratio?

10 What would you say is meant by the term 'break-even point'?

Self-assessment 4.9: Quick questions

1 Sales £50 per unit; variable costs £30 per unit; fixed costs £12,000; sale of 1,000 units.

(a) Calculate the profit.

(b) What would the position be if the selling price was reduced by 10 per cent?

(c) Using the selling price as in (b), calculate how many units will have to be sold to produce the same profit as in (a).

2 The fixed costs of Tubs Ltd are £24,000 per annum. The company is able to produce up to 30,000 tubs per year at a variable cost of 50p per tub. The selling price is £2 per tub.
Calculate the profit and the break-even point in value and volume.

3 Materials are limited in supply to 4,000 tons per period. A choice must be made between producing product T and product Z. Details are as follows:

	Product T	Product Z
	£	£
Selling price per unit	1 000	600
Variable cost per unit	600	360
Material required for one unit	8 tons	4 tons

4 Store Shed plc operates two stores. From the data given below calculate:

(a) the break-even point;

(b) the volume of sales required in each case to achieve a profit of 10 per cent on the capital invested.

	Buck & West	Brett 57
Fixed overheads	£50 000	£84 000
Profit volume ratio	40%	60%
Capital invested	£200 000	£240 000

Self-assessment 4.10: Iain Smoke Alarms Ltd

Iain Smoke Alarms Ltd has appointed Les Ward-Wick to take charge of its southern Scotland sales area. The alarms will be invoiced from head office at £9 plus £1 for carriage. It will cost £200,000 to acquire premises, fixtures and fittings in Edinburgh. Sales staff will be paid a commission of 25 per cent of the selling price, to encourage them to attract business. The recommended selling price is £20. Annual fixed costs are estimated at £25,000.

1 How many alarms must be sold to earn a return of 30 per cent on the initial investment of £200,000?

2 Calculate the break-even point.

3 If the head office decides that it must recover all expenses and the initial investment over two years, how many alarms must be sold over that period?

4 Les estimates that he could achieve a maximum level of sales of 15,000 alarms if the selling price were reduced by £1, or if £10,000 per annum were spent on advertising and promotion. Which would you recommend?

Self-assessment 4.11: Utreford Engineering plc

Utreford Engineering plc produces a microchip-controlled tool which sells at £40 per unit. Sales for the current period are expected to amount to 200,000 units. The costs are as follows:

Direct materials and direct labour £16 per unit
Commission payable at 5% of sales value

(£'000s)	Fixed costs	Variable costs
Factory indirect costs	320	80
Selling costs	340	160
Distribution costs	200	120
Administration costs	1 440	–

You are required to calculate:

1 The profit/loss and PV ratio for the current period.

2 The profit/loss and PV ratio if the selling price is reduced by 5 per cent and the sales increase by 12½ per cent.

3 The profit/loss and PV ratio if the selling price is reduced by 10 per cent and the sales increase by 25 per cent.

4 The break-even point for 1, 2 and 3 above.

You are *not* required to prepare a break-even chart.

Self-assessment 4.12: Break-even analysis

Discuss the contention that break-even analysis is based on a set of assumptions which totally invalidate any practical value it might have to an organization.

Self-assessment 4.13: Able Ltd and Cable Ltd

Two businesses, Able Ltd and Cable Ltd, sell the same type of product in the same type of market sector. Their budgeted profit and loss accounts for the year ending 31 March 19X9 are as follows:

	Able Ltd		Cable Ltd	
	£	£	£	£
Sales		300 000		300 000
Less				
Variable costs	240 000		200 000	
Fixed costs	30 000	270 000	70 000	270 000
Net budgeted profit		£30 000		£30 000

You are required to:

1 Calculate the break-even point for each business.

2 Prepare a break-even chart to show what the position would be if the actual sales made by both firms were £240,000 each.

3 State which business is likely to earn greater profits in conditions of:

(a) heavy demand for the product;

(b) low demand for the product.

Self-assessment 4.14: Step fixed costs

From the following data, see if you can produce a contribution approach type break-even chart which takes into account the step fixed costs:

Sales	5 000 units at £100 each	
Variable costs	£60 each	
Fixed costs up to 2 500 units		£90 000
Fixed costs over 2 500 units		plus a further £30 000

Total Absorption Costing Versus Marginal Costing

Having introduced you to both total absorption costing and marginal costing, we will now ponder awhile and take a step back and contrast the two methods. This will assist you to take a more critical view of them both and to appreciate the problems associated with their use. We will look particularly at their effects on stock valuations and profits or losses.

LEARNING OBJECTIVES

When you have read this chapter you should be able to:

- identify the principal differences between total absorption costing and marginal costing;
- describe the problems and dangers associated with them;
- understand why we use each of the systems;
- prepare and reconcile total absorption costing and marginal costing profit statements;
- appreciate how to use unit costs, unit gross profits or contribution per unit to prove the arithmetic accuracy of the gross profit or contribution;
- deal with problems involving the under- or over-absorption of fixed overheads;
- take a critical view of the two methods.

Marginal costing is far more realistic than absorption costing, because it includes only those costs which can be identified with the job or product, i.e. the variable costs, whereas absorption costing includes fixed overheads, many of which vary more with time than output. Marginal costing may be more suitable for internal reporting and decision-making purposes. However, for external reporting purposes SSAP 9 (Statement of Standard Accounting Practice) advocates the adoption of an absorption costing approach, recommending that an appropriate amount of the overheads be included in work-in-progress and finished stock valuations.

Method

Both methods rely on the predetermination of the costs which are to be used. Total absorption costing, it must be said, involves a great deal of subjective judgement. Methods by which the overheads and service department costs are to be apportioned to cost centres, the number of direct labour hours, machine hours, or production units, the choice of overhead absorption (recovery) rates, and the treatment of selling, distribution, administration, and R&D expenditure are all at the discretion of an individual or group of individuals. Marginal costing treats fixed costs as period costs, i.e. costs which are written off in the profit and loss account covering the period to which they belong. Thus, marginal costing does not involve as much subjective judgement, e.g. sorting out methods of apportionment, the selection of absorption (recovery) rates, etc.

Because of the way it is done, the absorption method frequently results in an under- or over-absorption of overheads. However, in marginal costing it is not always such an easy task to separate costs into variable costs and fixed costs, e.g. manufacturing labour being paid a fixed amount whether or not they produce anything. The answer is not always so clear cut, and may involve a judgement.

Dangers

It is dangerous to use absorption costing for decision making, because of the imprecise nature of the costs which it generates. Thus, marginal costing, because of its use of costs which can be traced to the product (or service), and the usefulness of the contribution in making assessments, is recommended for decision-making purposes.

Absorption costing just cannot do a realistic and fair share-out of the costs between jobs or products and between new and old product lines. Proof has been provided in that certain old products are made to bear a share of costs which are really incurred on behalf of new products, the effect being to overstate the profit made by the new product and understate the profit made by the old product. It has been known for such costing methods to result in management deciding to discontinue making old existing products which were really a lot more profitable than shown by the figures produced!

Three of the principal dangers of marginal costing are:

- **The assumption that fixed costs remain unchanged.** This means even in the short term, and that they are a given amount over which management has little or no control. Management must appreciate that step fixed costs do exist and that even in the short term they can exercise a degree of control. For example, they may be able to sublet some offices, retail, warehouse or factory space, or they may be able to reduce their inventory levels of raw materials, fuels, work-in-progress and finished goods, freeing space and fixed assets for other purposes, or they may be able to sell off surplus fixed assets.
- **Growth for the sake of growth.** This may be the result of believing that the only way to increase profitability is to increase the volume of sales. Some of those using marginal costing have assumed that if they increase their sales the profits will also increase. Again, they have failed to realize that certain fixed costs may also rise.
- **The danger of underpricing products.** It could well be, at the end of the day, that the contributions generated are insufficient to cover the fixed overheads. A special price given to a particular customer to land a contract could bring about demands for price cuts from other customers if they find out.

Calculations

Marginal costing calculations are much easier than total absorption costing calculations.

Stock valuations

Marginal costing valuations are more realistic, because they do not include fixed costs. Total absorption costing stock valuations carry forward a portion of the fixed overheads to the next accounting period.

Why use them?

Those who advocate the use of absorption costing point out that, despite its limitations, it is a serious attempt at trying to ensure that all costs are covered. Some justify the inclusion of fixed overheads by stating that production cannot take place without incurring certain fixed overheads. To their minds, absorption costing overcomes the illusion that fixed costs have nothing to do with production. There is also the 'matching' argument, i.e. the costs will be matched against sales revenue in the period in which the sale is made.

To conclude this comparison, it must be noted that whichever method is used to assist with the pricing decision, the likely reactions and prices of competitors, besides the company's own pricing strategy, must be taken into account. Also, marginal costing is advocated for decision-making purposes, but it should be used with care and in conjunction with other data.

Profit statements

We will now illustrate some of the principal differences between the two methods by looking at their effects on profit (or loss) calculations.

An **overhead absorption rate based on production units** will be used for all of the examples and self-assessments.

Unit costs and unit profits

Total absorption costing Values products at their total cost and arrives at a gross profit *en route* to the calculation of the absorption net profit.

Marginal costing Values products at their variable cost and looks at the contribution (as described and illustrated in Chapter 4) before deducting the fixed costs to arrive at the net profit.

Many of the problems which you are likely to encounter may be solved more easily and the calculations checked more quickly if you compute the total cost per unit and the gross profit per unit for total absorption costing; and the variable cost per unit and the contribution per unit for marginal costing.

This aspect should become clearer when you have worked through the following comprehensive example.

Total absorption costing and marginal costing profit statements

The data	Selling price	Variable cost	Fixed cost (overheads)
Per unit	£80	£50	£20
	Period 1 (Units)	Period 2 (Units)	
Opening stock	Nil	300	
Production	2 400	2 400	
Sales	2 100	2 200	
Closing stock	300	500	

The fixed overheads were based on a budget of 2,400 units (i.e. £48,000) for both periods. The actual fixed overheads for each of the periods was the same as the budget.

The marginal costing method uses a contribution approach and excludes the fixed costs from the product costs, the key being the calculation of the contribution as follows:

		Per unit
		£
	Selling price	80
Less	Variable cost	50
	Contribution	**30**

The total absorption costing method includes certain fixed costs which are assigned to products via a predetermined overhead absorption (recovery) rate. In this example the absorption rate is £20 per unit produced. Thus the total absorption method uses a gross profit approach, as follows:

		Per unit	
		£	£
	Selling price		80
Less Total cost:			
	Variable cost	50	
	Fixed cost	20	70
	Gross profit		**10**

The profit statements can now be prepared:

Marginal costing profit statement

	Period 1 £'000	Period 1 £'000		Period 2 £'000	Period 2 £'000
Sales (2100 × £80)		168	(2200 × £80)		176
Less production cost of sales:					
Opening stock	Nil		(300 × £50)	15	
Add Production (2400 × £50 variable cost)	120		(2400 × £50 i.e. the same)	120	
	120			135	
Less Closing stock (300 × £50)	15	105	(500 × £50)	25	110
Contribution (i.e. 2100 × £30)		**63**	(i.e. 2200 × £30)		**66**
Less Fixed costs		48			48
Profit		15	**Profit**		**18**

Total absorption costing profit statement

	Period 1 £'000	£'000		Period 2 £'000	£'000
Sales (as above)		168			176
Less production cost of sales:					
Opening stock	Nil		(300 × £70)	21	
Add Production cost					
2 400 × £50	120			120	
2 400 × £20	48		(the same)	48	
	168			189	
Less Closing stock					
(300 × (£50 + £20))	21	147	(500 × £70)	35	154
Gross profit		21	(2 200 × £10)		22
(i.e. 2 100 × £10)					

The differences in the profit figures are:

	Period 1 £'000	Period 2 £'000
Total absorption costing	21	22
Marginal costing	15	18
Difference in profits	**£6**	**£4**

The difference in the profits is caused by the different ways in which the fixed overheads are treated, and can be reconciled as follows:

	Period 1 £'000	Period 2 £'000
Fixed overheads included in closing stocks (300 × £20 and 500 × £20)	6	10
Less Fixed overheads included in the opening stocks (nil and 300 × £20)	Nil	6
Difference in profits	6	4

Note that in the marginal costing example all stock was valued at the variable cost of £50 per unit, and that with the total absorption costing method all stock was valued at the total cost (i.e. variable cost + fixed overheads) of £70 per unit.

Also note that we arrive at closing stock levels by adding the number of units of opening stock to the number of units produced, and then subtracting the number of units sold (quite a logical calculation). You need to appreciate that the profits were higher under total absorption costing because the amount of fixed overheads carried forward to the next accounting period was higher than that which was brought forward from the preceding accounting period. Therefore, don't automatically assume that profits under the total absorption costing method will always be higher. It all depends on the fixed overheads brought forward from the previous period and carried forward to the next period which have been included in the stock valuations.

Self-assessment 5.1: The Linz Company

The Linz Company had planned to produce and sell 2,000 units of product X for the last two months. However, the actual results obtained were as follows:

	January	February
Sales	1600 units	1400 units
Production	2000 units	2000 units

Additional information available shows that:

- the selling price was £40 per unit;
- the marginal/variable cost was £25 per unit;
- fixed overheads amounted to £16,000 per month (the absorption rate is therefore £8 per unit i.e. £16,000 divided by 2,000 production units);
- there were no opening stocks in January.

You are required to:

1 Compute the profits for January and February, using both the marginal and absorption costing methods.

2 Reconcile the two profit (or loss) figures.

Having completed the introduction examples we will now look at a more complex example involving the under- or over-absorption of overheads.

Letza Von McNeale Co. Ltd

The Letza Von McNeale Co. Ltd started trading on 1 November, 19X2. Their budget for each period is as follows:

			£'000	£'000
Sales	(25000 units)			600
Costs:				
	Fixed		150	
	Variable		250	400
		Gross profit		200
Less	Administration, selling and distribution expenses			60
		Net profit		£140

The following information for the first two trading periods is provided:

Period	Opening stock units	Production units	Sales units	Closing stock units
1	Nil	24 000	20 000	4 000
2	4 000	22 000	23 000	3 000

The fixed costs amounted to £150,000 in each of the periods.

Using the above information we will now prepare two profit statements, one using marginal costing and the other using total absorption costing, and then explain why the profit figures are different. It is assumed that in both of the methods, administration, selling and distribution costs are treated as period costs, i.e. written off in computing the profit (or loss).

Some useful figures:

				Per unit £
From the budget we ascertain the budgeted selling price	=	$\frac{£600\,000}{25\,000 \text{ units}}$	=	24
Less variable cost	=	$\frac{£250\,000}{25\,000 \text{ units}}$	=	10
		Contribution		**14**
Less fixed cost (absorption rate)	=	$\frac{£150\,000}{25\,000 \text{ units}}$	=	6
		Gross profit		**8**

The profit statements using the marginal costing method would be:

Marginal costing profit statement

	Period 1 £'000	£'000		Period 2 £'000	£'000
Sales (20 000 × £24)		480	(23 000 × £24)		552
Less Cost of sales:					
Opening stock	–		(4 000 × £10)	40	
Add Production (24 000 × £10)	240		(22 000 × £10)	220	
	240			260	
Less Closing stock (4 000 × £10)	40	200	(3 000 × £10)	30	230
Contribution		**280**			**322**
Less Fixed costs	150			150	
Administration, selling and distribution costs	60	210		60	210
Profit		**£70**			**£112**
Proof		£'000			£'000
20 000 units sold @ £14 contribution =		280	23 000 units sold @ £14 =		322
which agrees with the total contribution above					

Note that in the absorption costing method the fixed costs are absorbed by production at the rate of £6 for every unit produced. If we produce more units than budget we over-absorb, and if we produce less than the budgeted production units we under-absorb, provided that the actual fixed overheads are the same as the budgeted fixed overheads. The absorption costing profit statement could be drafted as follows:

Total absorption costing profit statement

	Period 1			**Period 2**	
	£'000	**£'000**		**£'000**	**£'000**
Sales (20 000 × £24)		480	(23 000 × £24)		552
Less Cost of sales:					
Opening stock	–		(4 000 × £16)	64	
Add Production cost:					
Variable (24 000 × £10)	240		(22 000 × £10)	220	
Fixed (24 000 × £6)	144		(22 000 × £6)	132	
	384			416	
Less Closing stock					
Variable (4 000 × (£10 + £6))	64	320	(3 000 × £16)	48	368
Gross profit		**160**			**184**
Less Under absorption					
(12000 @ £6)	6		(3 000 × £6)	18	
Administration, selling and distribution costs		66		60	78
	60				
Profit		£94			**£106**
Proof					
20 000 units sold @ £8 per unit gross profit £160 gross profit as above			23 000 @ £8 =		£184

The difference between the two sets of figures results from the carrying forward of fixed costs in the absorption method's stock valuations:

	Period 1	**Period 2**
	£'000	**£'000**
Total absorption costing profits	94	106
Less Marginal costing profits	70	112
	£24	(£6)

	Period 1		**Period 2**
	£'000		**£'000**
Fixed costs c/f in closing stock (4 000 × £6)	24	(3 000 × £6)	18
Less Fixed costs b/f in opening stock	Nil	(4 000 × £6)	24
	£24		(£6)

From this you can observe that we have to take account of the fixed overhead content of both the opening and closing stocks. Note that in practice it is likely that the actual amount of fixed overheads incurred could be more or less than the budgeted figure.

The method of valuation

You should note that any of the methods of stock valuation discussed earlier in this text could be used in the production of the profit statements, i.e. FIFO, LIFO, or AVE CO. The numbers in our illustrations and self-assessments have been kept simple to show you how to produce profit statements using both absorption and marginal costing, and why the results are different. To use FIFO/LIFO etc. would merely mean more complex calculations.

Finally, you should appreciate that over time the profits or losses are the same under both methods, because each method uses the same sales revenue and cost figures.

Now see if you can do the following self-assessment.

Self-assessment 5.2: Barry Bruk Ltd

The following data relate to Barry Bruk Ltd:

Budget	**Opening stock NIL 10 000 units £**	**Per unit £**
Direct materials	100 000	10
Direct wages	60 000	6
Prime cost	160 000	16
Variable overheads	40 000	4
Variable cost	200 000	20
Fixed cost*	50 000	5
Total cost	250 000	25
Sales	300 000	30
Profit	50 000	5
Selling and distribution expenses		£15 000

Period	**Production units**	**Sales units**
1	11 000	9 000
2	9 600	10 000

* Actual fixed costs were £50,000 in each of the periods, i.e. the same as those which were budgeted. There was no opening stock in period 1.

Draw up profit statements, using both absorption costing and marginal costing methods, then reconcile the profit or loss figures obtained by each method for each of the two periods.

Principal differences

Table 5.1 on p. 84 provides a concise review of the principal differences between total absorption costing and marginal costing.

Why do we use total absorption costing?

The arguments in favour of using total absorption costing are:

- To ensure that all costs are covered.
- Because production cannot be achieved without paying fixed overheads. Thus, fixed costs related to production should be included in the product costs. Marginal costing tends to give the impression that fixed costs have nothing at all to do with production.
- It provides a foundation upon which a pricing policy may be developed.
- It attempts to match the costs with the revenues in the period in which the goods are actually sold.
- There is no need to separate costs into fixed cost and variable costs.
- Its use is recommended by SSAP 9 for external reporting purposes *re* the valuation of stocks of work-in-progress and finished goods.

Why use marginal costing?

The reasons put forward for the adoption of marginal costing are:

- It is recognized as being useful for decision-making purposes because the costs generated are more accurate, i.e. the variable costs used can be identified with/ traced to the product/service.
- The contribution, i.e. sales revenue less variable costs, can be used for a multitude of problem-solving activities and the generation of information, e.g. break-even analysis, profit targets, etc.
- It does not involve any under- or over-absorption of overheads.
- Subjective judgements are avoided, e.g. deciding upon methods of apportionment, absorption rates and the estimation of figures such as the machine hours and direct labour hours of each production department/cost centre.

Table 5.1 The characteristics of total absorption costing and marginal costing

Criteria	Total absorption costing	Marginal costing
Makes use of budgeted figures	Yes.	Yes.
The separation of costs	Costs separated into those which can be traced to the cost centre (i.e. allocated costs) and those which cannot be traced, which have to be shared out (i.e. apportioned) using some arbitrary basis.	Costs need to be separated into variable costs and fixed costs. This is not always such an easy task.
Product costs:		
Variable costs	Included.	Included.
Fixed costs	Included (all/most). Some fixed costs may be written off direct to the profit and loss account, e.g. administration cost, selling cost and research and development expenditure.	Excluded. Fixed costs are treated as period costs, i.e. written off in the period to which they relate.
Stock valuation:		
Variable costs	Included.	Included.
Fixed costs	Included (all/most). (Carried forward to next accounting period.)	Excluded. (Not carried forward to next accounting period.)
Recovery of costs	Attempts to make sure that all costs are covered. However, there is likely to be an under- or over-recovery of overheads, because absorption rates have to be predetermined.	Uses only costs which can be traced to the product. Avoids having any under- or over-recovery of overheads.
Subjective judgement	Yes. The exercise of subjective judgement is necessary, *re* the selection of absorption (recovery) rates, choosing a method of apportionment, and dealing with service department costs, etc.	No (on the whole). The costs used can be identified and traced to cost centres/products. Those which cannot, i.e. the fixed costs, are treated as period costs.
Profit	Computed as gross profit and net profit.	Computed as a contribution and net profit.
Reporting	Advocated for external reporting by SSAP 9.	Advocated as being more meaningful for internal reporting.
Decision making	Unsuitable. The costs can never really be described as accurate.	Suitable. The costs used are realistic and more accurate.

- Fixed costs are treated as period costs, i.e. written off during the period in which they were incurred. This means that a lot of overheads which vary more with time than output are not included in the product costs, i.e. are not treated as part of the cost of the output.

Profit reconciliations

If the fixed overhead content of the opening stock is greater than the fixed overhead content of the closing stock, absorption costing will give a lower profit figure than marginal costing.

> **FURTHER READING**
>
> Chadwick L (1997) *Essence of Management Accounting* (2nd Edition), London: Prentice-Hall
>
> Drury C (1994) *Costing, An Introduction* (3rd Edition), London: Chapman and Hall

Total absorption versus marginal costing: additional self-assessments

Self-assessment 5.3: Absorption versus marginal costing multiple-choice test

Select the answers which you consider to be correct to the following multiple-choice problems:

1 Statement of Standard Accounting Practice 9 relating to stocks and work in progress recommended that a total absorption approach be used for:

A external reporting purposes

B internal reporting purposes

C internal and external purposes

D decision-making purposes

2 The budgeted production was 4,200 units per period. The opening stock for period 3 was 400 units, production was 3,700 units and sales 3,800 units. The closing stock for the period is:

A 300 units

B 800 units

3 The budgeted production was 3,000 units per period, the budgeted and actual fixed overheads for the period were £33,000. The actual production was 3,300 units. The fixed overhead absorption rate per unit is:

A £11

B £10

4 The actual and budgeted fixed overheads amounted to £84,000. The budgeted and actual production amounted to 20,000 units and 24,000 units respectively. This means that there will be:

A an under-absorption of £16,800

B an under-absorption of £14,000

C an over-absorption of £16,800

D an over-absorption of £14,000

5 Fixed costs of £18 per unit were included in the opening and closing stocks for absorption costing purposes. For the period under review there were 1,800 units opening stock and 1,200 units closing stock. The total absorption costing profit would be:

A £10,800 greater than the marginal costing profit

B £21,600 greater than the marginal costing profit

C £10,800 less than the marginal costing profit

D £21,600 less than the marginal costing profit

Self-assessment 5.4: Quick questions

1 Define the following terms, using your own words:

(a) period costs;

(b) under- and over-absorption of fixed overheads;

(c) the total or full cost of a product.

2 Why:

(a) did we use the number of production units to absorb the fixed overheads?

(b) is marginal costing considered to be more accurate than absorption costing?

(c) is there a lower degree of subjective judgement in marginal costing?

(d) do we talk about carrying forward fixed overheads in stock valuations under an absorption costing system?

3 (a) Explain briefly the principal differences between marginal costing and absorption costing.

(b) Explain how profit statements prepared using each of the methods can be reconciled.

Self-assessment 5.5: Jon Avi plc

Jon Avi plc commenced trading on 1 July 19X7 to manufacture and distribute a patented mountaineering product called the 'peakgrip'. The company's budget for each of two three-month periods is:

		£'000	£'000
Sales	25 000 units @ £20		500
Manufacturing cost:			
Variable costs @ £8		200	
Fixed overhead @ £7		175	375
	Gross profit:		125
Less Fixed selling & distribution costs			45
	Net profit:		80

The following data relates to the first two periods:

	Period 1 Units	Period 2 Units
Production	22 000	24 000
Sales	20 000	23 000

Assume that the actual fixed costs and actual fixed selling and distribution expenses are the same as the budget for each period. *You are required to*:

1 Prepare a total absorption profit statement for each period.

2 Prepare a marginal costing profit statement for each period.

3 Reconcile the profits.

Self-assessment 5.6: Clab & Co Ltd (I)

You have been supplied with the following information:
Budgeted fixed production overhead cost per unit £20 for each period.

This was computed: $\frac{\text{£500 000 budgeted fixed production overhead}}{\text{25 000 units budgeted production units for the period}}$

	Period 1 Units	Period 2 Units
Sales	20 000	24 000
Opening stock	Nil	7 000
Production	27 000	24 500
Closing stock	7 000	7 500
	£	£
Actual fixed production overheads	500 000	500 000
Variable cost per unit	40	40
Selling price per unit	116	116
Fixed selling and distribution expenses	730 000	730 000

You are required to:

1 Calculate the gross profit for each period using the total absorption costing method.

2 Calculate the contribution for each period using the marginal costing method.

3 For the total absorption method, calculate the under- or over-absorption for each period.

Self-assessment 5.7: Clab & Co Ltd (II)

Using the data supplied in 5.6, now see if you can prepare a profit statement for each period:

1 using the total absorption costing approach;

2 using the marginal costing approach; and

3 reconcile the two sets of figures.

6

Activity Based Costing

LEARNING OBJECTIVES

Having completed this chapter, including the self-assessments, you should be able to:

- appreciate why there is a need for ABC;
- understand how ABC works;
- define what is meant by:
  - resource cost
  - resource cost drivers
  - activity cost pools
  - activity cost drivers
  - cost objectives;
- select appropriate activity cost drivers for various activity cost pools;
- prepare activity based product cost computations and profit statements;
- appreciate the problems associated with using ABC.

Why is there a need for ABC?

As you may have observed from your review of the chapter on total absorption costing, that particular method of costing does have several problems and limitations. ABC (activity based costing) evolved as a result of the need to develop something which was more sophisticated and realistic compared with total absorption costing. It also developed in response to the changes which had, and were, taking place in the business environment. For example, production costs nowadays tend to include significant amounts spent on support activities such as setting, inspection and production scheduling. These costs tend to vary more with the range and complexity of the products which are being produced.

Activity based costing is a relatively new technique and was developed in the USA by R. Cooper and R. S. Kaplan during the late 1980s with the spread of advanced manufacturing technology (AMT). In an AMT environment it is acknowledged that production processes are far more complex in companies producing an increasingly diverse range of products for more sophisticated consumers. Greater variety in product ranges, more sophisticated and high-tech production processes, shorter product life cycles, higher quality expectations and increased competition have all played their part in increasing complexity. Thus there has been a need to recognize the importance of overheads. As a result direct labour costs represent a smaller proportion of total cost than they did in the past when material and labour costs were the dominant production costs.

Companies/departments/cost centres whose products are more diverse and complex than those of other companies/departments/cost centres, tend to make much more use of support services such as those mentioned in this chapter.

The technological support which is now available has made the use of systems such as ABC much more feasible than it was a number of years ago.

What is it?

CIMA has defined activity based costing as:

'cost attribution to cost units on the basis of benefit received from direct activities e.g. ordering, set-up, assuring quality'.

CIMA (Chartered Institute of Management Accountants) Official Terminology, 1991

ABC is concerned with the consumption of resources and the need to:

- understand the behaviour of overhead costs;
- ascertain which activities cause these overhead costs.

ABC states that activities cause costs and that the products/services consume the activities. It is used for the management of a firm's *output mix*, i.e. deciding what to produce via more accurate product costs, and their *activity mix*, i.e. ensuring that the products are produced in the most efficient way, e.g. improved design and the identification of surplus capacity.

How does ABC work?

ABC forces management to consider what causes the cost. It uses multiple *cost drivers* in order to attribute costs to activities and cost objects. Thus, overheads can be related to the activities which cause them, i.e. which drive them and make them happen. Figure 6.1 should help you to understand how this works.

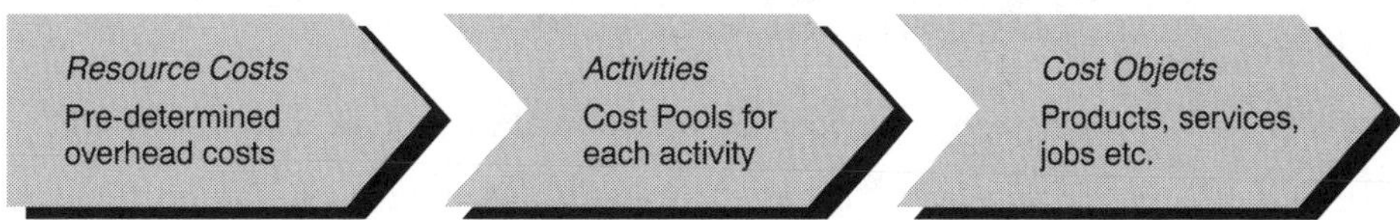

Figure 6.1 How activity based costing works

Resource costs

Direct costs such as direct materials, direct labour and direct expenses do not present a major problem. They can be charged directly to the product, service, contract or job concerned. The overheads, you may recall, consist of the indirect costs such as the rent and insurance of the premises, cleaners, wages, and expenditure on the maintenance of various fixed assets. As with total absorption costing the overheads still have to be estimated in advance by taking into account not only past performance, but also utilizing updated information about the future from the company's own budgets, plans and data received/collected.

Those overheads (described in ABC as resource costs) which can be identified and traced to a cost pool (described in ABC as an activity), can be allocated to the cost pool concerned. Those which cannot be identified with a cost pool will have to be *apportioned* to the cost pools by means of *resource cost drivers*, which could include:

- area of cubic capacity;
- the number of employees;
- the number of machine hours;
- the number of labour hours.

Costs such as short-term variable costs will vary with output and can therefore be shared out using a volume based cost driver such as direct labour hours. However as mentioned above, many overheads vary more with time than output. In addition, a significant proportion may also vary with various consuming activities, which are non-volume related. Thus, resource costs can be either allocated (identified with) cost pools or apportioned using an appropriate cost driver which measures the consumption/usage of the resource by the activities.

Activity cost drivers

Having shared out the resource costs between the various activities (cost pools), the next step is to assign the activity costs to the cost objects e.g. products, services, etc. This is done by using activity cost drivers to apportion such costs and/or allocating the whole of the cost pool in cases where it is specific to the particular product or service.

The activity cost drivers may be at the:

- *unit level* – i.e. activities performed every time a unit is produced;
- *product level* – i.e. activities which ensure that the product is produced;
- *batch level* – i.e. activities which are performed every time a batch is produced;
- *plant level* – i.e. activities which ensure that facilities are sustained, e.g. cleaning, insurance, etc.

It must be stressed once more that activities cause the costs, and the products and services, etc. consume those activities. It must also be pointed out that many of the activity cost drivers used are not related to output and reflect the fact that the transactions concerned have been incurred by the support departments. A summary of some of the better-known activity cost drivers is shown in Figure 6.2.

ACTIVITY COST POOL	ACTIVITY COST DRIVER (COST DRIVER)
Advertising	the value of sales in each sales area
Despatch	the number of despatch notes or number of deliveries to customers
Inspection	the number of inspections
Material handling	the number of times that the material is handled
Production scheduling	number of production runs
Purchasing	the number of purchase orders
Receiving (goods inwards)	the number of goods received notes/goods inward notes
Set-up costs	the number of set-ups, or number of production runs
Stores	the number of stores issue notes

Figure 6.2 Activity cost pools and cost drivers

Thus, as you should have observed from a review of Figures 6.1 and 6.2, ABC depends on how well it can assign the resource costs to activity pools via resource cost drivers, and assigns the activity cost pool costs to objects via the activity cost drivers. Some of the principal problems associated with this method are:

- the estimation of resources which will be consumed by cost objects e.g. products/ services, etc.;
- the choice of resource cost drivers;
- the identification of the activities;
- the selection of the appropriate activity cost drivers.

We will now review the content to date via the following self-assessment.

Self-assessment 6.1

1 Why is there a need for activity based costing?

2 How does ABC work?

3 Name two resource cost drivers which can be used to assign resource costs to activities.

4 Name three activity cost drivers which can be used to assign activity cost pools to cost objects.

5 Name, for ABC purposes, three cost objectives.

6 Circle the letter which you consider denotes the correct answer for the multi-choice questions which follow:

(a) In ABC costs are described as being caused by:

A activities

B resources

C cost objectives

D products or services

(b) In ABC which of the following can be described as cost objectives?

A activities

B products or services

C cost pools

D resource costs

(c) For short-term variable costs which vary with output the most likely cost driver to be used for sharing it out between the cost pools would be:

A direct labour hours

B indirect labour hours

C number of despatch notes

D number of inspectors

(d) Which of the following activity cost pools has been matched up correctly with an appropriate cost driver?

	Activity	*Cost driver*
A	receiving	number of goods inward notes
B	receiving	number of goods outward notes
C	material handling	number of goods inward notes
D	material handling	number of goods outward notes

Compare your attempts for questions 1–5 with the appropriate part of this chapter. The correct solutions will be found in Appendix 2.

A comprehensive example

The following comprehensive, yet simplified example, should help you to understand and appreciate the way in which the mechanics of ABC work.

We have deliberately used a small number of resource costs categorized into types according to their resource cost drivers for *JRC Ltd*, which are as follows:

Resource costs	**£'000s**	**Resource cost driver**
Type 1	110	Number of employees
Type 2	70	Number of labour hours
Type 3	50	Number of computer hours
	230	

The consumption of each resource cost by the activity cost pools is to be found by taking into account the following *information:*

	JRC Ltd ACTIVITY COST POOLS					
	Total	**Purchasing**	**Setting**	**Scheduling**	**Material handling**	**Despatch**
Number of:						
Employees	22	9	4	3	3	3
Labour hours	28 000	Nil	120 000	100 000	60 000	Nil
Computer hours	10 000	3 000	Nil	1 000	5 000	1 000
Allocated costs* (£000)	85	40	10	5	20	10

* These are the resource costs, which can be identified and traced to a particular activity cost pool. Knowing the above information we can now compute the amount of resource costs which are applicable to each activity cost pool, as shown below.

	JRC Ltd ACTIVITY COST POOLS					
	Total	**Purchasing**	**Setting**	**Scheduling**	**Material handling**	**Despatch**
	£'000	**£'000**	**£'000**	**£'000**	**£'000**	**£'000**
Allocated	85	40	10	5	20	10
Type 1	110	45	20	15	15	15
Type 2	70	Nil	30	25	15	Nil
Type 3	50	15	Nil	5	25	5
	315	100	60	50	75	30

We now need to know the activity cost driver information, which is as follows:

	JRC Ltd PRODUCTS			
	Total	**J**	**R**	**C**
Number of: Purchase orders	75 000	4 800	2 000	700
Set-ups	1 000	740	140	120
Production runs	400	240	120	40
Despatch notes	1 500	800	400	300

Knowing this, we can calculate the activity cost drivers, as follows:

	Purchasing	Setting	Scheduling	Material handling	Despatch
	£'000	**£'000**	**£'000**	**£'000**	**£'000**
Activity cost (*as above*)	100	60	50	75	30
Activity cost driver	7 500 orders	1 000 set-ups	400 production runs	400 production runs	1 500 notes
Activity cost	**£13.33 per order**	**£60 per set-up**	**£125 per run**	**£187.5 per run**	**£20 per note**

Finally, we can now calculate the consumption of the activity cost pools by the products:

	JRC Ltd PRODUCTS			
	J	**R**	**C**	**Total**
Purchasing @ £13.33 Per order	64 000	26 666	9 334	100 000
Setting @ £60 per set-up	44 400	8 400	7 200	60 000
Scheduling @ £125 per run	30 000	15 000	5 000	50 000
Material handling @ £187.5 per run	45 000	22 500	7 500	75 000
Despatch @ £20 per note	16 000	8 000	6 000	30 000
	£199 400	£80 566	£35 034	£315 000

Thus, it can be observed that the above costs do not vary with bases such as direct labour hours, machine hours or production units but with the activity which causes the cost. Note that the activity is divided between the various products by means of the activity cost drivers, as illustrated above.

For those who have to sit an examination which includes ABC, note that a vast number of the questions which tend to be set start with the costs already assigned to the activity cost pools. You should also note that in practice there would be many more resource costs and many more activity cost pools.

ABC and total absorption costing – a comparison

The total overhead costs in JRC Ltd which were allocated and distributed to activity cost pools amounted to £315,000.

In a total absorption costing system, these overheads would find their way into the product costs via a direct labour hours or machine hours absorption rate (or some other basis such as a percentage of prime cost).

If, in the JRC Ltd example, the direct labour hours applicable to each product were:

	J	R	C	Total
Direct labour hours	90 000	112 500	22 500	225 000
The overheads apportioned would be (see W1 below):	£126 000	£157 500	£31 500	£315 000

W1 $\frac{\text{£315 000 overhead costs}}{\text{225 000 direct labour hours}}$ = £1.4 per direct labour hour

	J	R	C	Total
Overheads assigned to product using ABC (as above)	£199 400	£80 566	£35 034	£315 000
Difference	(£73 400)	£76 934	(£3 534)	

Observations

It can be observed that in this example there are significant variations in the figures produced by the two methods. This is caused by the total absorption costing method using direct labour hours to charge the overheads to the products when in fact they are being driven by other cost drivers.

ABC profit statements

An ABC profit statement should not present a problem and the format for such a statement could be drafted along the following lines:

ABC profit statement six months to 30/6/XI				
	Product J £'000	Product R £'000	Product C £'000	Total £'000
Sales (a)				
Less product costs	£'000	£'000	£'000	£'000
Materials				
Labour				
Purchasing costs				
Setting				
Scheduling				
Material handling				
Despatch				
(b)				
Profit (a) − (b)				

The problems associated with ABC

- *Predetermination* As with total absorption costing the overheads still have to be estimated at the outset.
- *Selection of resource cost drivers and activity cost drivers* This is not such an easy task. A single cost driver may not be appropriate for dealing with all of the costs included in an activity cost pool.
- *The estimation of cost driver hours/runs/notes, etc.* Whether it is the number of direct labour hours, machine hours, computer hours, production runs, despatch notes or set-ups, etc. the fact remains that they *all* have to be predetermined and estimated before the start of the period to which they relate.
- *Cost/benefit* The increased cost of the sophistication needed should not outweigh the benefits of using such a system.
- *Managerial action* If management are to be effective via the use of ABC, they need to take action on certain outcomes revealed by the figures.
- *Direct costs* Certain costs such as direct labour are directly chargeable to the product and should not be included in the activity cost pools. Overheads consist of the *indirect* materials, labour and expenditure.
- *Questionable cost drivers* It is a matter of option, and questionable whether certain cost drivers do in fact provide a fair and equitable distribution of the activity being consumed e.g. the number of purchase orders, despatch notes, issue notes, etc. The true picture could reveal a much more complex situation, e.g. some orders take up far more time and effort than others.

Conclusion

As cost and management accounting systems go, ABC is still relatively new, and most definitely a step in the right direction. In the quest for realistic costs the author hypothesizes that there will be more multi-variable approaches developed, perhaps for each activity cost pool. However, ABC is a big improvement when compared with total absorption costing, providing costs which are more accurate and some degree of control over the activities which drive them.

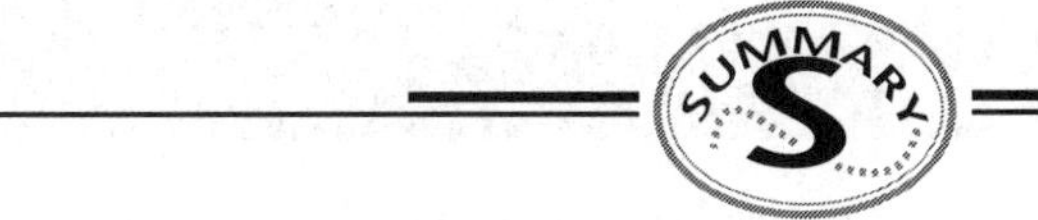

ABC (activity based costing) works on the premise that products/services (cost objects) do not cause costs and that *costs are caused by activities.* The products simply *consume* the activities.

In an environment in which labour costs are relatively low in proportion to the total product cost, production methods and processes have tended to become more and more complex. By recognizing this, and using resource cost drivers and activity cost drivers, ABC should provide more realistic and reliable product costs than those which are generated via total absorption costing. Many of the resource costs and activities are not volume based and for many of them the use of direct labour hours or machine hours could be totally inappropriate.

The use of ABC forces management to review and reappraise the way in which their business operates and to focus on clearly defined activity cost pools. However, it is not always an easy task to obtain such a clear focus and to identify appropriate cost drivers.

ABC is therefore, a system in which

- activities cause costs;
- products consume the activities;
- resource cost drivers and activity cost drivers provide the means by which overheads can be included in product/service costs;
- management can focus on what causes the demand for the resources; clearly defining their activity cost pools; and the identification of appropriate cost drivers;
- more realistic product costs are possible when compared with total absorption costing.

FURTHER READING

Drury C (1994) *Costing, An Introduction* (3rd Edition), London: Chapman & Hall

Ryan B (1995) *Strategic Accounting for Management*, London: Dryden

Weetman P (1996) *Management Accounting*, London: Pitman

Williamson D (1996) *Cost and Management Accounting*, London: Prentice Hall

There are also numerous very detailed US texts.

ABC: additional self-assessments

Self-assessment 6.2: Jonbur Ltd

Jonbur Ltd produce three products, J, O and N. The following budgeted overhead resource costs, together with their resource cost drivers, relate to the forthcoming period:

Resource cost	£'000	Resource cost driver
Indirect labour	60	Number of employees
Lighting heating & office space	300	Square metres
Computing	200	Computer hours

Details of the activity cost pools and resource cost drivers are as follows:

	Activity cost pools			
	Purchasing	Receiving	Despatch	Total
Number of employees	4	2	2	8
Square metres	4000	8000	8000	20000
Computing hours	20000	2000	3000	25000

The data relating to the activity cost drivers is:

Activity cost Pool	Activity cost Driver	Products			
		J	O	N	Total
Purchasing	No. of orders	5000	2000	1000	8000
Receiving	No. of received notes	4200	1000	840	6040
Despatch	No. of despatch notes	3000	500	500	4000

You are required to:

1 Using an ABC approach, calculate the overheads which will be assigned to each of the products.

Self-assessment 6.3: Vike Trading Co. Ltd

Activity cost pools for Vike Trading Co. Ltd for the period, have been computed and are as follows:

Material handling	Set-up costs	Scheduling	Purchasing	Total
£'000	£'000	£'000	£'000	£'000
32	40	36	20	128

Four product ranges are produced, V, I, K and E, and the prime cost (i.e. direct labour, materials and expenses) are:

V	I	K	E	Total
£'000	£'000	£'000	£'000	£'000
50	30	20	40	140

The activity cost drivers used to assign the activity cost pools, are as follows:

Activity	Driver	V	I	K	E	Total
Material handling	No. of production runs	4	6	4	2	16
Set-up costs	No. of set-ups	40	10	20	10	80
Scheduling	No. of production runs	4	6	4	2	16
Purchasing	No. of orders	100	180	40	80	400

The product sales revenue (assuming they are all sold) is:

V	I	K	E	Total
£'000	£'000	£'000	£'000	£'000
80	120	110	90	400

You are required to:

1 Calculate the profit or loss made by each product line using activity based costing.

Self-assessment 6.4: L.E. Tza plc

L.E. Tza plc manufactures three products, details of which are as follows:

Product	Volume units	Material cost per unit (£)	Direct labour per unit (hours)	Labour cost per unit (£)	Selling price per unit
BG	500	12	3	5	80.00
LT	8000	10	10	20	110.00
MD	700	8	5	9	90.00

The overheads for the period under review are as follows:

	£000
Material handling	85
Set-up costs	60
Maintenance costs	90
Despatch costs	75
Storage cost	200
	510

Details for the cost drivers which are to be used for activity based costing purposes are:

Activity	Cost drivers	BG	LT	MD	Total
Material handling	No. of requisitions	2000	1000	1000	4000
Set-up costs	No. of set-ups	75	50	75	200
Maintenance costs	No. of call outs	30	50	45	125
Despatch costs	No. of despatch notes	520	460	620	1600
Storage costs	Floor area (sq.m.)	1200	7400	1400	10000

You are required to:

1 Calculate the overhead which would be assigned to each product:

(a) using total absorption costing, based on direct labour hours, and

(b) using activity based costing.

2 Produce brief profit statements for each of the above methods.

3 Discuss the implications of the picture which is revealed by the review.

Budgetary Control

Budgeting is a vast and very important managerial accounting area. This chapter is intended as a gentle introduction to the subject. In order to make you aware of the fundamentals, it takes a key word approach to explain the planning, organization and control aspects of budgeting. It then uses an open-learning-type approach to introduce you to cash budgeting and the preparation of budgeted profit and loss accounts and balance sheets.

LEARNING OBJECTIVES

When you have read this chapter, you should be able to:

- understand the principles of budgetary control via a knowledge of the key words;
- prepare a cash budget and a budgeted profit and loss account and balance sheet;
- work out the closing stock figure from incomplete data;
- prepare a flexible budget.

Definitions

A *budget* has been defined by CIMA (Chartered Institute of Management Accountants) as:

> A plan expressed in money. It is prepared and approved prior to the budget period and may show income, expenditure and the capital to be employed. May be drawn up showing incremental effects on former budgeted or actual figures, or may be compiled by zero-based budgeting.

Budgetary control has been defined by CIMA as:

> The establishment of budgets relating the reponsibilities of executives to the requirements of a policy, and the continuous comparison of actual with budgeted results either to secure by individual action the objective of that policy or to provide a basis for its revision.

A *budget centre* is defined by CIMA as:

> A section of an entity for which control may be exercised and budgets prepared.

Having read the above definitions you may find that it is not so easy to pick out and identify key points. However, the key words outlined in the following pages should enable you to appreciate not only the importance of those which are present in the definitions, but also other key words which are not included.

From a budgeting point of view, planning tends to encompass the following activities.

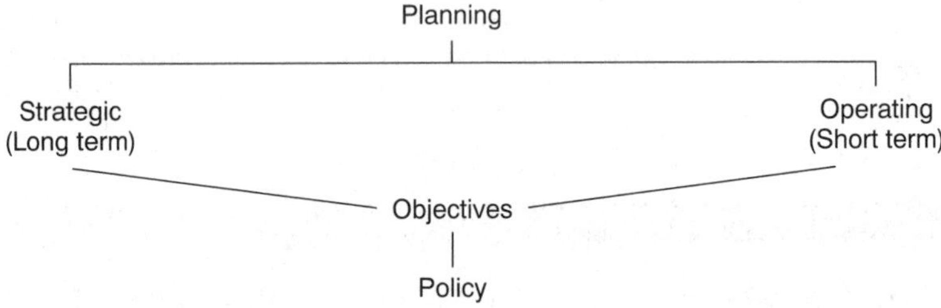

Figure 7.1 **The planning process**

Resource allocation The efficient use of the scarce resources which the company/ organization has at its disposal, e.g. finance, labour, equipment, etc.

Performance Planning not, for example, what sales, or costs or profits are going to be, but what they *should* be, given normal efficient operating conditions. This should involve the setting of targets against which to measure performance.

Monitoring The external and internal environments in which the company/organization operates must be monitored. Plans have to be based on a set of assumptions about the future. The monitoring needs to be a continuous process, so that budgets can be fine-tuned and amended to take account of environmental changes. This should help ensure that rolling (progressive) budgeting can be used, whereby budgets are reviewed and revised at regular intervals, e.g. monthly.

Strategic planning Strategic planning in relation to budgeting covers the long term and the medium term, and is concerned particularly with corporate objectives, which may be expressed in terms of profitability (return on capital employed), market share, take-over strategy, etc.

What is defined as long or medium term will to a great extent depend upon the nature of the industry. For example, in aerospace long term could be 15–20 years, medium term 5–15 years and short term under five years.

The limiting factor (also called the principal budget factor or key factor) This must be identified from the outset, before the commencement of the budget preparation process, e.g. production capacity or sales demand, as it dictates what a company/organization can or cannot do.

Operating planning This covers the short term and is usually broken down into periods of six or twelve months, and then further subdivided into weeks or months for control purposes.

The policy This is the means by which the objectives, long- and short-term, are to be achieved. Policies to be followed could relate to: the quality of products and/or service; marketing; R&D dividends; financing; take-overs, etc.

Note that in budgeting we are dealing with the future, for which we have to produce estimated forecasts. Thus, budgetary planning is about the predetermination of costs, revenues and profits, etc.

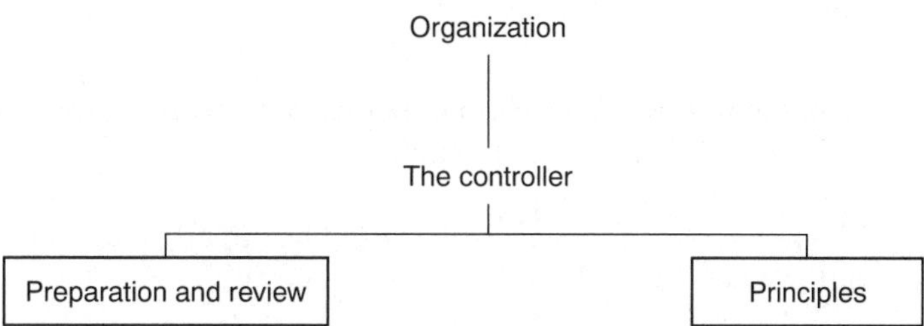

Figure 7.2 The organization of budgets

The controller To a large extent, the success of a budgetary control system depends upon the ability and energy of the controller. The controller should:

- be able to secure the co-operation and commitment of the personnel involved;
- produce a budget preparation timetable;
- organize meetings;
- provide information to appropriate personnel to assist them with their budget preparation task;
- communicate clearly to, and co-ordinate and motivate those involved to work together e.g. to review and revise budgets to ensure that objectives are achieved;
- see that the functional budgets, e.g. sales, production, etc. and master budget, i.e. budgeted profit and loss account and balance sheet are ready for implementation by the due date.

The controller and others charged with budgetary planning and organization process should try to consider the following factors if their budgets are to be effective:

Participation This frequently overlooked or ignored principle of good budgeting can save a lot of money, time and effort. By involving those who are 'in the know', the budgets or targets should be more realistic, relevant and acceptable. Some of the meetings should involve not only managers and supervisors, but also shop-floor workers.

Motivation Involving personnel in the budget preparation process, together with good clear communications and budget education, should improve employee motivation. The setting or imposing of unrealistic targets, which results from a lack of consultation, can have dramatic demotivating effects. Targets need to be negotiated, realistic and attainable.

Constraints The limiting factor/principal budget factor mentioned earlier must be recognized, and appropriate action decided upon. This is important, because budgets are interrelated. For instance, budgeted stocks or purchasing of materials is linked to the production budget, the production budget is closely related to the sales budget, and so on.

Behavioural aspects Human beings are involved in the budgeting process, and do not act in the same way to similar situations.

The following are areas which should be of particular concern to management because of their behavioural implications:

- The setting of targets and standards. This involves the setting of goals which are fair and attainable. Unattainable goals will only promote conflict and cause frustration.
- The budget as a 'whipping post', i.e. organizational problems or variances resulting from comparisons being blamed on 'the budget'. It is important that the cause of such problems and variances should be identified and communicated clearly to management.
- Budgets put people under pressure, as in the case of 'control by responsibility' (see p. 107) *re* production targets, sales targets and budgeted overhead expenditure.
- Some personnel may not be aware of what the budget is, or what it is trying to do. This is why staff education is necessary on a continuing basis.
- Budgets can lead to a 'blinkered' approach. This may be the case where a particular function or department achieves its budget targets, but at the expense of all/some of the other functions.
- Participation. This principle of good budgeting should be introduced and used with care. Problems can arise by the involvement of some employees and not others in the budget preparation process and the setting of targets, etc.

It is accepted that budgets are intended to affect human behaviour and that human behaviour cannot always be predicted. The human element must always be taken into account and carefully evaluated and monitored at frequent intervals.

Thus steps will need to be taken to eliminate personal bias and avoid false perceptions. Hence the need for clear communications of objectives, policies, reports and information.

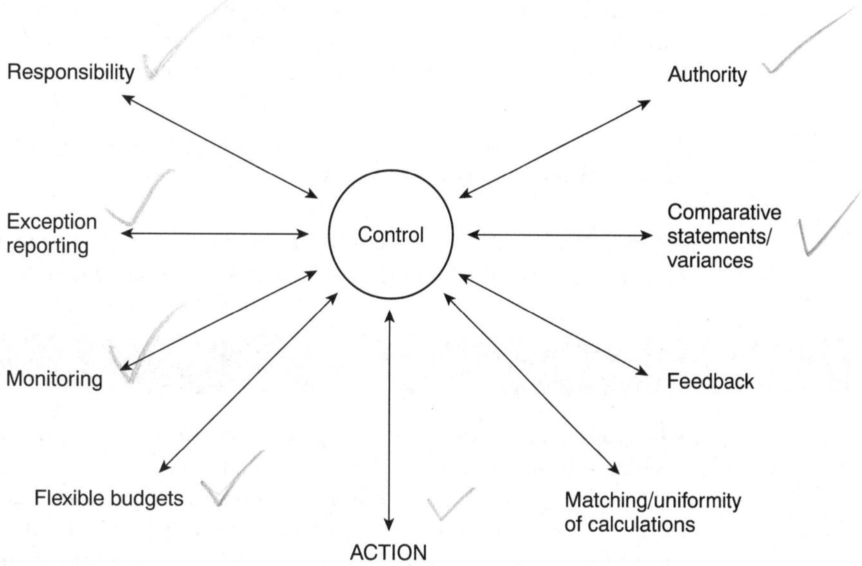

Figure 7.3 Control in budgeting

Responsibility Control by responsibility operates by making an individual (or group of people) responsible for the achievement of a particular target, e.g. sales or production, or responsible for the control of specific costs, e.g. capital expenditure, purchasing, etc.

Authority A sound budgeting system requires clear lines of authority. From an audit point of view, authority is also a very important key word. Authority needs to be delegated for budget preparation, cash flow management, materials management, the taking of action, e.g. to remedy an adverse situation revealed in a budget and actual comparative statement.

Exception reporting 'Management by exception' is a technique which highlights those items which are not going to plan. An exception statement or report simply draws the attention of management to specific problem areas, rather like saying, 'spend some of your valuable time putting right something which is going wrong.'

Budget and actual comparative statements These look at the position on a regular basis, e.g. each week or month. Adverse variances are highlighted and their causes investigated and reported on. In effect, it acts as an early warning system of deviations from planned performance.

Monitoring In addition to monitoring the environment in which the firm or organization operates, control systems should also be monitored to ensure that they are working properly and fulfilling their purpose.

Feedback It is essential that those who design, prepare and/or use budgets are provided with relevant feedback at frequent intervals. Feedback should be an integral part of any system of budgetary control.

Flexible budgets Budgets which are designed to change with the level of activity are considered to be better for control purposes. Budgeted and actual figures which are being compared should relate to the same levels of activity.

Matching/uniformity of calculations Budgeted figures and actual figures should be arrived at using the same content and calculations.

Action The final stage of control consists of taking appropriate corrective action in response to the information supplied in statements and reports.

Interrelationships

All budgets are really part of a jigsaw which forms the master budget. They are all very closely linked and interrelated. In the absence of some other limiting factor the usual starting point in the budgeting process is the sales budget, which is used as a basis for determining the production needed to meet the sales needs, which in turn is used to assess how much is needed by way of material requirements, labour requirements, capital expenditure requirements, and so on.

The following example should help to consolidate this point:

Single product
Budgeted sales 50 000 units @ £10 each
Budgeted opening stock 4 000 units
Closing stock 6 400 units
Components used to produce single product:

Ref	Per unit
X639Z	8
X665Z	5
N431P	2 litres

From this we can work out the production budget in terms of units, by *working back* firstly using calculation 1 and then calculation 2, as follows:

		Units	
	Opening stock	4000	
Add	Production (2)	52400	(56400 − 4000) = 52400 (calculation 2)
	(1)	56400	(50000 + 6400) = 56400 (calculation 1)
Less	Closing stock	6400	
	Units sold:	50000	

* Production budget = 52400 units

The material requirements would therefore be:

Material ref	X639Z	X665Z	N431P
Usage	8 × 52400	5 × 52400	2 litres × 52400
Materials budget	419200 units	262000 units	104800 litres

Having achieved a matching in terms of quantity, the quantities could then be priced and valued.

Note that this process may reveal a limiting factor/principal budget factor if this is not already known, i.e. a constraint which places a limitation on what can be done. Thus, the real starting point in the budget preparation process should be to identify the limiting factor/principal budget factor and to decide what action, if any, has to be taken. It is no use making the starting point sales, if there is insufficient production capacity!

Cash budgets

The cash budget is a period-by-period account of the cash which is expected to come in, and the cash which is expected to go out. In arriving at the balance at the end of the period, the previous period's balance has to be brought forward. The figures used have to be forecast in advance, hence cash budgeting's other name, cash flow forecast. You will find that many organizations prepare month-by-month cash budgets, working several months ahead.

You should note that the purpose of a cash budget is to:

- ensure that cash is available when needed;
- identify when there is going to be a shortage of cash;
- identify when there is going to be surplus cash.

* First, (calculation 1) add together the budget sales units of 50,000 to the budgeted closing stock units of 6,400 which equals 56,400 units. Then, (calculation 2) deduct the opening stock of 4,000 units from the 56,400 units to arrive at the 52,400 production units as illustrated above.

The cash graph

You can plot the estimated monthly cash or bank balances on a cash graph. In addition to showing negative and positive balances, the bank overdraft limit will also be shown on the cash graph. Figure 7.4 is an example.

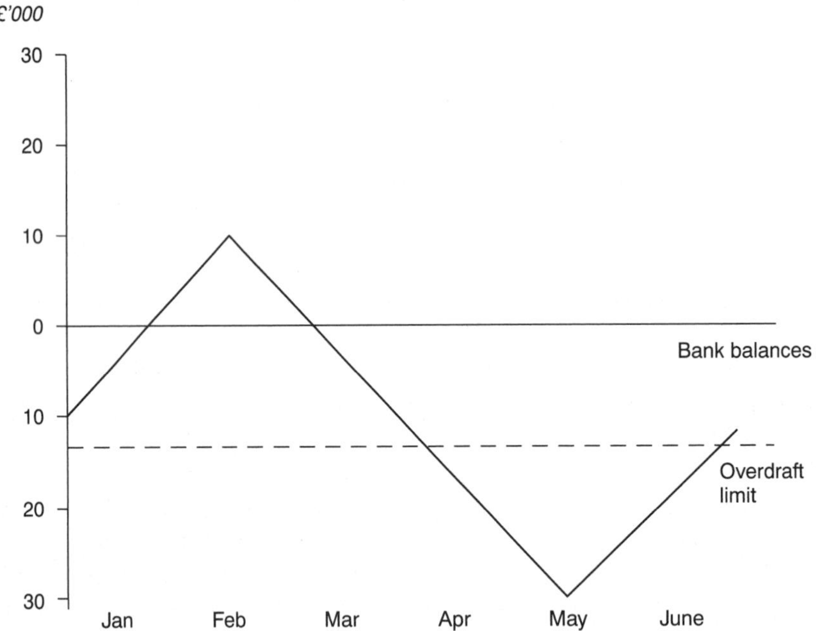

Figure 7.4 The cash graph

You can see at a glance that if action is not taken, the overdraft limit will be exceeded in May. Forecasting this position well in advance will enable the business concerned to take early remedial action.

Self-assessment 7.1: Dacroo Ltd cash graph

Using the information provided, can you now plot the balances for the following six months on the cash graph provided below and briefly comment on the position disclosed?

Estimated bank balances

	£'000
Balance brought forward	(5) i.e. an overdraft
July	5
Aug	(10)
Sept	10
Oct	25
Nov	20
Dec	5

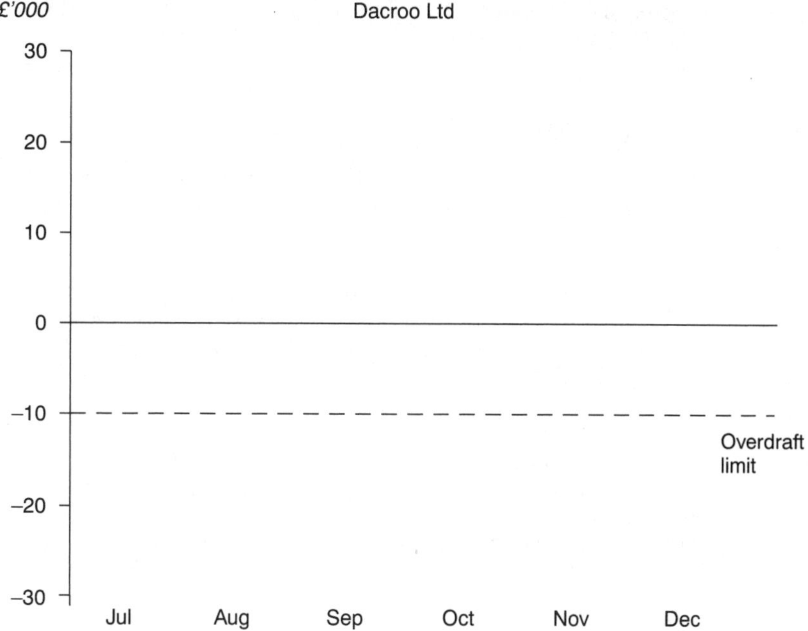

Action

If the cash budget reveals a future shortage of funds the company may:

- renegotiate their overdraft limit, or put a case to their bankers for a temporary increase in their overdraft limit; or
- take action themselves, such as: improving credit control; taking longer credit periods from suppliers; delaying paying for a fixed asset; disposing of surplus stocks; selling some of their investments, etc.

Where the cash budget indicates a surplus, it may be possible to invest the surplus short term, rather than leave it to earn nothing in a bank current account.

Cash budget computations

The principal rules which you should follow when preparing cash budgets are as follows:

- Pick up the opening balance at the start of the budget period.
- Calculate the amounts expected to be received from customers or paid out to creditors by taking into account the periods of credit which are allowed.
- You must not include non-cash items, such as depreciation, in the cash budget.
- You need to remember that the closing balance which you calculate for one month becomes the opening balance of the next month. Thus, what really matters is when

the cash is expected to flow in or out, not the period covered by the receipt or payment.

Activity: Mr and Mrs Rice

We will now apply the principles described above to the following, somewhat over-simplified example.

Mr and Mrs Rice will be opening their new business, a retail shop selling beers, wines and spirits, in January 19X4. They have provided you with the following information and have asked if you can produce a cash budget which has been requested by their bank manager.

	£
They will pay £50 000 cash into the business on 1 January 19X4	
Rent on premises, payment due on 1 January 19X4 and 1 April 19X4 (per quarter)	500
Cash outlay on equipment received in January, payable in February 19X4	60 000
Monthly planned purchases of stock for resale:	
January	20 000
February	24 000
March to June (per month)	30 000
All stock is bought on one months' credit	
Monthly planned sales are:	
January	10 000
February	16 000
March	28 000
April–June (per month)	40 000
All sales are on two months' credit	

Monthly cash outlay on general expenses is expected to be £650.
Wages and salaries are expected to be £1 200 per month.
Depreciation of equipment in the first half-year is estimated at £3 000.
The closing stock of beers, wines and spirits amounts to £48 000 at 30 June 19X4.
It is hoped that any temporary excess of payments over receipts will be financed by a bank overdraft.
(There are no missing figures in this example.)

See if you can follow these step by step instructions as we complete their cash budget.

1. First, you should have observed that there are no missing figures.
2. You simply ignore the depreciation, as it is a non-cash item.
3. Next you pick up the opening balance at bank on 1 January 19X4, which in this case is the initial capital introduced of £50,000.
4. You then enter the sales, taking into account the fact that there are two months' credit; for example, the January sales cash will not be received until March, and so on.
5. Next you enter the purchases in which there is a one-month credit period. This means the January purchases will be paid for in February.
6. You then enter the rent paid in January and April, the months in which the rent is actually paid in cash. You also complete the wages and salaries column and the

general expenses column. Finally you record the equipment in the fixed assets column as being paid for in February.

7 Having completed inserting all of the information, vertical column by vertical column, you now start with January and work out the closing balance, horizontal column by horizontal column. The closing balance in each calculation becomes the opening balance of the next column, and so on until you reach the end of June. Note that the opening balance, plus inflows less outflows, equals the closing balances. However, if your opening balance is an overdraft, take care!

Mr and Mrs Rice Cash budget (cash flow forecast) (steps (3) to (6))*

	INFLOWS		OUTFLOWS					
19X4	Opening balance	Sales (4)	Purchases (5)	Rent (6)	Wages and salaries (6)	General expenses (6)	Fixed assets (6)	Closing balance
	£	£	£	£	£	£	£	£
Jan. (3)	50000	–	–	500	1200	650	–	______
Feb.	–	–	20000	–	1200	650	60000	______
Mar.	–	10000	24000	–	1200	650	–	______
Apr.	–	16000	30000	500	1200	650	–	______
May	–	28000	30000	–	1200	650	–	______
Jun.	–	40000	30000	–	1200	650	–	

* Step numbers are shown in brackets.

You should have completed your answer as follows:

Mr and Mrs Rice Cash Budget (cash flow forecast) (step (7))

	INFLOWS		OUTFLOWS					
19X4	Opening balance (7)	Sales	Purchases	Rent	Wages and salaries	General expenses	Fixed assets	Closing balance (7)
	£	£	£	£	£	£	£	**£**
Jan.	50000	–	–	500	1200	650	–	47650
Feb.	47650	–	20000	–	1200	650	60000	(34200)
Mar.	(34200)	10000	24000	–	1200	650	–	(50050)
Apr.	(50050)	16000	30000	500	1200	650	–	(66400)
May	(66400)	28000	30000	–	1200	650	–	(70250)
Jun.	(70250)	40000	30000	–	1200	650	–	(62100)

OVERDRAFT

The budgeted profit and loss account and balance sheet

You can project the cash budget figures to produce a master budget (i.e. budgeted final accounts, that is to say, a budgeted profit and loss account and budgeted balance sheet). This should help you to develop a clearer understanding of accounting concepts; for example, to explain why profits have gone up and cash has gone down.

To convert the cash budget information to provide the information we need for the budgeted final accounts, you need to do the following:

- First, add up each vertical cash budget column, except the opening and closing balance columns.
- Second, add on the two months of sales on credit, i.e. debtors 2 × £40,000 = £80,000 and the one month's purchases on credit at £30,000 to the sales and purchases respectively.
- Third, taking into account the closing stock and depreciation, complete the budgeted profit and loss account.

	INFLOWS	OUTFLOWS				
	Sales	**Purchases**	**Rent**	**Wages and salaries**	**General expenses**	**Fixed assets**
Totals	94 000	134 000	1 000	7 200	3 900	60 000
Debtors/ creditors	80 000	30 000				
	174 000	164 000				

Mr and Mrs Rice Budgeted profit and loss account for the half-year ending 30 June 19X4

	£	£
Sales (as above)		174 000
Less cost of sales:		
Opening stock	–	
Add Purchases (as above)	164 000	
	164 000	
Less Closing stock (given)	48 000	116 000
Gross profit (gross profit/sales % = $33\frac{1}{3}$ %):		58 000
Less expenses:		
Rent	1 000	
Wages and salaries	7 200	
General expenses	3 900	
Depreciation (given)	3 000	15 100
Net profit:		£42 900

Note that the sales figure includes all the sales made during the period, even though £80,000 has not yet been received in cash. The purchases include all the purchases made during the period, including those which are still to pay for, i.e. all the cash and credit sales and purchases for the period.

- Fourth, complete the balance sheet. Include all of the amounts owing, fixed assets adjusted for depreciation, current assets, current liabilities and capital:

Mr and Mrs Rice Budgeted balance sheet as at 30 June 19X4

Employment of capital	**£**		**£**
Fixed assets:	60000		
Equipment			
Less Depreciation	3000		57000
Working capital:			
Current assets			
Stock		48000	
Debtors (2 months' sales on credit)		80000	
Cash and bank		–	
		128000	
Current liabilities:	**£**		
Creditors	30000		
Bank overdraft (per cash budget)	62100	92100	35900
			£92900
Capital employed			**£**
Capital (The amount introduced by Mr and Mrs Rice)			50000
Add Net profit (as per trading and profit and loss account)			42900
			£92900

Note that the capital employed represents the amount invested in the business by Mr and Mrs Rice, i.e. £50,000 plus their ploughed-back profits.

Missing figures

The data from which you may have to produce your cash budget and/or budgeted profit and loss account and balance sheet may be incomplete. For example, the closing stock of raw materials or the purchases figure may not be given.

If for example, the closing stock figure had not been given in our Mr and Mrs Rice illustration, we could work it out, provided that we knew the average mark-up, i.e. the gross profit/sales percentage of $33\frac{1}{3}$ per cent.

To find the closing stock figure:

1 Work out the gross profit (£174,000 × $33^1/_3$%) = £58,000.

2 Take the gross profit of £58,000 from the sales figure of £174,000. This gives us the cost of sales (cost of materials consumed) figure of £116,000.

3 From the opening stock plus purchases figure of £164,000, take away the cost of sales figure of £116,000. The difference of £48,000 is the closing stock figure.

You may be interested to learn that this method is frequently used in cases where stock has been damaged, destroyed or stolen, for the purposes of estimating the closing stock for insurance claims. Also, please take care with mark-ups. The one we have just used was based on selling price. You may be provided with a mark-up which is based on cost price. This should not present you with any problems; all you have to do is convert it to a mark-up on selling price, using the following guidelines:

Mark-up on cost price		Mark-up on selling price
$^1/_4$ (25%)	=	$^1/_5$ (20%)
$^1/_3$ ($33^1/_3$%)	=	$^1/_4$ (25%)
$^1/_2$ (50%)	=	$^1/_3$ ($33^1/_3$%)

and so on.

To find the purchases figure In cases where we know the opening and closing stocks and the cost of sales (cost of materials consumed) figure, the purchases figure may have to be calculated. For example, we may have figures for opening stock of £120, closing stock £140, and cost of sales £210:

	£
Cost of sales	210
Plus closing stock	140
This figure represents the total of opening stock plus purchases	350
Less opening stock	120
Therefore purchases	= **£230**

Self-assessment 7.2: Latin & Co.

Latin & Co. is starting up a new business on 1 January 19X4. They provide the following information:

	£
Quarterly rent of premises, payment due on 25 March and 25 June	300
Cash outlay on equipment – payable 25 January	60000
Monthly planned purchases of stock for resale:	
January	30000
February	20000
March to June (per month)	16000
All stock is bought on two months; credit (i.e. January purchases are paid for in March)	
Monthly planned sales are:	
January	10000
February	16000
March to June (per month)	26000

- Planned gross profit each month is on average 25 per cent of sales.
- All sales are on one month's credit. No bad debts or arrears of payment are expected.
- Monthly cash outlay on general expenses is expected to be £500.

- Salaries are expected to be £1,400 per month.
- Depreciation of equipment on the first half-year is estimated at £3,000.
- Latin and Co. will pay £65,000 cash into the business. They do not plan to withdraw any money from the business during the year.

You are required to:

1 Using the work sheets provided and the data supplied, prepare a monthly cash budget for the half-year, and a budgeted profit and loss account for the half-year, and closing balance sheet, as at 30 June 19X9.

You will need to use the mark-up in order to estimate the budgeted closing stock at 30 June 19X9.

Latin & Co. Cash budget

19X9		**INFLOWS**	**OUTFLOWS**					
	Opening balance	**Sales**						**Closing balance**
Jan.								
Feb.								
Mar.								
Apr.								
May								
Jun.								

Latin and Co.
Budgeted profit and loss account for the year ending . . . 19X9

		£	£
	Sales		
Less	Cost of sales:		
	Opening stock	–	
Add	Purchases		
Less	Closing stock		
	Gross profit:		
Less	Expenses:		
	Rent		
	Wages & Salaries		
	General expenses		
	Depreciation		
	Net profit:		

Budgeted balance sheet

as at 19X9

	£	£
Employment of capital:		
Fixed assets		
Less Depreciation	____	
Working capital:		
Current assets		
Stock		
Debtors		
Cash and bank	____	
Less current liabilities		
Creditors		
Bank overdraft	____	____
Capital:		
Capital		
Add Net profit	____	____

Self-assessment 7.3: Adobo plc

The following forecast data relating to Adobo plc has been provided for you:

19X6	April	May	June	July	August
	£'000	£'000	£'000	£'000	£'000
Cost of sales	140	160	180	220	200
Wages/salaries	66	66	66	84	60
Depreciation of machinery	16	16	16	16	16
Rent and rates	7	7	7	7	7
Selling expenses	25	30	24	28	20
Distribution expenses	38	38	44	40	40
Administration expenses	10	10	10	8	8
Sales (all on credit)	350	380	420	550	320
Stock of raw materials at month end	150	175	160	120	100

You are also informed that:

- The opening bank balance on 1 June is expected to be £40,000.
- Suppliers allow one month's credit.
- Customers are allowed two months' credit.
- Selling expenses are paid during the following month.
- Distribution expenses are paid 50 per cent in the actual month and 50 per cent in the following month.
- Rent and rates will be paid £21,000 in April and £21,000 in July.
- All other expenses are paid during the month in which they are incurred.

You are required to:

1 Prepare a cash budget for the three months to 31 August 19X6. (Note that you are not asked to prepare a budgeted profit and loss account and balance sheet.)

Comparative statements

Budgetary control relies heavily on budget and actual comparative statements. It is important that in addition to communicating the variances, such statements also report on the reasons for significant adverse variances.

Simple budget and actual comparative statement				
		[Details of purpose, etc.]		Date ....
Item	Actual	Budget	Variance	Reasons for the variance
	£	£	£	

Figure 7.5 Comparative statement

Note that the chart in Figure 7.5 could also include the previous year's details, for further comparison.

Fixed and flexible budgets

Fixed budget A budget which is designed to remain unchanged, irrespective of the level of activity actually attained.

Flexible budget A budget which, by recognizing the difference between fixed, semi-variable and variable costs, is designed to change in relation to the actual level of activity attained.

Monthly departmental flexible budget					
	£'000	£'000	£'000	£'000	£'000
Sales	100	120	140	160	180
Direct costs (e.g. finished goods, wages)	40	48	56	64	72
Variable overheads	10	12	14	16	18
Semi-variable overheads	15	16	17	18	19
Fixed overheads	20	20	20	24	24
	85	96	107	122	133
Profit	15	24	33	38	47

Figure 7.6 The flexible budget

For comparison purposes it is essential that the actual and budgeted levels of activity are the same. Therefore, flexible budgets should be used if comparisons are to be realistic and valid.

Flexible budgets should not present you with any problems. All you have to do is work out a budget for the actual level of activity which has been attained taking into account cost behaviour.

Self-assessment 7.4: Brimells plc – flexible budgeting

You are provided with the following information for period 3:

		Budget	Actual
Output/sales (units)		500 000	460 000
		£'000	£'000
Sales	(A)	60 000	57 500
Cost of sales:			
Materials		12 500	10 120
Labour		10 000	9 660
Manufacturing overheads		5 000	3 450
	(B)	27 500	23 230
Other expenses:			
Selling expenses		8 000	7 220
Distribution expenses		9 000	8 232
Administration expenses		4 000	4 000
	(C)	21 000	19 452
Net profit (A) – ((B) + (C))		**£11 500**	**£14 818**

Note that the budget was based on:

- selling expenses being 50 per cent fixed and 50 per cent variable;
- distribution expenses being $33\frac{1}{3}$ per cent fixed and $66\frac{2}{3}$ per cent variable;
- administration expenses being all fixed.

You are required to:

1 Compare the actual figures with a budget based upon an output/sales level (i.e. a level of activity) of 460,000 units. (You do *not* need to compute the variances.)

Zero-based budgeting

Another approach to budgeting, which has been found to be particularly useful for dealing with non-revenue-earning cost centres is zero-based budgeting, or ZBB for short. Each cost centre has to justify its budget. What may have happened in the past is simply treated as history, and not relevant. The executives/groups concerned all start from a nil base and have to sort out their priorities and put forward their reasons for wanting funds. The aim is to do away with inefficient and obsolete activities.

If you know something about each of the key words below, you should know a lot about the principles of budgeting and budgetary control:

- a budget;
- action;
- authority;
- behavioural aspects;
- budget education;
- budget and actual comparative statements;
- budget centres;
- co-operation and commitment;
- communication and co-ordination;
- constraints;
- continuous comparison;
- control by responsibility;
- environmental change;
- feedback;
- flexible budgets;
- functional budgets;
- goals;
- interrelationships;
- limiting factor;
- management by exception;
- master budgets;
- matching;
- meetings;
- monitoring;
- motivation;
- objectives;
- operating planning;
- organization;
- participation;

- performance;
- planning;
- policy;
- predetermination;
- principal budget factor;
- resource allocation;
- strategic planning;
- targets;
- the controller;
- the future;
- the provision of information.

Cash budgets Record when the cash/bank transactions actually take place, i.e. when the money comes in or goes out. They take into account the periods of credit received from suppliers/granted to customers.

The master budget Tends to consist of a budgeted profit and loss account and budgeted balance sheet. The information used to produce the cash budget can be extended or adjusted to assist in the preparation of the master budget. Comparing the cash budget with the budgeted profit and loss account helps you to understand questions such as: Why, if our profits have gone up by £164,000, has cash only gone up by £23,000?

Missing figures It is possible to compute missing figures, e.g. purchases or closing stocks by taking the average mark-up, i.e. the gross profit/sales percentage into account.

Flexible budgets These are used to ensure that budget and actual comparisons are made using the same level of activity.

Zero-based budgeting (ZBB) Managers/executives have to justify why they need the budget.

FURTHER READING

Chadwick L (1997) *The Essence of Management Accounting* (2nd Edition), London: Prentice-Hall

Dyson J R (1994) *Accounting for Non-Accounting Students* (3rd Edition), London: Pitman

Ryan B (1995) *Strategic Accounting for Management*, London: Dryden

Williamson D (1996) *Cost & Management Accounting*, London: Prentice Hall

Budgetary control: additional self-assessments

Self-assessment 7.5: Budgeting multiple choice test

Select the answer which you consider to be correct to the following multiple-choice problems:

1 Where goods are to be sold on which customers are given three months' credit, goods sold on credit in June would be included in the cash budget for:

A June

B August

C September

D October

2 New equipment is expected to be purchased by cheque in June of the forthcoming period, details of which are as follows:

Cost: £16,000

Life: five years

Scrap value at the end of its life: £4,000

Depreciation using the straight-line basis (i.e. a percentage of cost per year/month)

The amount of depreciation which will be included in the cash budget for the month of June will be:

	£
A	Nil
B	200
C	266
D	12,000
E	16,000

3 You have been provided with the following information:

	£
Sales	24,000
Mark-up on selling price	20%
Opening stock	£1,600
Closing stock	£1,950

The purchases figure amounts to:

£

A 18,000

B 18,350

C 19,200

D 19,550

4 You have ascertained that the budgeted selling and distribution expenses are 40 per cent fixed and 60 per cent variable, and for a budgeted output of 80,000 units amounted to £160,000. The selling and distribution figure which should be used in a flexible budget for 60,000 units should be:

£'000

A 112

B 120

C 136

D 160

5 The sales figure in a budgeted trading and profit and loss account will only include:

A cash sales for the period

B credit sales for the period

C cash and credit sales for the period

D cash sales and cash from credit sales for the period

Self-assessment 7.6: Quick questions on budgeting

1 Explain the difference between 'a budget' and 'budgetary control'.

2 Explain how the following key words apply to budgetary control:

- monitoring;
- predetermination of costs and revenues;
- the principal budget factor;
- participation;
- control by responsibility;
- management by exception.

3 Draw a cash graph and explain briefly how it helps to illustrate the purpose of cash budgeting.

4 Draft a simple budget and actual comparative statement, for production departments or sales.

5 Explain briefly why it is important to use flexible rather than fixed budgets.

Self-assessment 7.7: A. Walley

A. Walley has just won £10,000 on the football pools and decided to set-up in business. It is intended to commence trading on 1 October, 19X3 and anticipated that sales and purchases for the first six months will be as follows:

	Sales £	Purchases £
October	5 000	6 000
November	7 000	7 000
December	9 000	8 000
January	10 000	9 000
February	11 000	10 000
March	12 000	11 000

Due to the highly competitive nature of market forces, planned gross profit will only be about 10 per cent of sales. Walley also feels that it will be necessary to offer generous sales credit terms of three months. (So, cash from October's sales will be received in January.) Suppliers of goods for resale will have to be paid in the month following that of purchase. It is thought that the bank manager will authorize an overdraft.

Walley will work from home and expects that business electricity consumption will be £350 per quarter, payable December and March. General expenses will be approximately £50 a month, payable in the month they are incurred.

The budgeted closing stock at 31 March 19X4 is £2,400.

You are required to:

1 Calculate a cash budget for the six months to 31 March 19X4.

2 Calculate a budgeted profit and loss account for the six months to 31 March 19X4.

3 Calculate a budgeted balance as at 31 March 19X4.

4 Discuss briefly: 'A cash budgeting system may force management into action.'

Self-assessment 7.8: Basil Felix & Co

Draw up a cash budget for Basil Felix & Co from the following information for the six months ended 30 June 19X6:

- Opening cash (including bank) balance £78,600.

- Production in units:

19X5		19X6					
Nov.	Dec.	Jan.	Feb.	Mar.	Apr.	May	Jun.
5000	6000	5000	8000	6000	5000	5000	6000

- Raw materials used in production cost £10 per unit. Of this 25 per cent is paid in the same month as production and 75 per cent in the month following production.
- Direct labour costs of £1 per unit are payable in the same month as production.
- Variable expenses are £6 per unit, payable 50 per cent in the same month as production and 50 per cent in the month following production.
- Sales at £50 per unit:

19X5		19X6						
Oct.	Nov.	Dec.	Jan.	Feb.	Mar.	Apr.	May	Jun.
200	600	600	768	720	640	500	500	560

Debtors take an average credit period of two months.

- Fixed overheads are £18,000 per month, payable each month.
- New equipment received in January 19X5 costing £84,000 is to be paid for in February 19X5.
- Rent of £6,000 per quarter is due to be received in March and June.

Self-assessment 7.9: Bankend Electronics plc

The following data has been supplied to you for the company's year ended 31 December 19X1:

	Budget	Actual
Level of activity	75%	60%
	£'000	**£'000**
Direct costs:		
Materials	120	91
Labour	150	132
Variable overheads	60	51
	330	274
Fixed overheads	50	56
	£380	£330

You are required to:

1 Prepare a flexible budget for the actual level of activity, and compute the variances.

Standard Costing and Variance Analysis

Standard costing is another example of predetermined costing, involving costs which look forward rather than backwards and can be used for planning and control purposes.

LEARNING OBJECTIVES

When you have read this chapter, you should be able to:

- appreciate how standards are set;
- know why businesses use standards;
- compute material and labour variances and suggest reasons for those which are adverse, or which are interrelated;
- prepare a reconciliation of the standard and actual profits.

This chapter introduces you to standard costing by looking at a comprehensive tabulation of how standards are set, followed by a series of questions and answers, numerical examples and self-assessments.

How standards are set

The management accountant wanted a standard price for a new component which was to be incorporated into a product. He provided the chief buyer with the parts number; the chief buyer just looked at his price list and said, 'Oh, call it £10.25 per unit.'

Is standard setting so simple? The way in which it is sometimes done in real life may not always reflect good practice. The setting of standards, if they are to be useful, involves much more. Table 8.1 should help you to appreciate some of the considerations.

All business functions should be involved in the setting of standards which have an impact upon their function. It is essential that meetings are held to discuss, evaluate, review and amend standards at regular intervals. With the world as it is, standards cannot remain in use and unchanged for long periods of time.

Table 8.1 *The setting of standards*

Item	Quantity	Price
Sales	Information from marketing, taking into account the entry into new target markets/ segments. Records of past performance updated by data about the future. Information from monitoring the environment/product markets.	Information from marketing, taking into account the prices of competitors and the firm's own pricing policy. Again, based on past experience and future expectations.
Direct materials	Data relating to usage would be supplied by the production department and via stores records and the materials analysis. You should note that a business can keep an analysis of the way in which it uses its direct materials. Levels of anticipated qualities, waste/scrap, as well as changes in production methods, labour skills, product lines and designs, would also need to be considered.	Information would come from the buying office. The information should take into account anticipated qualities, price fluctuations and inflation.
Direct labour	One of the principal sources of information is the payroll analysis of direct labour. Another important source of data comes via time and work study, e.g. to establish the time allowed to complete a task. Account should also be taken of changes in working practices, production methods, factory organization, product lines, designs, etc.	Here also, a lot of information can be obtained from a study of the payroll analysis for direct labour. Add to this, the input from the personnel and production departments, for example concerning anticipated pay increases and pay settlements, grades of labour to be used etc.
Direct expenses	Historic records updated to take account of changes in activity levels, policies, inflation, product lines, product design, etc.	
Variable overheads	As above, per the direct expenses plus information from the materials and payroll analysis for those items of materials and labour which are not direct to the product but vary with the level of activity. The prices and rates of pay would use the same criteria as described for direct materials and direct labour.	
Fixed overheads	The historic data would be adjusted to take into account anticipated increases/ decreases, e.g. caused by inflation, changes in activity levels causing 'step fixed costs', leasing new premises, buying new machines and equipment. All functions should be consulted, e.g. marketing, finance, production, research and development, welfare, etc.	

Why use standards?

A standard costing system should:

- provide management with frequent variance reports which highlight when costs and/or revenues are not going according to expectations. Thus, management can take appropriate corrective action as early as possible;
- provide management with an early warning about possible losses and inefficiencies;
- help to ensure the control of all the elements of cost and revenue in terms of price and volume;
- work well in small, medium and large-scale businesses;
- help to achieve uniformity in the costing of jobs and/or products.

However, it will be necessary to prepare a reconciliation between the cost accounts and the financial accounts, e.g. stocks valued at standard cost will have to be revalued for financial accounting purposes.

Which standard should be used?

There are a number of standards which could be adopted, some of which are as follows.

Basic standard A standard which is established for use unaltered over a long period of time.

Current standard A standard related to current conditions, and which is established for use over a short period of time.

Normal standard The average standard which it is anticipated can be attained over a future period of time.

Ideal standard The standard which can be attained under the most favourable conditions possible.

To be of any real use to management, a standard has to be realistic. Thus, the current standard and the normal standard are recommended. However, both should be flexible enough to be revised and amended to reflect environmental changes which take place from time to time, even in the short term. Thus, if current conditions change significantly, then the standard should also be changed.

What is a standard time?

In standard costing, standard hours or standard minutes are used to indicate how long it should take a production worker to perform a task or operation. These standard times may also be used as a principal element in incentive or productivity schemes, e.g. in the calculation of the bonus earnings.

Variance analysis

Figure 8.1 lists a number of variances which, in aggregate, affect the profit variance. However, you should note that there are many more variances than those which are illustrated, for instance, the overhead and sales variances can be divided up even further, into subvariances.

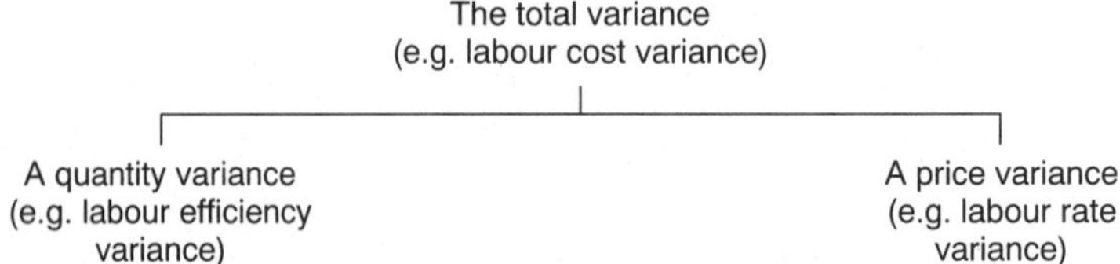

Variances in total sales or total materials, labour or overheads are caused by two factors:

- a quantity (or volume) variance; and
- a price variance.

An adverse (or negative) variance If the actual expenditure exceeds the planned (i.e. standard) expenditure, the variance may be described as an adverse or negative variance.

A favourable (or positive) variance If the actual expenditure is less than the planned expenditure, the variance will then be classed as a favourable or positive variance.

Variance reports Comparative reports or statements should be presented to management at regular intervals. They should highlight significant adverse variances, as well as providing explanations of why they have occurred. This should help management to decide upon the appropriate action needed to put right anything which has gone wrong.

Materials and labour variances

In their simplest form, materials and labour variances can be computed as follows:

The total variance

This is the overall variance and results from a comparison of the actual quantity in terms of material or labour hours with the standard set for the actual level of activity attained:

	Materials	**Labour**
Standard quantity (SQ) at standard price (SP) (for actual level of activity)	SQ × SP	SQ × SP
Less Actual quantity (AQ) at actual price (AP)	AQ × AP	AQ × AP
=	Material cost (total) variance	Labour (wages) cost (total) variance

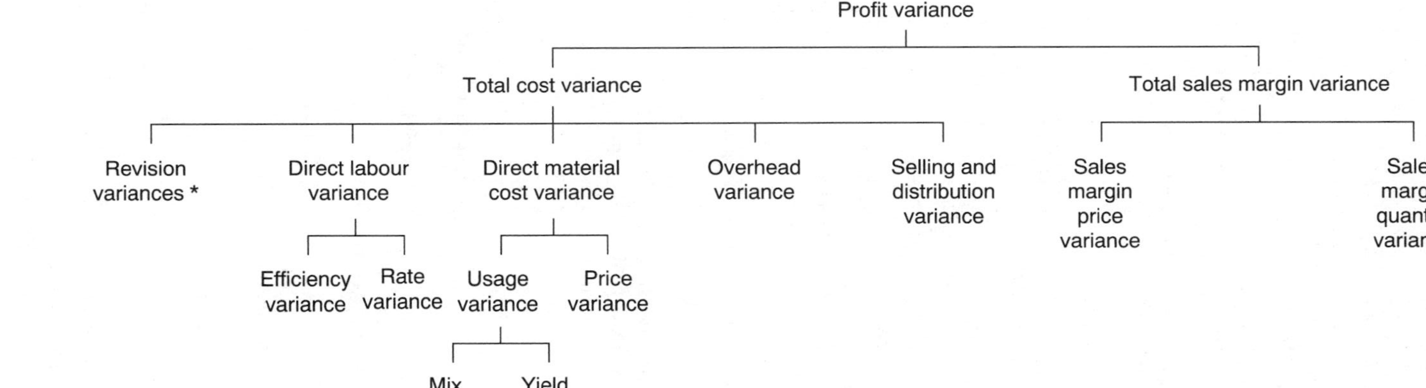

Figure 8.1 Variance analysis

* The revision variance refers to the amount by which the budget/standard has had to be revised.

Example labour variances

We will use the following information to calculate the labour variances:

Standard labour rate	£8 per component
Hours	2 per component
Actual production data was:	
1 000 components produced	
Labour rate paid	£8.40 per hour
Hours worked	1 950 hours

The labour variances could be calculated as follows:

Labour cost variance (i.e. the total variance)
(Actual hours × actual rate) less (standard hours × standard rate for actual production)
(1 950 × £8.40) = £16 380 less (2 000 × £8 = £16 000) = £380 Adverse

Labour rate variance
(Actual rate − standard rate) × actual hours
(£8.40 − £8) = 40p × 1950 = £780 Adverse

Labour efficiency variance
(Actual hours − standard hours for actual input × standard rate per hour)
(1 950 − 2 000) = 50 hours × £8 = £400 Favourable

Summary	**£**	
Labour rate variance	(780)	(A)
Labour efficiency variance	400	(F)
Labour cost variance	(380)	(A)

Layout of the above may be improved by presenting calculations as follows:

	£	
Actual labour cost (1 950 × £8.40)	16 380	
Less Standard labour cost (2 000 × £8)	16 000	
= Labour cost variance	£380	Adverse

Another approach for calculating the same variances is shown below:

	Labour cost or wages variance		**Labour rate or wages rate variance**		**Labour efficiency variance**	
	£		**£**		**£**	
Actual hours at actual rate (1 950 at £8.40)	16 380		16 380			
Standard hours at standard rate (2 000 at £8) for the actual level of activity	16 000				16 000	
Actual hours at standard rate (1 950 at £8)			15 600		15 600	
	£380	(A)	£780	(A)	£400	(F)

Summary (proof)	£	
Labour rate variance	(780)	(A)
Labour efficiency variance	400	(F)
Labour cost variance	£(380)	(A)

Labour cost variance This is the total variance which arises from comparing the actual labour cost with the standard labour cost, for the actual level of activity achieved. In the example, the actual was greater by £380 than the standard cost, which means the variance is adverse, representing an overspend.

Labour rate variance This is calculated by multiplying the actual hours, 1,950, by the difference in the wage rate paid:

	Hours	**Rate**		
	Actual 1 950	× £8.40 actual	= 16 380	
Less	Actual 1 950	× £8.00 standard	= 15 600	
	= Actual 1 950	× 40p (difference) = Variance	780	(Adverse)

The variance is adverse because it cost the company 40p per hour more than it had planned. Thus, every actual hour worked costs the company 40p more than planned.

Labour efficiency variance This is an evaluation of the time lost or saved at the standard rate.

		Hours		**Standard rate**		**£**
(Time allowed)	Standard	2 000	×	£8	=	16 000
(Time taken)	Actual	1 950	×	£8	=	15 600
Hours saved		50	×	£8	= Variance	£400 (Favourable)

This variance was favourable, because the work performed was done in 50 hours less than the standard time allowed.

Note that variances can be interrelated; a favourable labour efficiency variance could arise at the expense of poor material usage, i.e. an adverse material usage variance.

Material variances for price and usage are computed in a similar manner.

The diagram in Figure 8.2 should help you to appreciate how the two labour variances are arrived at, and why they are calculated in such a way.

Self-assessment 8.1: Material variances

You have been provided with the following information about the use of materials:

- standard price £88 per litre;
- standard usage 8 litres per unit of product;
- actual price £95 per litre;
- actual usage for 1000 units of product was 9 200 litres.

You are required to work out the material:

- cost (total) variance;
- price variance;

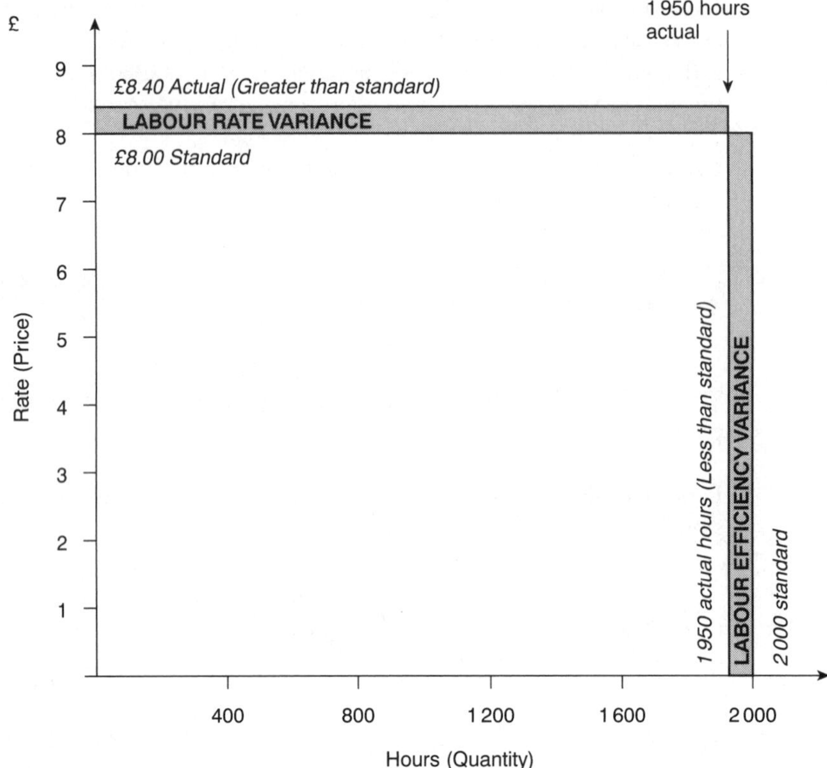

Figure 8.2 Labour variances

- usage variance; and
- suggest possible reasons for the variances.

Material mix and yield variances

As indicated in Figure 8.1, the material usage variance can be subdivided into two component parts, a mix variance and a yield variance.

Mix variance The mix we are talking about is the mix of materials (rather like a cookery recipe) which has to be combined to produce a product. The mix variance is due to the actual mix of materials used being different from the standard mix. It can be computed by subtracting the standard cost of the standard yield from the actual quantity at the standard price.

Yield variance A yield in manufacturing terms is the expected output from a given input of materials. The yield variance is attributable to producing an actual yield which is lesser or greater than the standard yield, e.g.:

Standard yield	485 kilos
Actual yield	475 kilos
Less than the standard	10 kilos

Multiply this by the standard cost per kilo and you have the yield variance.

However, note that there are several different ways and formats in use for the computation of variances.

The following example should help you to better understand mix and yield variances.

Example: IWC plc

IWC plc manufactures a product containing materials in the following proportions and at the standard cost shown:

30% material X at £50 per kilo
70% material Y at £60 per kilo

A standard loss of 5% is expected in production.

During a period when 96 kilos of the product were produced, 32 kilos of material X at an actual cost of £49 per kilo, and 68 kilos of material Y at an actual cost of £63 per kilo, were used.

We shall now calculate the material cost variances (using the tabular method which we looked at earlier) i.e.:

- price;
- mix;
- yield;
- total (cost);
- usage.

Abbreviations:

AQ = actual quantity

SQ = standard quantity

AP = actual price

SP = standard price

SC = standard cost

SY = standard yield

AY = actual yield

IWC PLC

Standard cost of 95 kilos				**£**
Material X	30 kilos at £50 per kilo			1 500
Material Y	70 kilos at £60 per kilo			4 200
	100			
Less loss	5			
Standard yield	95 kilos at £60 per kilo standard cost			£5 700

			£	
		(AQ × AP)	£	
(a) *Actual cost of kilos produced*	X	(32 × £49)	1 568	
	Y	(68 × £63)	4 284	5 852
		(AQ × SP)		
(b) *Actual quantity at standard price*	X	(32 × £50)	1 600	
	Y	(68 × £60)	4 080	5 680
(c) *Standard cost of standard yield* (95 × £60) (SY × SC)		as above		5 700
(d) *Standard cost of actual yield* (96 × £60) (AY × SC)				5 760

		£
Price variance	(a − b)	172 (A)
Mix variance	(b − c)	20 (F)
Yield variance	(c − d)	60 (F)
Total/material cost variance	(a − d)	92 (A)

Material usage variance	£
= Mix variance	20 (F)
Yield variance	60 (F)
	£80 (F)

Proof

		£
(AQ × SP)	(b)	5 680
Less (SC × AQ)	(d)	5 760
	(b − d)	£80 (F)

The reconciliation of standard and actual profits

Variances can be used to explain the difference between the standard profit and the actual profit. The following example and specially designed statement should help to illustrate this.

Example: Gilleard Ltd

Gilleard Ltd make a single product, which requires 3 kilos of material normally costing £5 per kilo, and takes one standard hour's labour to produce. Labour employed on this process should be paid £8 per hour.

During the month, it is estimated that 1,000 units will be sold at £56 each. Overheads (all fixed in relation to output) are budgeted to be £1,800 per month.

It can be assumed that no stocks of raw materials or finished products are carried.

The actual wages paid for the period were £9,180, representing 1,080 hours at £8.50 per hour.

Materials purchased during the month were as follows:

Kilos	£
2500 at £5.50 per kilo	13750
700 at £5 per kilo	3500
	£17250

A total of 1,080 hours were taken on the process to produce 1,100 units, all of which were sold. Units were sold at £52 each.

The actual overheads incurred were £2,100.

We will now prepare a product standard cost statement and monthly operating statement, showing clearly any variances.

Gilleard Ltd
Actual profit and loss account for 1100 units

		£	£
Actual sales			57200
1100 at £52			
	Less actual costs:		
Materials			
	2500 at £5.50	13750	
	700 at £5	3500	
		17250	
Labour			
	1080 hours at £8.50	9180	
Overheads		2100	28530
	Net profit		**£28670**

Standard cost statement

		£
Budgeted sales	1000 at £56	56000
Sales volume variances	100 at £56	5600
	= 1100 at £56	61600

Standard costs for 1100 units

	£	
Materials 1100 × 3 kilos × £5 =	16500	
Labour 1100 at £8 =	8800	
Overheads =	1800	27100
Standard profit for 1100 units		**£34500**

Reconciliation

			£
Standard profit (as calculated)			34 500
Variances	(Favourable)	(Adverse)	
	£	£	
Sales price variance: £52 − £56 = £4 × 1 100		4 400	
Material price variance: £17 250 − 3 200 kilos × £5		1 250	
Material usage variance: 3 300 − 3 200 = 100 × £5	500		
Labour rate variance: £9 180 − 1 080 hours × £8		540	
Labour efficiency variance: 1 080 − 1 100 hours = 20 × £8	160		
Overheads variance: £2 100 − £1 800		300	
	660	6 490	(5 830) Adverse
		Actual profit	**£28 670**

Further proof of the material and labour variances can be computed as follows:

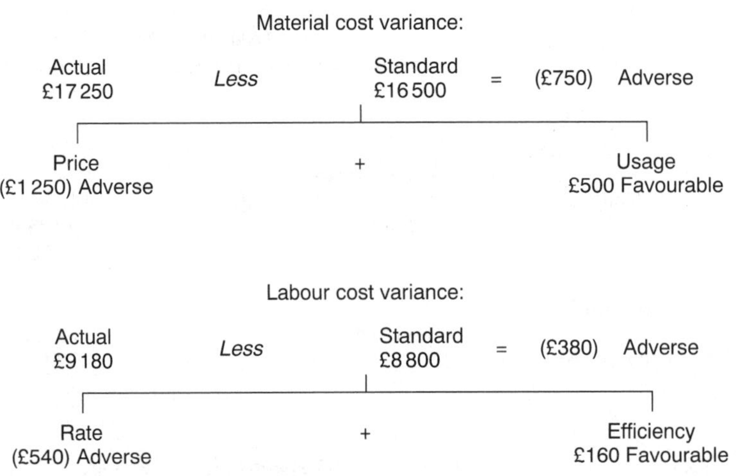

Self-assessment 8.2: Ingham plc

Ingham plc make a single product. The product requires 2 litres of material normally costing £6 per litre, and takes two standard hours of labour to produce. Labour employed on this process should earn £9.00 per hour.

During the month, it is estimated that 1,000 units will be sold at £40 each. Overheads (all fixed in relation to output) are budgeted to be £1,000 per month.

It can be assumed that no stocks of raw materials or finished products are carried.

The actual wage rate paid was £9.25 per hour. Other 'actual' data for the period are:

- Materials purchased and used during the month were 2,300 litres at £5.75.
- 2,200 hours were taken to produce 1,200 units, all of which were sold. Units were sold at £42 each.
- Overheads incurred were £1,150.

You are required to:

1 Prepare a product standard cost statement and monthly operating statement and a reconciliation statement showing clearly any variances.

Setting standards Standards are set using a combination of historic data and information about the future, plus contributions from appropriate functons, e.g. work study, product design, production, quality control, marketing, etc.

The use of standards Standards are used for control purposes and are designed to promote efficiency. The way in which this is achieved is via variance analysis. Variance reports are produced at regular intervals, highlighting to management significant adverse variances. This is another example of the principle of management by exception.

Adverse or favourable? A cost variance in terms of price or quantity is adverse if the actual exceeds the standard, and favourable if the position is reversed.

A revenue variance, e.g. sales in terms of price and quantity (i.e. volume) is favourable if the actual exceeds the standard and adverse if the position is reversed.

A variance can be classified thus:

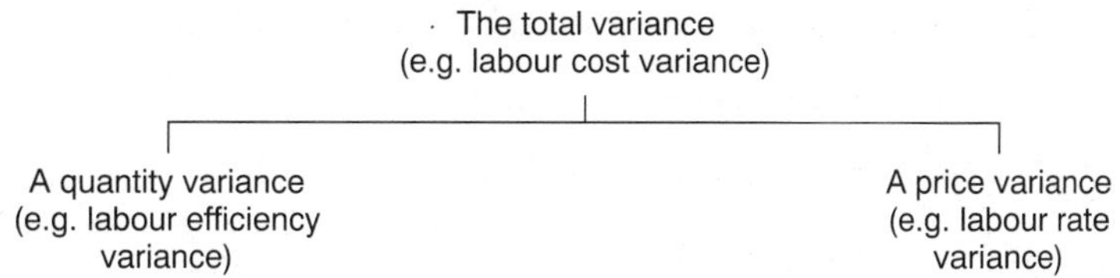

Interrelated variances A single factor could well be the reason why two variances occur. For example, if material of a quality lower than standard is used, the material price variance could be favourable, i.e. a lower price than planned is paid, but the material usage variance could be adverse, i.e. more material than planned could be used.

Reconciliations of standard and actual profits The logic behind the calculations are that:

The standard profit (for the actual level of activity)
less adverse variances
plus favourable variances
equals the actual profit

Other variances Finally, remember that this chapter was intended as an introduction to the subject and that there are many, many more variances and subvariances.

FURTHER READING

Atrill P & McLaney E (1994) *Management Accounting, An Active Learning Approach*, Oxford: Blackwell

Drury C (1994) *Costing, An Introduction*, London: Chapman & Hall

Dyson J R (1994) *Accounting for Non-Accounting Students*, London: Pitman

Williamson D (1996) *Cost and Management Accounting*, London: Prentice Hall

Standard costing: additional self-assessments

Self-assessment 8.3: Standard costing multiple choice test

Select the answer which you consider to be correct to the following multiple-choice problems:

1 Which standard did we recommend should be used in practice?

A The basic standard

B The normal standard

C The expected standard

D The ideal standard

2 The direct material cost variance can be divided between:

A A usage and a price variance

B A mix and a yield variance

C A usage and a rate variance

D An efficiency and a mix variance

3 You are provided with the following data:

Standard hours:	Standard hours for actual level of activity:	Actual hours:
2750	2400	2650

The standard wage rate per hour was £6.50.
The actual wage rate per hour was £7.00.

(a) The adverse labour rate variance amounts to:

A £1200

B £1325

C £1375

(b) The labour efficiency variance is:

A £650 favourable

B £1625 favourable

C £650 adverse

D £1625 adverse

4 You have been supplied with the following tabulation:

	Standard	**Actual**	**Standard for actual level**
Usage (units)	5000	6400	6000
Cost of materials:			
	(at £4.50)	(at £4.25)	(at £4.50)
	£22500	£27200	£27000

The material cost variance can be divided into:

	Price variance of:	**Usage variance of:**
A	£1500 favourable	£1800 adverse
B	£1600 favourable	£1700 adverse
C	£1500 favourable	£1700 adverse
D	£1600 favourable	£1800 adverse

Self-assessment 8.4: Standard costing quick questions

1 Explain briefly which data would be used to help set the standard for:

- direct material usage;
- direct material price;

- direct labour efficiency;
- direct labour rate.

2 List three reasons why companies use standard costing.

3 In your own words, define what is meant by the term 'standard time', and how it is arrived at.

4 The Coombs Bakery employs a standard costing system and provides you with the following data:

- actual hours worked: 5600 hours;
- standard rate per hour: £5;
- actual wages paid: £25200 (at £4.50 per hour);
- standard hours: 4000 hours.

You are required to define and calculate:

(a) The labour cost variance (wages variance).

(b) The labour rate variance.

(c) The labour efficiency variance.

5 See if you can think of five probable causes of an adverse material usage variance, and write them down.

6 Why could a favourable labour rate variance be linked to an adverse material usage variance?

Sellf-assessment 8.5: Ivan and Co plc

Ivan & Co plc manufacture a product containing materials in the following proportions and at the standard cost shown for 100 kilos input:

40 per cent material XL90 at £53 per kilo
60 per cent material Z007 at £33 per kilo

A standard loss of 18 per cent is expected in production.

During the period under review, 80 kilos of the product were produced, using 42 kilos of material XL90 at an actual cost of £50 per kilo, and 58 kilos of material Z007 at an actual cost of £35 per kilo.

Calculate the material variances, i.e.:

1 price;

2 usage;

3 mix;

4 yield;

5 total (cost).

Self-assessment 8.6: Scholes Nut and Screw Co.

As management acountant of the Scholes Nut and Screw Co., you are responsible for collecting the following data for December 19X8.

Prepare a statement for your board of directors reconciling the budget (target) operating profit with the actual operating profit.

	Target (Standard)		Actual
Sales (units)	10000		8000
Sales	£120000		£99516
	£		£
Cost of sales:			
Materials (60000 kilos at 50p)	30000	(52000 kilos)	24118
Labour (20000 hours at £2.50)	50000	(18000 hours)	47560
Operating costs	80000		71678
Operating profit	£40000		£27838

Self-assessment 8.7: Jackson Ltd

Jackson Ltd make a single product. This article requires 2 kilos of material normally costing £6 per kilo, and takes two standard hours of labour to produce. Labour employed on this process is expected to earn the standard rate of £7.50 per hour.

During the month, it is estimated that 1000 units will be sold at £32 each. Overheads (all fixed in relation to output) are budgeted to be £1200 per month.

It can be assumed that no stocks of raw materials or finished products are carried.

Shortly after the period commences, operators receive a 50p per hour increase in their hourly rate of pay. Other 'actual' data for the period are:

- Materials purchased and used during the month 2100 kilos at £5.60 per kilo.
- 2000 hours were taken on the process to produce 1100 units, all of which were sold. Units were sold at £30 each.
- Overheads incurred were £1700.

Prepare a product standard cost statement and monthly operating statement, and a reconciliation statement, showing clearly any variances.

9

Decision-making and Relevant Cash Flows

Before we move on to study capital investment appraisal, it is necessary for you to have a good understanding of what is meant by relevant cash flows (also called incremental cash flows).

LEARNING OBJECTIVES

When you have read this chapter, you should be able to:

- ▶ understand how to apply the concept of relevant cash flows;
- ▶ appreciate further how marginal costing techniques can be used in decision-making.

Relevant cash flows

Which cash flow?

The cash flows which one should select and use for decision-making purposes are the *relevant* cash flows (sometimes referred to as 'incremental cash flows'). Relevant cash flows use only relevant inflows, i.e. revenues, and relevant outflows, i.e. costs.

When is a cost or revenue a relevant cash flow?

A cost or revenue is a relevant cash flow if it has arisen as a direct consequence of going ahead with a particular project. Expenditure which would be paid out whether or not the project goes ahead is irrelevant to the decision.

For example:

- Fixed costs already paid out are *sunk costs*, i.e. paid out and gone forever, and are irrelevant.
- Fixed costs which are only paid out if the project goes ahead, i.e. additional fixed costs, are relevant.
- Wages or salaries of new employees who will be taken on if the project goes ahead are relevant.
- The wages paid to existing employees who are unaffected by whether or not the project goes ahead are irrelevant.
- Expenses incurred either to the project or other projects if the project goes ahead are relevant.

The following self-assessment should help you come to terms with this concept.

Self-assessment 9.1: Relevant costs and relevant revenues

Indicate whether the item is relevant or irrelevant by ticking the appropriate column, and indicate whether or not it will increase or decrease the cash flow.

If the project goes ahead:	*A relevant cash flow*	*An irrelevant cash flow*
1 Two new employees will be taken on at a cost of £18,000 each per annum.		
2 One employee earning £12,000 per annum will be made redundant, but		
3 will receive £6,500 redundancy pay.		
4 Sales of one of the company's products will go down by £100,000, which		
5 would cost £68,000 to produce.		
6 Fixed costs would remain at their usual level, £110,000.		
7 One supervisor earning £24,000 would not be paid more, but would be expected to spend 25 per cent of his/her total time on the new project.		
8 Material will have to be specially ordered at a cost of £19,600.		
9 Material already in stock which cost £13,400 and has no other use and no residual value will be used.		
10 Material already in stock which would cost £1,450 to dispose of will be used.		
11 Material already in stock, original cost £8,500, replacement cost £11,200, will be used.		

A relevant cash flow
An irrelevant cash flow

12 Three existing employees who are on fixed salaries will have to be transferred from other departments, and
13 overtime costing £43,000 will have to be worked.
14 A machine, currently lying idle, which cost £120,000 four years ago can be used on the project;
15 this machine could be sold now for £30,000, or
16 at the end of the project for £12,000.
17 Sales of one of the company's products will generate an additional contribution of £79,000.
18 A highly skilled operative who is paid £32,000 per annum will have to be transferred from another department, and
19 that department will have to lose an order destined to yield a contribution of £26,000.
20 Safety work will have to be carried out costing £17,000.

Example: relevant cash flows

An organization is contemplating the purchase of a new machine and has provided us with the following information:

An old machine which cost £144,000 some years ago and has a book value of £36,000 can be traded in now for £25,000. At the end of year 5 it could be sold for £8,000.

The new machine would cost £465,000 now, and at the end of year 5 could be sold for £70,000.

Maintenance/running costs have been estimated as follows:

Year	Old machine £	New machine £
1	24 000	18 000
2	16 000	18 000
3	16 000	18 000
4	18 000	20 000
5	17 000	20 000

Sales would increase by £120,000 per year.

Costs would increase by £45,000 per year.

Two employees earning £19,000 per year each would be made redundant, each receiving £24,000 redundancy pay.

Materials already in stock which have no other use and no disposal value and which originally cost £14,000 can be used on the project.

New packaging materials will have to be bought at a cost of £7,000 per year.

The relevant cash flows are:

Year **(£'000)**	**0 (i.e. now)**	**1**	**2**	**3**	**4**	**5**
Inflows						
Additional sales	–	120	120	120	120	120
Residual value (new machine)	–	–	–	–	–	70
Maintenance savings (old 24–new 18)	–	6	–	–	–	–
Labour savings	–	38	38	38	38	38
(A)	Nil	164	158	158	158	228
Outflows						
New machine (465–trade in £25)	440	–	–	–	–	–
Old machine, lost residual value	–	–	–	–	–	8
Additional maintenance	–	–	2	2	2	3
Additional costs	–	45	45	45	45	45
Redundancy pay (assumed paid now)	48	–	–	–	–	–
Packing materials	–	7	7	7	7	7
(B)	488	52	54	54	54	63
Net incremental cash flows						
(A) – (B)	(£488)	£112	£104	£104	£104	£165

From your observations of the above net incremental cash flows calculation you should have noted that:

- The cost and book value of the old machine are irrelevant. Past expenditures and incomes of whatever category cannot be changed, whether or not a new project goes ahead. It is in effect 'water under the bridge'.
- If the project goes ahead, a trade-in of £25,000 will be received now but the residual value of £8,000 in year 5 will be lost.
- Making the two employees redundant results in a saving each year of £38,000 and a one-off payment immediately of £48,000.
- The expense of the material costing £14,000 which is already in stock is irrelevant because it has no other use or disposal value. If it had a disposal value, this would appear as a loss of revenue.

One of the most important key words in this area is the word *additional*. The item in question is relevant if, as a result of the project going ahead, it generates additional income or gives rise to additional costs.

Now see if you can compute the relevant cash flows by attempting the self-assessment which follows.

Self-assessment 9.2: Linzburg Mlilo plc

The company has been invited to supply a large batch of electrical components over a period of six months at a contract price of £300,000.

The costs of the batch are made up as follows:

Materials XZXL90 and TZX131 will have to be ordered specially and will cost £180,000.

YYYY631 cost £43,000 and is already in stock; it has no other use, but could be resold for £18,000.

A further supply of YYYY631 will have to be acquired at a cost of £11,000.

Labour Existing employees currently paid £68,000 in total will be used to produce the components. They will have to work some overtime, which should work out at £16,000 in total.

A number of new employees will have to be taken on and paid a total of £45,000. The additional work will be handled by existing supervisory staff who are currently paid £40,000 for all of the work they supervise.

Another department will have to subcontract some of their production to another company, at a cost of £34,000.

Overheads Fixed production overheads for the period are £29,000.

Variable production overheads for the period applicable to the contract would be £18,000. Other fixed overheads for the period amount to £36,000.

You are required to compare the relevant cost with the contract price.

Decision-making

Decision-making tends to rely heavily on marginal costing, and makes good use of the techniques concerned with:

- comparing alternative scenarios;
- profit targets;
- limiting (or key) factors.
- break-even analysis.

However, in addition to the financial information, consideration must also be given to a number of non-financial factors such as:

- changes in the internal and external environment;
- behavioural factors;
- feedback from appropriate personnel;
- internal control;
- various other non-financial factors.

(See also Chapter 4)

Relevant cash flows (also called incremental cash flows) arise as a direct result of a project going ahead. If a cost happens whether or not a project goes ahead, it is irrelevant, for instance a sunk cost such as the rent of the factory, i.e. it is paid whether or not the project goes ahead.

Marginal costing techniques used to compare alternatives, to deal with profit targets and to take account of key factors, and/or break-even analysis, have been found to be very useful when it comes to the provision of financial information for decision-making purposes.

FURTHER READING

Atrill P & McLaney E (1994) *Management Accounting, An Active Learning Approach,* Oxford: Blackwell

Chadwick L & Kirkby D (1996) *Financial Management*, London: Routledge

Drury C (1994) *Costing, An Introduction*, London: Chapman & Hall

Pike R & Neale B (1996) *Corporate Finance and Investment*, London: Prentice Hall

Decision-making and relevant cash flows: additional self-assessments

See if you can apply your knowledge of marginal costing to solve this self-assessment.

Self-assessment 9.3: Nederwick – to close or not to close

The annual flexible budget of Nederwick plc is as follows:

Production capacity	**40%** **£**	**60%** **£**	**80%** **£**	**100%** **£**
Costs:				
Direct labour	16 000	24 000	32 000	40 000
Direct material	12 000	18 000	24 000	30 000
Production overhead	11 400	12 600	13 800	15 000
Administration overhead	5 800	6 200	6 600	7 000
Selling and distribution overhead	6 200	6 800	7 400	8 000
	£51 400	£67 600	£83 800	£100 000

Because of trading difficulties the company is operating at 50 per cent capacity. Selling prices have had to be lowered to what the directors maintain is an uneconomic level, and they are considering whether or not their single factory should be closed down until the trading conditions improve.

A market research consultant has advised that in about twelve months' time there is every indication that sales will increase to about 75 per cent of normal capacity, and that the revenue to be produced in the second year will amount to £90,000. The present revenue from sales at 50 per cent capacity would amount to only £49,500 for a complete year.

If the directors decide to close down the factory for a year it is estimated that the following costs will have to be paid:

	£
Fixed costs	11 000
Closing down costs	7 500
Maintenance	1 000
Re-opening costs	4 000

You are required to:

1 From the information provided calculate whether or not it is better to close the factory or keep it open.

In order to do this you have to calculate the fixed costs by comparing the variable costs with the total costs.

10

Capital Investment Appraisal

One of the main tasks facing management is to decide on the allocation of the scarce resources at their disposal between competing activities or projects, and to do this in line with the corporate objectives. The financial information relating to the possible courses of action will be just one of many factors which have to be taken into account in coming to a decision. Numerous other quantitative and qualitative factors also need to be considered.

The financial manager will be making proposals and recommendations geared to maximizing the financial objectives of the firm, which in most cases comes down to maximizing the wealth of the business. This maximization will not only be reflected in a direct benefit to the shareholders by way of an increase in the value of their shares, but ultimately can be regarded as beneficial to most, if not all, the wider group of 'stakeholders'.

LEARNING OBJECTIVES

The aims of this chapter are to introduce you to:

- the characteristics of capital investment appraisal/project appraisal and the judgements which are involved;
- financial management;
- cost/benefit analysis;
- the way in which the relevant cash flows are arrived at, including an insight into the tax factor;
- the following methods of assessing capital projects:
  - payback
  - net present value (NPV)

- discounted payback
- internal rate of return (IRR)
- cost benefit/profitability index
- accounting rate of return.

Characteristics

The capital investment decision is no different in principle from any other decision. However, the capital investment decision does possess certain distinctive features:

- It will normally involve relatively high levels of expenditure.
- It will be made for the medium/long term, with estimates and future activity over a long time-scale.
- Once taken, the decisions can be difficult to reverse – for example building the Channel Tunnel or an aerospace project.
- If not easily reversible, then, at least for all but the largest companies, such decisions have to be taken relatively infrequently.

As with all management processes, a framework is required to provide proper control over the activity. For capital investment decisions, this will have the following prerequisites:

- The setting of a long-range capital investment plan.
- The systematic search for investment opportunities.
- An objective process for collecting information and for carrying out the forecasting of future costs and benefits, for example:
  - marketing (competition, pricing, product advantage);
  - production (teething problems, cost behaviour);
  - macro-economic (inflation, interest rates, politics, societal issues, geographical problems).
- Evaluation procedures, for example:
  - application of appropriate techniques;
  - comparison with alternatives;
  - comparison with desired yardsticks – accept/reject criteria.
- Proper documentation, review and examination of proposals, for example:
  - a prescribed format for proposals;
  - an investment committee.

- Assessment of logistics, such as:
  - timings;
  - scheduling of deliveries and installations;
  - critical paths.
- Evaluation of outcomes:
  - diagnosis of problems/successes;
  - identification of remedies.

Financial management

Decision-making in the financial management area breaks down into two basic components:

- The investment decision – what to invest in.
- The financing decision – how best to get the finance for it.

The investment decision

The activities requiring decisions may be very diverse, ranging from whether or not to invest in a new product, whether to move to more efficient or less expensive premises, whether or not to adopt a new administrative procedure, to whether or not to spend money on new equipment and/or people in a particular area or to accomplish a particular end. We can perhaps classify our types of investment opportunity as follows:

- Replacement of obsolete or worn-out equipment in order to maintain current operating capacity in an existing business.
- Expansion by the acquisition of new production capacity, either in an existing business or line of products, or in new business/products.
- Mergers with or acquisitions of different or complementary businesses (for diversification or greater integration).
- Other investment in e.g.:
  - improved systems for cost control;
  - improved production systems;
  - governmentally prescribed changes in, for example, health and safety measures or pollution control, etc.

Cost/benefit analysis

One common cry in all these situations will always be: 'What will it cost and what will we get out of it?' Every major decision involving the outlay of resources needs, at the outset, an analysis of the likely costs and benefits – hence the use of the term 'cost/benefit analysis'.

Almost immediately we encounter the first problem: not all costs and benefits can be easily quantifiable in financial terms. What value would you place, for instance, on the destruction of beautiful countryside by the building of a motorway or power station; or how would you seek to quantify the goodwill engendered by the joint construction of a hospital in a deprived area of the Third World?

'Public interest' issues tend to arise in major projects and require identification so that their impact can be separately assessed, whether or not an attempt is made to quantify them in financial terms. The next problem then emerges – it is more difficult to quantify some of the costs and benefits than others. The directly attributable major outlays are usually easy enough to identify and to quantify, for example:

- the salaries and wages payable to personnel totally involved in the activity;
- the expenditure on plant and equipment required;
- the establishment and other overhead costs of separate premises and operations.

Other situations are much more difficult to assess:

- where facilities will have to be shared;
- where overall management time will have to be apportioned;
- where there are operational implications for other parts of the organization.

Nevertheless, estimates must be made in all these areas and the results of the analysis must then be reviewed.

It is therefore important, at this stage, to determine which costs and benefits we should be considering – in other words those which are relevant to the decision. We can identify these as the future costs or benefits which will arise as a result of the decision, if taken. These will be the:

- differential, incremental or avoidable costs or benefits of *taking* a particular course of action (*see Chapter 9*);
- the opportunity costs of *forgoing* another course of action.

Cost-saving or income-generating?

At this stage in the exercise, it is important to determine whether the project being analysed is one which is intended to benefit the business by cost reduction or by income generation, or in certain cases a combination of the two. It cannot be overlooked that what starts out by being considered a cost-saving exercise, e.g. the installation of a computer to handle some previously labour-intensive clerical task, can have a powerful income-generating function also, e.g. perhaps by the leasing out of spare processing time on the machine.

The message here is threefold:

- There is a powerful, psychological, morale-boosting effect to income generation which does not attach to cost reduction, particularly when the latter may have connotations of job losses, redundancies, closures and so on.
- It is important in presenting any case which may be competing with others, to maximize the potential plus points and therefore to keep a look-out for beneficial side-effects which may enhance the main issue.
- The development within an organization of entrepreneurial flair is almost always linked to the concept of income generation – having an eye to *making* money, rather than saving it. Although the latter can have a very significant impact on the overall financial position, it is usually perceived as the function of the accountants and 'control-mongers' and to being aimed at essentially the short-term rather than the long-term expansion and development of the business.

All this is not to say that the process of development through income-generating activity should take place in an uncontrolled way. The philosophy that declares 'you have to spend it in order to make it' can be fraught with pitfalls – hence, the need for evaluation.

The financing decision

One corollary of the 'spend it to make it' school of thought is that before you can spend it, you have to *get* it. So where do we get it and what is it going to cost us?

The sources from which businesses obtain the finance to carry out their activities can basically be divided into two:

- The business itself – from shareholders' funds and retained earnings.
- Other people – that is to say, borrowing it.

Each of these can in turn be subdivided into several individual sources but in each case the cost of obtaining the funds will, or *should*, be defrayed from the cash generated by the profitable activity.

Examples of the range of options are as follows:

Leasing Costs charged directly against profits for which there is no repayment of amounts borrowed and no depreciation of the acquired fixed assets.

Issue of shares The costs of finance are incurred by way of increased dividends – either on ordinary shares or by way of a fixed rate on preference shares. Assets acquired are written off against profit by way of depreciation.

Bank or other borrowing The costs of finance are interest costs, charged directly against profits. Assets acquired are treated as above (per issue of shares); amounts borrowed are repaid out of the cash proceeds of profitable operations.

Trade credit Deferred payment terms (if you can get them) will usually absorb the money cost in the price of the asset acquired, and this will be written off against profit by way of depreciation.

But what about the cash-rich company with plenty of reserves that can just go out and buy what it needs without having to negotiate any form of finance with anyone else? Well, we call the money costs in this case '*opportunity costs*' – in other words, the cost of forfeiting income from investing the money we are planning to put into our project. An opportunity cost represents the forgoing of some benefit or other, usually expressed in terms of 'if we hadn't done this, we would have been benefiting from that.'

The actual cost of financing or 'the cost of capital', is one input into the assessment of the required 'rate of return' for any project.

Estimating the relevant cash flows

The cash flows which are to be used in capital investment appraisal have to be estimated in a similar way to that in which a cash budget is arrived at. However, capital investment appraisal uses incremental cash flows consisting of relevant costs and revenues. Thus, as mentioned in Chapter 9, outflows of cash which would have occurred regardless of whether or not the project goes ahead are irrelevant to the decision, and should be excluded from the cash flows.

Being a non-cash item, depreciation should also be excluded from the cash flows. The cash moves when the asset concerned is bought or sold.

The effects of taxation, however, should be taken into account in estimating the cash flows. Many textbook-type problems on this area ignore taxation. Taxation cannot be ignored because it can and does have a significant impact on the estimated cash flows.

Methods of evaluation

The examples which follow will all use the net (tax adjusted) incremental cash flows for Project 2066:

Year	1	2	3	4	5	6
£(000s)	59	122.6	62.2	58.5	16.92	14.38

The project has a net cost of £228,000.

The payback method

This method of capital investment appraisal simply looks at how long it takes the incremental net cash flows to recover the initial investment. Using the tax-adjusted cash flows from our example, we can compute the payback period as follows:

Project 2066		
Year	**Cash flow £'000**	**Cumulative cash flow £'000**
1	59	59
2	122.6	181.6
3	62.2	243.8
4	58.5	302.3

From the information it can be observed that the payback takes more than two years, but less than three. Assuming that the cash flows accrue evenly throughout Year 3, we can work out how long it takes to generate the amount needed to take the Year 2 cumulative of £181,600 to equal the initial investment of £228,000:

	£'000
Initial investment	228
Less Year 2 cumulative	181.6
Amount needed to be generated in Year 3	46.4
$\therefore \frac{46.4}{62.2 \text{ (Year 3 cash flow)}} \times 12$ months =	say 9 months

Thus, the payback period is 2 years 9 months.

Thus, the payback method asks how quickly will the positive cash-flow from profitable operation result in the recovery of the up-front capital investment. It merely totals cash inflows against outflows, until such time as the cumulative net total overtakes the original cash outlay. The payback method considers the project acceptable if the payback period is equal to or less than a predetermined acceptable yardstick. For competing projects, choose the one with the quickest payback. The longer the project goes on the greater the uncertainty and, therefore, the greater the risk.

Problems with the payback method

In addition to ignoring the timing of the cash flows, the payback method has the following weaknesses:

- It does not take the 'time value' of the cash flows into account.
- It ignores cash flows beyond the payback period.
- It may lead to adopting projects with a higher inherent risk.
- It may lead to the rejection of good, wealth-creating projects.
- It does not provide any measure of overall profitability.

Having said this, the payback method possesses the merit of simplicity, and is widely used in many organizations. Its drawbacks are probably not so significant where it is used to assess relatively short-term, lower value projects.

The net present value (NPV) method

The payback method takes no account of the well-observed fact that 'a bird in the hand is worth two in the bush'. In other words, money which you collect now can be made to work to your advantage immediately, and is, therefore, inherently more 'valuable' than the same nominal amount of legal tender which you are due to receive this time next year. A simple example shows the reasoning behind this:

If we have £1,000 now we can invest it at – say – 10 per cent for one year, so at the end of the year we will possess £1,100 – wealth creation of £100. So the 'future value' in one year's time of £1,000 at an interest rate of 10 per cent is £1,100. It follows that the 'present value', at a rate of 10 per cent of £1,100 in one year's time is £1,000.

- Future value at 10 per cent of £1,000 = £1,000 × 1.1 = £1,100.
- Present value at 10 per cent of £1,100 in one year = £1,100 × 1/1.1 = £1,000.

What is the present value of £1,000 in one year? £1,000 × 1/1.1 = £909.

The calculation of future value, by the way, is not the same thing as allowing for inflation (which is about the fact that a given nominal amount won't buy the same quantity of goods this time next year, for various reasons) although it has the same sort of effect and is another reason why 'future' money is not worth as much as 'present' money.

The net present value method (also called the discounted cash flow method) does take into account the 'time value' of the cash flows. It works on the principle that over time, the value of money goes down, i.e. £1 today will be worth less in one year's time. The cash flows are converted to their present value equivalents by multiplying them by an appropriate net present value discount rate.

Which discount rate should be used? To a great extent, this depends upon the subjective judgement of the selector. There are a number of rates which could be used, for example:

- the cost of capital;
- a 'cut-off rate';
- a risk-adjusted rate.

Whichever is used, if the net present value is positive the project is worthy of further consideration. If the net present value is negative, the project should be rejected, because it is not wealth-creating.

The net present value is calculated as follows: the total of the present value of the cash flows *less* the initial investment equals the net present value.

Assuming a cost of capital of 10 per cent for our example, we can use the present value tables in Appendix 1 to discount the cash flows as follows:

Project 2066				
Year	Cash flows £'000	10% discount rate	Present value £'000	Cumulative present value £'000
1	59	.909	53.63	53.63
2	122.6	.826	101.27	154.90
3	62.2	.751	46.71	201.61
4	58.5	.683	39.96	241.57
5	16.92	.621	10.51	252.08
6	14.38	.564	8.11	260.19
			260.19	
	Less initial cost		228.00	
	NPV	=	£32.19	

The project has a positive net present value, which indicates that it is wealth-creating and therefore worthy of consideration. On the basis of the above information alone, however, the project cannot be accepted, because there are various other considerations which enter into the decision. Remember, the above financial information is just one piece of the decision-making jigsaw. The decision rule advocated by numerous other texts is that if the project's net present value is positive, then it should be accepted because it is creating wealth. However, this approach is a little too naïve for real life situations. There are numerous non-financial factors which must also be taken into account.

The discounted payback method

When we computed the net present value for the tax-adjusted incremental cash flows for Project 2066, we added a cumulative present value column. From this we can compute the discounted payback, an improvement on the payback method because it does take account of the time value of money.

We can see at a glance that our initial investment is paid back during Year 4. The discounted payback works out as follows:

	£'000
Initial investment	228
Less Present value of cash flows to end of Year 3	201.61
Amount needed to be generated in year 4:	26.39

$$\therefore \frac{26.39}{39.96} \times 12 \text{ months} = \text{say } 8 \text{ months}$$

Thus, the discounted payback is 3 years 8 months.

The internal rate of return (IRR)

The discount rate which will produce a net present value of nil is called the internal rate of return. It represents the actual rate of return on a project. It is the point at which the present value of all the cash flows are equal to the initial investment in the project. For example, with Project 2066, the present value of all the cash flows would have to be equal to the initial cost of £228,000.

Having already worked out the NPV of the project using a 10 per cent discount rate, we automatically know that the internal rate of return is greater than 10 per cent. Why? Because using a 10 per cent discount rate produces a positive NPV. To end up with a nil NPV will take a higher discount rate.

The story to date tells us that the IRR is +£32,190 away from the 10 per cent discount rate. Using a trial and error method, we now look for a higher discount rate which will give us a negative NPV.

We will try a 20 per cent present value discount factor, as follows:

Project 2066			
Year	**Cash flow £'000**	**20% Discount rate**	**Present value £'000**
1	59	.833	49.15
2	122.6	.694	85.08
3	62.2	.579	36.01
4	58.5	.482	28.20
5	16.92	.402	6.80
6	14.38	.335	4.82
			210.06
	Less Initial investment		228.00
		NPV	(£17.94)

Having found a negative NPV, we now know that the IRR is greater than 10 per cent but less than 20 per cent.

Our picture of the IRR can be set out as in Fig. 10.1.

Thus, the IRR is:

$$10\% + \left(\frac{£32\,190}{50\,130} \times 10 \right) = 10\% + 6.42\% = 16.42\%$$

Some organizations employ 'cut-off' internal rates of return relative to the risk category of the project. Thus if the IRR on a project falls short of that which is required, the project will be dropped.

For example, if the IRR required for project 2066 was 15 per cent, it should be considered further. If, however, the IRR required was 24 per cent it should be shelved.

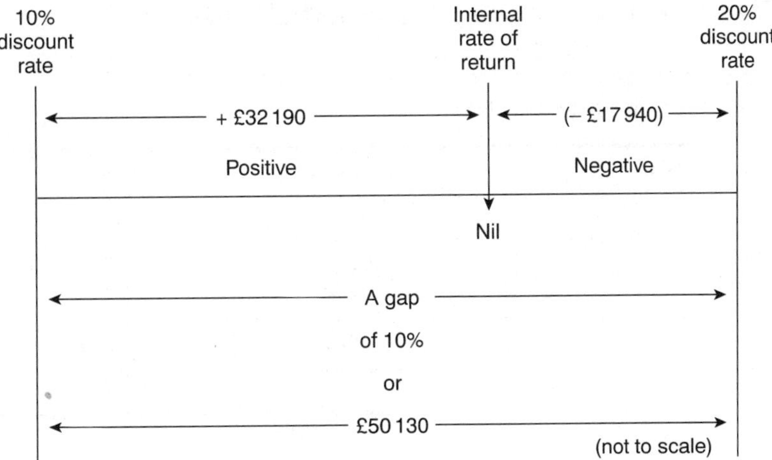

Figure 10.1 Finding the IRR

The cost benefit (profitability index)

This is just another way of looking at the present value of the cash flows, and is computed as follows:

$$\frac{\text{Present value of the cash flows}}{\text{Initial cost of the project}}$$

For Project 2066 the profitability index (PI) using our 10% discount factor would be:

$$\frac{£260\,190}{£228\,000} = 1.14$$

It can form a convenient way of ranking alternative projects. In this case for every £1 invested £1.14p's worth of present value cash flows are generated.

Accounting rate of return

The above evaluations have concentrated on cash flows, but it may be important for political reasons, or to satisfy perceptions in the market-place, to consider the 'accounting rate of return' – the idea of return on capital employed being measured in terms of accounting profit.

This is calculated for a project as a whole to compare the overall achievement against a predetermined yardstick, or on a year-by-year basis in order to measure the effect on the overall company return on capital.

The following example illustrates the method:

Original cost: £50 000
Length of project: 4 years

Year	Incremental cash flows £	Depreciation £	Accounting profit £
1	10 000	12 500	(2 500)
2	20 000	12 500	7 500
3	40 000	12 500	27 500
4	30 000	12 500	17 500
	£100 000	£50 000	£50 000

Average accounting profit over four years = £12,500

Average capital employed = £50,000 ÷ 2 = £25,000

Therefore accounting rate of return = 50%

Year by year, the figures calculate thus:

Year 1	(2 500)	÷	43 750	=	Negative
Year 2	7 500	÷	31 250	=	24.00%
Year 3	27 500	÷	18 750	=	146.67%
Year 4	17 500	÷	6 250	=	280.00%

You should note that the computation of the accounting profit does take depreciation into account.

Problems with accounting rate of return

- Overall assessment ignores timing of earnings flow.
- Selection of target rate often arbitrary.
- Uncertainty over definition of 'profit' and 'capital employed'.

The average capital employed is based on the fact that at the start of the project £50,000 is invested, but at the end of the project there is nil invested, because the asset has been written down to nil.

Judgement

As with all financial estimating techniques, let us remind ourselves that once again we are dealing with a technique which, while on the face of it is extremely mathematical and precise in its operation, it nevertheless depends heavily on the exercise of judgement. Points at which this judgement has to be exercised include:

- Identification and estimation of both the costs and the benefits of the proposed project.
- Decisions as to whether it is possible, and if so how, to measure the financial effect of the 'social' or 'public interest' implications of the plan.
- Estimation of the relevant financing 'costs' of the proposal, particularly in the context of the timing of any required repayments.
- Estimation of the timing of the 'absolute' cash flows in order to enable calculation of the 'payback' period.
- Identification of the expected rate of return to be used in discounting the future net cash flows back to present values – calculation of the 'discounted cash flows', or DCF. This includes assessment of a 'riskless' rate of return which might otherwise be received for the money invested, assessment of the 'cost of capital', compensation for inflation (other than already 'bundled' in the going rate of interest) and a judgement of the 'business risk' involved in the project in order to determine some sort of 'risk premium'.

Sensitivity analysis

Sensitivity analysis may be applied to test the extent to which the resultant figures which relate to a capital investment project may change as a result of a change in one or more of the assumptions on which the figures are based. Assumptions made for a project involving the purchase of new plant and machinery could include: the cost of the plant and machinery; its life and residual value; running costs; etc. Sensitivity analysis will provide an indication about what could happen to the expected rate of return etc. as a result of changes in basic assumptions. It does therefore, help management to appreciate a range of possible outcomes in their quest to cope with uncertainty.

Capital investment appraisal and the tax factor

The illustration which follows has been designed to provide you with an insight into the way in which tax is dealt with in producing the net after tax cash flows. The assumptions about the rates of taxation and other tax matters which we will be using are:

- Capital allowances at 25 per cent, reducing balance method.
- A rate of Corporation Tax of 50 per cent.
- Tax payable and tax allowances receivable – a one year time lag e.g. those payable or receivable for one year will affect the cash flows of the next year.
- Cash received from the residual value of machinery or equipment will be received in the year following that in which the sale takes place.
- Tax relating to balancing allowances and balancing charges (profits or losses on the sale of fixed assets as computed for tax purposes) will affect the cash flows of the year following that in which the sale takes place.

- For existing assets which will be replaced if the project goes ahead, you will either be provided with the tax written down value and sale proceeds, or the balancing allowance or balancing charge, or sufficient information to calculate them using 25 per cent Capital Allowances.

Please note:
Where a machine or equipment is to be replaced if a project goes ahead, do not ignore the tax aspects relating to the old machine when computing the *relevant cash flows*, e.g. the tax on the balancing allowance or balancing charge.

Example: Tahir plc

Tahir plc is considering whether or not to replace a machine purchased a few years go with a new machine.

You have been provided with the following information:

Old machine	**£**
Cost in 19X2	64 000
Scrap value at the end of 19X8	8 000
Trade-in value (now) 19X5	24 000
Taxation written down value (now)	nil

Depreciated at 20 per cent reducing balance for financial accounting purposes.

New Machine	**£**
Cost (now) in 19X5 (project life 4 years)	124 000
Scrap value at the end of 19X8	16 000

Depreciated at 25 per cent per annum for financial accounting purposes. This new machine will generate incremental (relevant) cash flows of £48,000 per annum. Plant replacement decisions of this type are expected to produce an IRR (Internal Rate of Return) of 20 per cent.

Should the new machine be purchased?

	Capital allowances computations*		
19X5	**Cost/W.D.V. b/f**	**W.D. allowance @ 25%**	**W.D.V. c/f**
	£	£	£
New machine	124 000	31 000	93 000
19X6			
Balance b/d	93 000	23 250	69 750
19X7			
Balance b/d	69 750	17 438	52 312
19X8			
Balance b/d	52 312	13 078	39 234
19X9 The machine is sold for scrap – proceeds:			16 000
	Balancing allowance (BA)		

The above allowances are incorporated into the cash flows, taking into account a corporation tax rate of 50 per cent and a one year time lag.

*Old machine = £24,000 BC @ 50 per cent = £12,000. It is assumed that the £12,000 tax on the old machine's BC (balancing charge) will affect the 19X6 cash flows.

	Incremental cash flows (year)						
	19X5	19X6	19X7	19X8	19X9	19X0	
Inflows (£'000s)							
From new machine	48	48	48	48	–	–	
Scrap value of new machine					16		
Tax on BC (old machine)						4	(A saving)
Capital allowances	–	15.5	11.625	8.719	6.539	11.617	(BA)
(A)	48.0	63.5	59.625	56.719	22.539	15.617	
Outflows (£'000s)							
Tax on BC (old machine)	–	12	–	–	–	–	
Scrap value (old machine)					8		(A loss)
Tax on cash flows	–	24	24	24	24	–	
(B)	–	36	24	24	32	–	
Net cash flow							
(A)−(B) × by	48.0	27.5	35.625	32.719	(9.461)	15.617	
Discount factor @ 20%	.833	.694	.579	.482	.402	.335	
PV=	39.984	19.085	20.627	15.771	(3.803)	5.232	96 896
Less initial investment		124 000 − 24 000					100 000
					NPV		(£3 104)

The net present value (NPV) is less than the required internal rate of return (IRR). According to the company's decision rule it should, therefore, be rejected.

In earlier chapters of this text, the terms 'cost' and 'benefit' were treated in their profit and loss account context with only a relatively brief mention of the cash requirements demanded by the need to repay borrowed money and to show a final 'net return', in cash terms, by way of reward for the investment in the particular activity or project.

It is important to remind ourselves again of this difference between profit and cash, and to realize two important truths:

- If a project does not yield cash for a long time, then the 'money costs' will mount up. This is the case even if the activity is inherently profitable (and cash-generating) in the longer term.
- The quicker the cash starts rolling in, the more attractive the particular project will be when compared with other competing proposals of equal profitability but with slower cash inflows.

As well as a positive 'cost/benefit' assessment, it is therefore important to have an analysis of the estimated net cash flows generated by the activity, since, ultimately, wealth creation will be measurable in terms of total cash accruing to the business. The methodology of drawing these up is the same as for any cash forecasting exercise. The forecast cash flows will, of course, exclude any non-cash expenses charged for the purpose of measuring 'accounting profit' – in particular depreciation – but should take the tax factor into account.

The methods of capital investment appraisal

The payback method

This looks at how long it takes to recover the cost of the initial investment from the incremental (relevant) cash flows.

Methods using discounted cash flows

The concept of the future value of money, and the discounting calculation to reflect it, leads us to ask: what do the total net cash flows, spread over the life of the project or activity, come to when converted back into 'present day' money?

This approach has the attraction that we can assess all of our competing projects on the same basis – namely, the present values of their individual future cash flows, no matter when they are actually generated.

The actual conversion to present values is done using discounting tables.

These provide factors for calculating the present value of £1 if received at various periods in the future, and assuming a specified rate of return, e.g. the cost of capital or a 'cut-off' rate.

The net present value (NPV) method This method uses the calculation: the present value of the cash flows *less* the initial cost of the project equals the NPV.

The discounted payback method This simply looks at how long it takes to recover the initial cost of the project, from the present values of the cash flows.

The internal rate of return This looks for the discount rate which will produce a net present value of nil, i.e. the point at which the present value of the cash flows is equal to the cost of the initial investment in the project.

The cost benefit (profitability index) This is used for ranking projects and is computed by dividing the present value of the cash flows by the initial cost of the project.

Other methods

Accounting rate of return This takes the accounting profit which has been computed after taking depreciation into account:

$$\frac{\text{Average accounting profit}}{\text{Average capital employed}} \times 100 = \text{The accounting rate of return (as a percentage).}$$

Alternatively it can be calculated on a year-by-year basis.

FURTHER READING

Atrill P & McLaney E (1997) *Financial Management for Non-Specialists*, London: Prentice Hall

Chadwick L (1997) *The Essence of Management Accounting* (2nd Edition), Hemel Hempstead: Prentice-Hall

Chadwick L & Kirkby D (1996) *Financial Management*, London: Routledge

Pike R & Neale B (1996) *Corporate Finance & Investment*, London: Prentice-Hall

Weetman P (1996) *Management Accounting, An Introduction*, London: Pitman

Williamson D (1996) *Cost and Management Accounting*, London: Prentice-Hall

Capital investment appraisal: additional self-assessments

Self-assessment 10.1: Quick questions

1 Why is depreciation not deducted in computing the cash flows?

2 What is meant by the term 'incremental' or 'relevant' cash flow?

3 When is a cost an irrelevant cash flow?

4 Using the present value of £1 table, calculate the present value of:

(a) £5,000 receivable in ten years' time using a discount rate of 15 per cent;

(b) £12,000 receivable in five years' time using a discount rate of 10 per cent;

(c) £2,500 receivable in seven years' time using a discount rate of 12 per cent.

5 Using the present value of an annuity table, calculate the present value of:

(a) receiving a cash flow of £4,000 per year for five years at a 10 per cent rate;

(b) receiving a cash flow of £12,000 per year for six years at a rate of 8 per cent;

(c) the cost of an annuity of £2,000 per annum for ten years at 6 per cent.

Self-assessment 10.2: Marsoakland plc

The managing director of your company has obtained terms on which four different companies would supply almost identical fabric-printing equipment. These are:

Fabprint plc	£20,000 payable on delivery and £5,000 payable at the end of each of the following five years.
Texcop Inc	£10,000 payable on delivery, £15,000 payable at the end of four years, and £20,000 payable at the end of five years.
Chonso Print	£8,000 at the end of each of the following four years, and £13,000 at the end of the fifth year.
Vogel Bochum	£5,000 payable on delivery, and £10,000 payable at the end of each of the following four years.

(a) Using the following annuity and NPV figures below, where appropriate, calculate the equivalent cash price which could be offered, if payment were to be made in full at the time of delivery, compound interest being taken into account at 10 per cent per annum:

- The cost of an annuity of £1 for:
  - four years is £3.170;
  - five years is £3.791.
- An annuity of £1 per annum amounts to:
  - £4.641 in four years;
  - £6.105 in five years.
- The present value of £1 is:
  - £0.683 if payable in four years' time;
  - 0.621 if payable in five years' time.

(b) State which other factors and practical considerations ought to be taken into account before arriving at a final decision to purchase the fabric-printing equipment.

Self-assessment 10.3: Robpell plc

Robpell plc are considering the following project:

Project **Year**	**1**	**2**	**3**	**4**
Incremental:	**£'000**	**£'000**	**£'000**	**£'000**
Receipts	20	30	20	16
Payments	16	25	17	14
(including depreciation of £8,000 per annum)				

The initial outlay on the project is £38,000. The company's cost of capital is 12 per cent.

Calculate:

1 the payback;

2 the discounted payback;

3 the NPV of the project.

Self-assessment 10.4: Risky Business plc

The directors of Risky Business plc are considering the acquisition of a new machine, which could generate incremental cash inflows and outflows as follows:

Year	1	2	3	4	5
	£'000	£'000	£'000	£'000	£'000
Income	85	110	150	120	40
Expenditure (excluding depreciation)	65	80	100	90	25

The immediate initial outlay needed to acquire the machine is £100,000.

For financial accounting purposes the new machinery is depreciated on a straight-line basis.

The corporate planning team has categorized all projects as follows:

	Risk	Required rate of return %
A	Low	12
B	Average	18
C	High	25

The project is of the average risk category. Do you think the company is likely to accept this project?

Self-assessment 10.5: Which twisting machine?

Jim Hodgson has been considering the problem of the replacement of one of the twisting machines, and has discussed the matter with the financial manager, Pat Bessell. Apparently there are three possible alternative machines which could be purchased:

- A Quad-twist, a new automated version of the present machine, manufactured by Chad-tex of Huddersfield.
- An Auto-twist 85, manufactured by a German company.
- A Twita 66 Twisting Machine, made in Japan.

In discussion Pat stressed the need for a proper evaluation of the alternatives and made the point that the first step was accurately to estimate the incremental cash flows for each of the alternatives. Jim Hodgson and Pat Bessell had done this, and produced the following figures:

	UK Quad-twist £	**German Auto-twist £**	**Japan Twita 66 £**
Initial outlay (approx.)	100 000	100 000	100 000
Cash inflows:			
Year 1	10 000	40 000	30 000
Year 2	20 000	30 000	30 000
Year 3	30 000	30 000	30 000
Year 4	30 000	10 000	30 000
Year 5	30 000	5 000	20 000
Year 6	34 000	5 000	10 000

You are required to: prepare your evaluation (assuming a cost of capital of 10 per cent), using:

1 The packback method.

2 The discounted payback method

3 The net present value method

4 The profitability index

5 The internal rate of return.

Comment briefly on your findings.

11

Strategic Issues

The principal objective of this, the final chapter, is simply to introduce you briefly to some of the newer applications of cost and management accounting and to highlight its strategic importance.

LEARNING OBJECTIVES

Having read this chapter you should understand what is meant by:

- strategic management accounting;
- activity-based cost management;
- attribute costing;
- benchmarking;
- life cycle costing;
- quality costing;
- target costing;
- competitor assessments;
- the balanced scorecard.

More cost and management accounting techniques

It was not the objective of this text to cover cost and management techniques such as process costing, contract costing, operating costing which it could be argued is well within the domain of the professional management accountant.

Strategic management accounting (SMA)

In addition to assessing internal performance and reviewing and monitoring internal costs and revenues, SMA is also concerned with reviewing the external environment in which the firm operates. For example, producing and generating information and reports on competitors, customers, markets, suppliers, the impact of social changes/green issues, economic matters etc. However, the role of management accounting always has been and always will be the provision of appropriate and relevant managerial information which will help with planning, monitoring, control and decision making.

Activity-based cost management

This becomes a reality when management focus on the resource consuming activities which cause the costs in the first place. This involves monitoring, evaluating, reporting and controlling such costs. Thus, there is some effort involved in managing the forces that cause the activities.

Attribute costing

This involves trying to assign a cost to a product/service attribute that is valued and appeals to customers, e.g. warranty arrangements, after sales service, operating performance, etc.

Benchmarking

This is the process by which an organisation attempts to measure its operations, products and services against those of its competitors/market leaders.

Life cycle costing

Life cycle costing is defined by CIMA as 'The practice of obtaining, over their lifetimes, the best use of physical assets at the lowest total cost to the entity.' This will involve a review of costs and revenues throughout the life cycle which is illustrated in Figure 11.1.

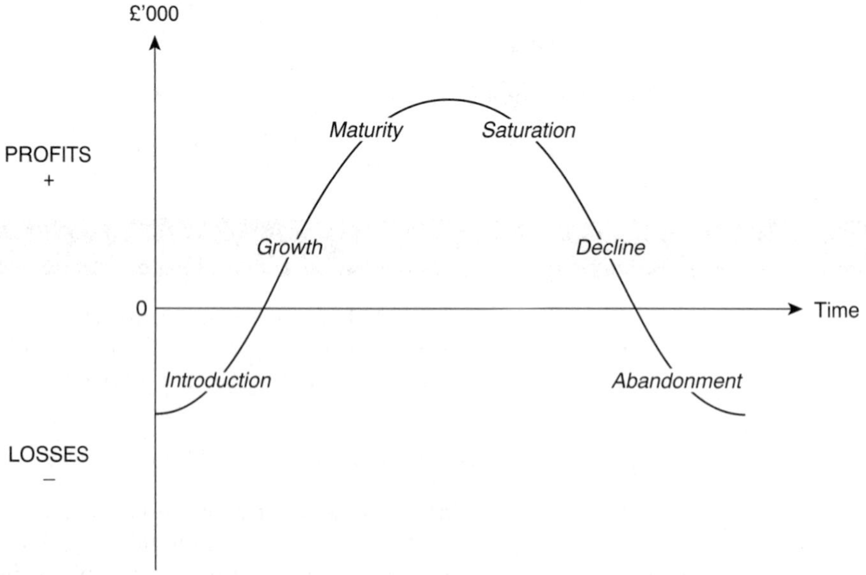

Figure 11.1 The product life cycle

The stages are, the introduction (which as illustrated in Figure 11.1 can be affected by start-up expenditure), the growth stage, the maturity stage, saturation (in which profits level off and start to fall because of increased competition), the decline stage and abandonment.

Quality costing

Quality costing deals with the costs associated with the identification of defects in terms of prevention costs, failure costs and appraisal costs, and reporting them to management. Management can then take corrective/appropriate action to ensure that the quality of the product in terms of its manufacture/assembly/component parts, etc. improve.

Target costing

This technique works by setting a selling price designed to attract a particular market share of a particular target market/market segment. The product has then to be designed so as to realize a desired profit. Its cost must not, therefore, exceed the set selling price less the desired profit.

Other strategic issues

The balanced scorecard

The balance scorecard is an approach that leads a management to focus on achieving current financial results and on creating future value through strategic activities. The scorecard translates an organization's mission and strategy into a set of performance measures built around the following perspectives: financial, customer, internal processes, and innovation and improvement.

Competitor assessment

This involves monitoring the performance of competitors in terms of sales, market share and estimates of their unit costs. It also involves reviews of financial performance via published financial reports and accounts, all of which can assist in the quest for gaining a competitive advantage.

Strategic management accounting takes a very keen interest in a company's external environment. Cost and management accounting covers a very wide field of techniques and activities. There are many different types of costing many of which are strategic in their outlook.

FURTHER READING

Atrill P A & McLaney E (1994) *Management Accounting, An Active Learning Approach*, Oxford: Blackwell

Ryan B (1995) *Strategic Accounting for Management*, London: Dryden

Williamson D (1996) *Cost and Management Accounting*, London: Prentice Hall

Appendix 1

Present Value Discount Tables

PRESENT VALUE OF £1

Year	5%	6%	7%	8%	9%	10%	11%	12%	13%	14%	15%	16%	17%	18%	19%	20%	21%	22%	23%	24%	25%	26%	27%	28%	29%	30%	35%	40%
0	1.000	1.000	1.000	1.000	1.000	1.000	1.000	1.000	1.000	1.000	1.000	1.000	1.000	1.000	1.000	1.000	1.000	1.000	1.000	1.000	1.000	1.000	1.000	1.000	1.000	1.000	1.000	1.000
1	.952	.943	.935	.926	.917	.909	.901	.893	.885	.877	.870	.862	.855	.847	.840	.833	.826	.820	.813	.807	.800	.794	.787	.781	.775	.769	.741	.714
2	.907	.890	.873	.857	.842	.826	.812	.797	.783	.769	.756	.743	.731	.718	.706	.694	.683	.672	.661	.650	.640	.630	.620	.610	.601	.592	.549	.510
3	.864	.840	.816	.794	.772	.751	.731	.712	.693	.675	.658	.641	.624	.609	.593	.579	.564	.551	.537	.524	.512	.500	.488	.477	.466	.455	.406	.364
4	.823	.792	.763	.735	.708	.683	.659	.636	.613	.592	.572	.552	.534	.516	.499	.482	.467	.451	.437	.423	.410	.397	.384	.373	.361	.350	.301	.260
5	.784	.747	.713	.681	.650	.621	.593	.567	.543	.519	.497	.476	.456	.437	.419	.402	.386	.370	.355	.341	.328	.315	.303	.291	.280	.269	.223	.186
6	.746	.705	.666	.630	.596	.564	.535	.507	.480	.456	.432	.410	.390	.370	.352	.335	.319	.303	.289	.275	.262	.250	.238	.227	.217	.207	.165	.133
7	.711	.665	.623	.583	.547	.513	.482	.452	.425	.400	.376	.354	.333	.314	.296	.279	.263	.249	.235	.222	.210	.198	.188	.178	.168	.159	.122	.095
8	.677	.627	.582	.540	.502	.467	.434	.404	.376	.351	.327	.305	.285	.266	.249	.233	.218	.204	.191	.179	.168	.157	.148	.139	.130	.123	.091	.068
9	.645	.592	.544	.500	.460	.424	.391	.361	.333	.308	.284	.263	.243	.225	.209	.194	.180	.167	.155	.144	.134	.125	.116	.108	.101	.094	.067	.048
10	.614	.558	.508	.463	.422	.386	.352	.322	.295	.270	.247	.227	.208	.191	.176	.162	.149	.137	.126	.116	.107	.099	.092	.085	.078	.073	.050	.035
11	.585	.527	.475	.429	.388	.350	.317	.287	.261	.237	.215	.195	.178	.162	.148	.135	.123	.112	.103	.094	.086	.079	.072	.066	.061	.056	.037	.025
12	.557	.497	.444	.397	.356	.319	.286	.257	.231	.208	.187	.168	.152	.137	.124	.112	.102	.092	.083	.076	.069	.062	.057	.052	.047	.043	.027	.018
13	.530	.469	.415	.368	.326	.290	.258	.229	.204	.182	.163	.145	.130	.116	.104	.093	.084	.075	.068	.061	.055	.050	.045	.040	.037	.033	.020	.013
14	.505	.442	.388	.340	.299	.263	.232	.205	.181	.160	.141	.125	.111	.099	.088	.078	.069	.062	.055	.049	.044	.039	.035	.032	.028	.025	.015	.009
15	.481	.417	.362	.315	.275	.239	.209	.183	.160	.140	.123	.108	.095	.084	.074	.065	.057	.051	.045	.040	.035	.031	.028	.025	.022	.020	.011	.006
16	.458	.394	.339	.292	.252	.218	.188	.163	.141	.123	.107	.093	.081	.071	.062	.054	.047	.042	.036	.032	.028	.025	.022	.019	.017	.015	.008	.005
17	.436	.371	.317	.270	.231	.198	.170	.146	.125	.108	.093	.080	.069	.060	.052	.045	.039	.034	.030	.026	.023	.020	.017	.015	.013	.012	.006	.003
18	.416	.350	.296	.250	.212	.180	.153	.130	.111	.095	.081	.069	.059	.051	.044	.038	.032	.028	.024	.021	.018	.016	.014	.012	.010	.009	.005	.002
19	.396	.331	.277	.232	.194	.164	.138	.116	.098	.083	.070	.060	.051	.043	.037	.031	.027	.023	.020	.017	.014	.012	.011	.009	.008	.007	.003	.002
20	.377	.312	.258	.215	.178	.149	.124	.104	.087	.073	.061	.051	.043	.037	.031	.026	.022	.019	.016	.014	.012	.010	.008	.007	.006	.005	.002	.001
25	.295	.233	.184	.146	.116	.092	.074	.059	.047	.038	.030	.025	.020	.016	.013	.011	.009	.007	.006	.005	.004	.003	.003	.002	.002	.001	.001	.000
30	.231	.174	.131	.099	.075	.057	.044	.033	.026	.020	.015	.012	.009	.007	.005	.004	.003	.003	.002	.002	.001	.001	.001	.001	.000	.000	.000	.000
35	.181	.130	.094	.068	.049	.036	.026	.019	.014	.010	.008	.006	.004	.003	.002	.002	.001	.001	.001	.001	.000	.000	.000	.000	.000	.000	.000	.000
40	.142	.097	.067	.046	.032	.022	.015	.011	.008	.005	.004	.003	.002	.001	.001	.001	.000	.000	.000	.000	.000	.000	.000	.000	.000	.000	.000	.000
45	.111	.073	.048	.031	.021	.014	.009	.006	.004	.003	.002	.001	.001	.001	.000	.000	.000	.000	.000	.000	.000	.000	.000	.000	.000	.000	.000	.000
50	.087	.054	.034	.021	.013	.009	.005	.003	.002	.001	.001	.001	.000	.000	.000	.000	.000	.000	.000	.000	.000	.000	.000	.000	.000	.000	.000	.000

Note: The above present value factors are based on year-end interest calculations

CUMULATIVE PRESENT VALUE OF £1 PER ANNUM
(i.e. present value of an Annuity of £1)

Year	5%	6%	7%	8%	9%	10%	11%	12%	13%	14%	15%	16%	17%	18%	19%	20%	21%	22%	23%	24%	25%	26%	27%	28%	29%	30%	35%	40%
1	.952	.943	.935	.926	.917	.909	.901	.893	.885	.877	.870	.862	.855	.847	.840	.833	.826	.820	.813	.807	.800	.794	.787	.781	.775	.769	.741	.714
2	1.859	1.833	1.808	1.783	1.759	1.736	1.713	1.690	1.668	1.647	1.626	1.605	1.585	1.566	1.546	1.528	1.510	1.492	1.474	1.457	1.440	1.424	1.407	1.392	1.376	1.361	1.289	1.224
3	2.723	2.673	2.624	2.577	2.531	2.487	2.444	2.402	2.361	2.322	2.283	2.246	2.210	2.174	2.140	2.106	2.074	2.042	2.011	1.981	1.952	1.923	1.896	1.868	1.842	1.816	1.696	1.589
4	3.546	3.465	3.387	3.312	3.240	3.170	3.102	3.037	2.974	2.914	2.855	2.798	2.743	2.690	2.639	2.589	2.540	2.494	2.448	2.404	2.362	2.320	2.280	2.241	2.203	2.166	1.997	1.849
5	4.329	4.212	4.100	3.993	3.890	3.791	3.696	3.605	3.517	3.433	3.352	3.274	3.199	3.127	3.058	2.991	2.926	2.864	2.804	2.745	2.689	2.635	2.583	2.532	2.483	2.436	2.220	2.035
6	5.076	4.917	4.767	4.623	4.486	4.355	4.231	4.111	3.998	3.889	3.784	3.685	3.589	3.498	3.410	3.326	3.245	3.167	3.092	3.021	2.951	2.885	2.821	2.759	2.700	2.643	2.385	2.168
7	5.786	5.582	5.389	5.206	5.033	4.868	4.712	4.564	4.423	4.288	4.160	4.039	3.922	3.812	3.706	3.605	3.508	3.416	3.327	3.242	3.161	3.083	3.009	2.937	2.868	2.802	2.508	2.263
8	6.463	6.210	5.971	5.747	5.535	5.335	5.146	4.968	4.799	4.639	4.487	4.344	4.207	4.078	3.954	3.837	3.726	3.619	3.518	3.421	3.329	3.241	3.156	3.076	2.999	2.925	2.598	2.331
9	7.108	6.802	6.515	6.247	5.995	5.759	5.537	5.328	5.132	4.946	4.772	4.607	4.451	4.303	4.163	4.031	3.905	3.786	3.673	3.566	3.463	3.366	3.273	3.184	3.100	3.019	2.665	2.379
10	7.722	7.360	7.024	6.710	6.418	6.145	5.889	5.650	5.426	5.216	5.019	4.833	4.659	4.494	4.339	4.192	4.054	3.923	3.799	3.682	3.571	3.465	3.366	3.269	3.178	3.092	2.715	2.414
11	8.306	7.887	7.499	7.139	6.805	6.495	6.207	5.938	5.687	5.453	5.234	5.029	4.836	4.656	4.486	4.327	4.177	4.035	3.902	3.776	3.656	3.544	3.437	3.335	3.239	3.147	2.752	2.438
12	8.863	8.384	7.943	7.536	7.161	6.814	6.492	6.194	5.918	5.660	5.421	5.197	4.988	4.793	4.610	4.439	4.278	4.127	3.985	3.851	3.725	3.606	3.493	3.387	3.286	3.190	2.779	2.456
13	9.394	8.853	8.358	7.904	7.487	7.103	6.750	6.424	6.122	5.842	5.583	5.342	5.118	4.910	4.715	4.533	4.362	4.203	4.053	3.912	3.780	3.656	3.538	3.427	3.322	3.223	2.799	2.469
14	9.899	9.295	8.745	8.244	7.786	7.367	6.982	6.628	6.302	6.002	5.724	5.468	5.229	5.008	4.802	4.611	4.432	4.265	4.108	3.962	3.824	3.695	3.573	3.459	3.351	3.249	2.814	2.478
15	10.380	9.712	9.108	8.559	8.061	7.606	7.191	6.811	6.462	6.142	5.847	5.575	5.324	5.092	4.876	4.675	4.490	4.315	4.153	4.001	3.859	3.726	3.601	3.483	3.373	3.268	2.825	2.484
16	10.838	10.106	9.447	8.851	8.313	7.824	7.379	6.974	6.604	6.265	5.954	5.669	5.405	5.162	4.938	4.730	4.536	4.357	4.190	4.033	3.887	3.751	3.623	3.503	3.390	3.283	2.834	2.489
17	11.274	10.477	9.763	9.122	8.544	8.022	7.549	7.120	6.729	6.373	6.047	5.749	5.475	5.222	4.990	4.775	4.576	4.391	4.219	4.059	3.910	3.771	3.640	3.518	3.403	3.295	2.840	2.492
18	11.690	10.828	10.059	9.372	8.756	8.201	7.702	7.250	6.840	6.467	6.128	5.818	5.534	5.273	5.033	4.812	4.608	4.419	4.243	4.080	3.928	3.786	3.654	3.529	3.413	3.304	2.844	2.494
19	12.085	11.158	10.336	9.604	8.950	8.365	7.839	7.366	6.938	6.550	6.198	5.877	5.584	5.316	5.070	4.844	4.635	4.442	4.263	4.097	3.942	3.799	3.666	3.539	3.421	3.311	2.848	2.496
20	12.462	11.470	10.594	9.818	9.129	8.514	7.963	7.469	7.025	6.623	6.259	5.929	5.628	5.353	5.101	4.870	4.657	4.460	4.279	4.110	3.954	3.808	3.673	3.546	3.427	3.316	2.850	2.497
25	14.094	12.783	11.654	10.675	9.823	9.077	8.422	7.843	7.330	6.873	6.464	6.097	5.766	5.467	5.195	4.948	4.721	4.514	4.323	4.147	3.985	3.834	3.694	3.564	3.442	3.329	2.856	2.499
30	15.372	13.765	12.409	11.258	10.274	9.427	8.694	8.055	7.496	7.003	6.566	6.177	5.829	5.517	5.235	4.979	4.746	4.534	4.339	4.160	3.995	3.842	3.701	3.569	3.447	3.332	2.857	2.500
35	16.374	14.498	12.948	11.655	10.567	9.644	8.855	8.176	7.586	7.070	6.617	6.215	5.858	5.539	5.251	4.992	4.756	4.541	4.345	4.164	3.998	3.845	3.703	3.571	3.448	3.333	2.857	2.500
40	17.159	15.046	13.332	11.925	10.757	9.779	8.951	8.244	7.634	7.105	6.642	6.234	5.871	5.548	5.258	4.997	4.760	4.544	4.347	4.166	3.999	3.846	3.703	3.571	3.448	3.333	2.857	2.500
45	17.774	15.456	13.606	12.108	10.881	9.863	9.008	8.283	7.661	7.123	6.654	6.242	5.877	5.552	5.261	4.999	4.761	4.545	4.347	4.166	4.000	3.846	3.704	3.571	3.448	3.333	2.857	2.500
50	18.256	15.762	13.801	12.234	10.962	9.915	9.042	8.305	7.675	7.133	6.661	6.246	5.880	5.554	5.262	5.000	4.762	4.545	4.348	4.167	4.000	3.846	3.704	3.571	3.448	3.333	2.857	2.500

Note: The above present value factors are based on year-end interest calculations.

Appendix 2

Suggested Answers for Self-assessments

The elements of cost

2.1: Stock-holding costs

1 Stocks of materials, fuels, work-in-progress and finished goods cost money to buy or produce. A business does therefore have to finance its investment in such stock. Stock which is held by a business represents capital tied up. The capital is untied when the stock is sold.

2 In addition to the cost of the stocks of materials, etc. there are also holding costs. Holding costs are all the other costs associated with acquiring and keeping of stocks.

3 Holding costs consist of acquisition costs, the stores function, inventory control, handling, and administration costs, etc. (see Fig. 2.1)

4 Management can keep stock-holding costs to a minimum by:

- using the regular delivery system and JIT (just in time);
- using subcontractors;
- Pareto analysis;
- improving the coding and classification system;
- adopting a policy of standardization.

For other ideas, see Chapter 2.

5 The advantages of keeping stock levels to acceptable minimums are:

- less capital tied up in stocks;
- a reduction in holding costs;
- making better use of factory and warehouse space.

However, note that if reducing stocks causes a stock-out, this could result in lost production and lost orders.

6 If the business sells surplus stocks this will mean that there is less stock to manage and control, and will free valuable storage space for other purposes. The space freed may even be available for production purposes, or to sublet.

7 The financial benefits of employing a subcontractor are:

- they provide the fixed assets and the labour used for production purposes;
- they may have to finance the purchase and holding of the materials and components used, work-in-progress and stocks of finished goods.

Provided that the price and quality are right, the use of subcontractors can prove a very worthwhile option.

8 Variety is expensive because more materials will have to be stocked, tying up more capital. Capital is expensive, so holding costs will therefore be increased.

Stores ledger *Turbo Wheels Ref. SS193*

Date	Details	Receipts			Issues			Balance		
		Qty	Price	£	Qty	Calc	£	Qty	Price	£
1 *FIFO*			£						£	
March	Balance b/f							100	12	1 200
March	Received	100	15	1 500				200	–	2 700
April	Issued				160	100×£12 +60×£15	2 100	40	15	600
May	Received	200	6	3 200				240	–	3 800
June	Issued				180	40×£15 +140×£16	2 840	60	16	960
July	Received	100	20	2 000				160	–	2 960
Aug.	Issued				120	60×£16 +60×£20	2 160	40	20	800
2 *LIFO*										
March	(as above)(opening balance plus units received)							200	–	2,700
April	Issued				160	100×£15 +60×£12	2 220	40	12	480
May	Received	200	16	3 200				240	–	3 680
June	Issued				180	£16	2 880	60	40×£12 +20×£16	800
July	Received	100	20	2 000				160	–	2 800
Aug.	Issued				120	100×£20 +20×£16	2 320	40	12	480
3 *AVE CO*										
March	(as above)(opening balance plus units received)							200	13.50*	2 700
April	Issued				160	13.50	2 160	40	13.50	540
May	Received	200	16	3 200				240	15.58	3 740
June	Issued				180	15.58	2 805	60	15.58	935
July	Received	100	20	2 000				160	18.34	2 935
Aug.	Issued				120	18.34	2 201	40	18.34	734

*Average Price: $\frac{£2\,700}{200}$ = £13.50

2.2: Pricing methods

You will find many cost and management accounting texts cover this area. Although the questions set may be longer and the numbers more difficult to deal with, the principles remain unchanged.

2.3: Labour

1 An analysis of time sheets, time cards and time recorded via computer terminals can give a breakdown of:

- direct and indirect labour;
- productive and non-productive (idle) time;
- overtime worked;
- machine hours per operative, machine, machine group, department, etc;
- the cost per cost entre, e.g. department, subsection, service, operation or product, etc.

2 The payroll analysis is helpful in assisting management with the preparation of budgets and standards. It is also useful in providing control information, e.g. the idle time analysis and machine utilization information.

3 Productivity deals are popular with employers because they prefer pay increases to be self-financing.

4 The cost per unit came down in the Thirsk Antics Ltd example:

- because the incentive scheme paid £8 per unit, as opposed to £10 per unit paid under the current system;
- because the overtime payments are being spread over a greater number of units.

5 If employees produced seventy-five units in 51 hours (including 12 hours of overtime) their earnings would be:

	£
75 units × £8 =	600
Overtime premium	
12 hours × £5 =	60
	£660

6 The rate of labour turnover, i.e. the rate at which employees leave an organization, is calculated as follows:

$$\frac{\text{number of persons leaving in the period}}{\text{average number of persons on the payroll during the period}} \times 100$$

7 The costs which should be included in the cost of labour turnover are shown in Chapter 2.

8 Management can reduce the cost of labour turnover by ensuring that every leaver has an interview to find out why they are leaving. The reasons for leaving then need to be reported to management and acted upon accordingly.

Management can take other action to reduce labour turnover, e.g. using works committees, suggestion schemes, welfare and social activities, perks, employee share schemes and profit sharing, and the continuing education and training of their personnel.

2.4: Direct and indirect expenses

1 Indirect – the payments can be traced directly to the cost centre, i.e. the canteen, but are still an overhead.

2 Indirect – it can be traced to the cost centre, the robotic machine department, as a production overhead.

3 Indirect – it cannot be traced to specific products or services.

4 Indirect – for all cost centres.

5 Direct – hired for the packing department.

You will observe that what is direct or indirect is not always so clear cut. It all depends upon the circumstances, in particular on the traceability for the expense to the service, product or process, and whether it forms part of the product or service.

2.5: Quick questions

1 Direct materials: those materials which form part of the product.

2 Materials management: concerned with the planning and control of materials, including ordering, inventory control, internal control, etc.

3 Acquisition costs: the costs involved in the ordering, purchasing, receiving and inspection of materials in terms of staff costs, fixed assets used, and associated overheads.

4 JIT: a production system in which the material becomes available during a very short period before it is needed.

5 Pareto analysis: Pareto invented the 80–20 rule, e.g. 20 per cent of your stock could account for 80 per cent of its value. Thus, if you identify the relevant 20 per cent and subject those items to more frequent controls, you are in effect controlling a vast percentage of the value of the stock held.

   It has been found that the 80–20 rule does offer numerous applications; e.g. 20 per cent of your stock could account for 80 per cent of production hold-ups! Pareto analysis uses A, B, C classifications, e.g.

A items-control daily;

B items-control weekly;

C items-control monthly; and so on.

This is why Pareto Analysis is sometimes called ABC analysis.

6 FIFO: a method of pricing or valuing stock issued to production or for resale and in stock. The issues are valued in the same order as that in which the stock came in.

FIFO should also be used as the physical issue system, to avoid stock losses, irrespective of the method of stock valuation.

7 Direct labour: the labour which is used to transform raw material into finished goods in a manufacturing environment.

8 Idle time: idle time is also called waiting time or non-productive time. Employees may be non-productive because they are waiting for work, materials or a setter, or because of a machine breakdown.

9 The payroll analysis: an analysis of the wages and salaries paid, according to direct and indirect labour, departments, cost centres, products, etc. It is a very useful source of data for absorption costing systems and budget preparation.

10 The rate of labour turnover. The rate at which employees leave a company or organization in a given period for pastures new.

2.6: Methods of stock valuation

		£	£
1 Sales	(140 units)		11 760
Less FIFO value of stock sold:			
	50 at £60	3 000	
	80 at £76	6 080	
	10 at £72	720	9 800
	FIFO profit:		£1 960
Value of closing stock (£15 180 − £9 800) =			£5 380

		£	£
2 Sales	(140 units)		11 760
Less LIFO value of stock sold:			
	20 at £65	1 300	
	30 at £64	1 920	
	40 at £72	2 880	
	50 at £76	3 800	9 900
	LIFO profit:		£1 860
Value of closing stock (£15 180 − £9 900) =			£5 280

		£	£
3 Sales	(140 units)		11 760
Less AVE CO value of stock sold:			
	140 at £69*		9 660
	AVE CO Profit:		£2 100
Closing stock (15 180 − 9 660) = (or 80 units at £69)			£5 520

$$\text{Average cost} = \frac{£15180}{220 \text{ units}} = £69 \text{ per unit}$$

The illustrations in the text so far were all concerned with the valuation of stock issued to production. This example was taken from a wholesaling environment. However, whatever the type of business, the operation of the valuation methods remain the same.

2.7: FIFO LIFO AVE CO

Stores ledger

Date	Receipts			Issues			Balance		
FIFO	**Qty**	**Price**	**£**	**Qty**	**Price**	**£**	**Qty**	**Price**	**£**
1 Jan	1 000	5	5 000				1 000	£5	5 000
5 Jan				500	5	2 500	500	£3	2 500
20 Feb	800	6	4 800				1 300		7 300
25 Feb				1 000	500×£5 +500×6 }	5 500	300		1 800
4 Mar	700	8	5 600				1 000		7 400
16 Mar				500	300×6+ 200×£8 }	3 400	500	£8	4 000
LIFO									
20 Feb	(as above)						1 300		7 300
25 Feb				1 000	800×£6 +200×£5 }	5 800	300	£5	1 500
4 Mar	700	8	5 600				1 000		7 100
16 Mar				500	£8	4 000	500	300×£5 +200×£8 }	3 000
AVE CO									
20 Feb	(as above)						1 300	5.62*	7 300
25 Feb				1 000	5.62	5 620	300		1 680
4 Mar	700	8	5 600				1 000	7.28†	7 280
16 Mar				500	7.28	3 640	500		3 640

* $\frac{\text{£7 300}}{\text{1 300 units}} = \text{£5.62}$

† $\frac{\text{£7 280}}{\text{1 000 units}} = \text{£7.28}$

Overheads and total absorption costing

3.1: Direct and indirect expenditure

Direct: 1, 4, 5, 6, 9, 10*

Indirect: 2, 3, 7, 8, 10*

* It all depends upon whether or not the supervisor concerned is actually producing anything. If they simply supervise other workers then the salary paid will be regarded as indirect (except where there is a single product environment).

In practice, whether an item will be treated as direct or indirect will depend to a great extent upon the individual or group of individuals who have to make that decision. You must appreciate therefore, that the treatment of certain items of expenditure will depend upon the subjective judgement of the decision maker. Any item which is really direct may be treated as indirect on materiality grounds i.e. if the item in question is of insignificant value.

3.2: Methods of apportionment

1 = A; 2 = A (the replacement value of machinery is not appropriate); 3 = B; 4 = B (in practice, estimates should be based on an estimate of the time spent in each cost centre by the supervisor); 5 = D (if the kilowatt hours figures were not available, then floor area or cubic capacity would have to be used).

3.3: Calculating the absorption (recovery) rates

1 Machine Group I $\dfrac{\text{£26880}}{\text{19200 machine hours}}$ = £1.40 per machine hour

Machine Group II $\dfrac{\text{£27000}}{\text{21600 machine hours}}$ = £1.25 per machine hour

Assembly $\dfrac{\text{£18120}}{\text{10000 direct labour hours}}$ = £1.812 per direct labour hour

2 The whole factory $\dfrac{\text{£72000}}{\text{24000 direct labour hours}}$ = £3.00 per direct labour hour

The rate you have calculated for the whole factory is called a *blanket rate* i.e. one rate which covers every department. This overall rate is not to be commended, because it fails to take account of departmental differences. For highly mechanized departments, machine hour rates are considered to be the most appropriate.

3.4: Costing a job

Job cost for job no. XYP 008165

	£	£
Materials		*67.00*
Labour:		
Machine Group I (£8 × 6 hours)	48.00	
Machine Group II (£9 × 8 hours)	72.00	
Assembly (£7 × 5 hours)	35.00	155.00
Overheads		
Machine Group I (£1.40 × 20 m/c hours)	28.00	
Machine Group II (1.25 × 21 m/c hours)	26.25	
Assembly (£1.812 × 5 direct lab hours)	9.06	63.31
		£285.31

Note that you would add a mark-up to the £285.31 in order to set a selling price or produce a quotation.

3.5: Total absorption costing Cut Gate plc

Parts (a) and (b) are on pp. 186–7.

(c) Quotation for Job 16783 RBP

		£	£
Materials			2941.00
Direct labour:			
Dept.			
X	(17 hrs × £9)	153.00	
N	(10 hrs × £11)	110.00	
Q	(5 hrs × £8)	40.00	303.00
Overheads:			
Dept.			
X	(30 mach. hrs × £1.60)	48.00	
N	(10 hrs × £2.25)	22.50	
Q	(5 hrs × £3.10)	15.50	86.00
			3330.00
Add mark up at 40 per cent on cost			1332.00
Quote:			£4662.00

Note that to recover department X's overheads we use the number of machine hours, because we are using a machine hour absorption rate.

3.6: Total absorption costing multiple-choice test

1 A

2 C

3 A

4 D

5 D which is calculated as follows:

	£
Materials and labour	336
Overheads:	
Assembly (8×£2.25)	18
Machine Dept. (20×£3.50)	70
	£424

3.5(a) *Departmental overhead distribution summary*

Overhead expenditure	Basis of apportionment	Total	Production departments			Service departments	
			X	N	Q	Maintenance	Stores
		£	£	£	£	£	£
			(30%)	(20%)	(20%)	(10%)	(20%)
Rent and rates	Floor	36000					
Light and heat	Area	26000					
Insurance of buildings		12000					
		7400	22200	14800	14800	7400	14800
			(10%)	(40%)	(40%)	(5%)	(5%)
Welfare and canteen £21000 Works manager's salary £19000	number of employees	40000	4000	16000	16000	2000	2000
			(60%)	(15%)	(15%)	(5%)	(5%)
Insurance of machinery	Replacement values	6400	3840	960	960	320	320
Indirect labour	allocated	69000	12000	7700	8300	18000	23000
Depreciation of machinery & equipment	allocated	38080	24500	5500	4000	2580	1500
Other overheads	allocated	10520	3460	2240	1140	1300	2380

		£238 000	70 000	47 200	45 200	31 600	44 000
Stores apportioned	(given)		8 800	17 600	13 200	4 400	−44 000
						36 000	
Maintenance apportioned	(given)		25 200	7 200	3 600	−36 000	
	c/fwd	£238 000	104 000	72 000	62 000		

3.5(b)	*Production departments*		
	X	N	Q
Overheads b/f	104 000	72 000	62 000
Machine hours	65 000		
Direct labour hours		32 000	20 000
Absorption rates:	*£1.60* per machine hour	*£2.25* per direct labour hour	*£3.10* per direct labour hour

Suggested Answer

3.7: Total absorption costing quick questions

1

'T' Section Machine hour rate	'Q' Section Direct labour hour rate
$\frac{£134\,400}{56\,000}$ = £2.40 per machine hour	$\frac{£57\,600}{32\,000}$ = £1.80 per direct labour hour

2 A 'blanket' overhead absorption rate:

$$\frac{£192\,000}{48\,000 \text{ hours}} = \textit{£4 per direct labour hour}$$

A blanket rate avoids the problems of allocating and apportioning overheads to the sections. However, it will not reflect departmental differences, which could prove to be quite significant.

3 For the limitations of total absorption costing, please refer to p. 46.

4 For a concise description of how total absorption costing works, see p. 34, Fig. 3.3, etc.

5 For the reasons why it is difficult to distinguish between direct and indirect expenditure, see pp. 32–3.

3.8: Mason Van Chad Construction Ltd

1	**Basis**	**Total £**		**A**		**B**		**C**
Rent	Area	31 000	30%	9300	36%	11 160	34%	10 540
Indirect labour	DLH	19 500	6/12	9750	4/12	6500	2/12	3250
Depreciation	Value of plant	11 000	20/44	5000	18/44	4500	6/44	1500
Repairs & maintenance	Tech. est.	6000		2700		1890		1410
Consumable stores	DLH	4500	6/12	2250	4/12	1500	2/12	750
Canteen	No. of employees	10 000	40/80	5000	25/80	3125	15/80	1875
Works manager's salary	Direct	13 000		3500		5500		4000
National Insurance	No. of employees	2000	40/80	1000	25/80	625	15/80	375
General administration	Est.	30 000	5/12	12 500	4/12	10 000	3/12	7500
		127 000		51 000		44 800		£31 200
2 *Direct labour hours*				6000		4000		2000
Absorption rate (Per DLH)				£8.5		£11.2		£15.6

3			£	£	£
	Direct materials			856	
	Direct labour	A 24×5	120		
		B 10×4.50	45		
		C 6×4		24	189
	Overheads	A 24×8.5	204		
		B 10×11.2	112		
		C 6×15.6	93.6	409.6	1 454.6
	+ mark up at 20%				290.9
					£1 745.5

3.9: Techtex plc

1 Departmental overhead distribution summary:

Quarter ending 31 December, 19X3

Expense	Total	Base used	Production Machining	Production Assy.	Service Mtce.	Service Handling
	£		£	£	£	£
Indirect labour	80 500	Actual	20 000	8 800	39 700	12 000
Supervision	6 000	No. of employees	2 000	3 000	750	250
Canteen	7 200	No. of employees	2 400	3 600	900	300
Rent and rates	25 000	Floor area	12 000	9 000	3 000	1 000
Fuel and light	7 500	Floor area	3 600	2 700	900	300
Other costs	5 270	Actual	4 230	420	300	320
Plant insurance	1 880	Plant cost	1 200	400	200	80
Plant depreciation	23 250	% of cost	15 000	6 250	1 250	750
	156 600		60 430	34 170	47 000	15 000
Mtec. department		Tech. estimate	12 690	29 610	−47 000	4 700
						19 700
Handling department		Tech. estimate	7 880	11 820		−19 700
	£156 600		£81 000	£75 600	–	–

2 Machine hour rate:

$$\frac{£81\,000}{6\,750 \text{ machine hours}} = £12 \text{ per machine hour}$$

£75 600 hours

Direct labour hour rate: $\dfrac{}{15\,120 \text{ direct labour hours}}$ = £5 per direct labour hour

3 Quotation for a job:

			£	£
				1 186
Direct material				
Direct labour	M/C dept.	5 × £6	30	
	Assy.	8 × £5	40	70
Overheads				
M/C dept.		7 × £12	84	
Assy.		8 × £5	40	
Cost			124	
			1 380	
			414	
			£1 794	
Add Profit at 30% on cost				

Marginal costing and break-even analysis

4.1: Giessen plc I

The effect on the contribution

	Strategy		
	(1)	(2)	(3)
	£	£	£
Selling price	25	24	25
Less Variable cost	23	20	20
Contribution	2	4	5
Contribution needed:	**£'000**	**£'000**	**£'000**
Profit target	36	36	36
Fixed costs	90	90	90
Advertising	-	-	15
	126	126	141
	126	126	141
Number of units which must be sold:	2	4	5
Contribution needed	63 000 units	31 500 units	28 200 units
	£'000	**£'000**	**£'000**
Sales value (units × selling price)	1 575	756	705

Management will have to decide which is the most feasible.

4.2: Giessen plc II

Acquiring the new semi-automatic machine would generate a contribution per unit of:

	£	
Selling price	25.00	
Less Variable cost	17.50	
Contribution	£7.50	(or £5 existing contribution + £2.50 reduction in variable cost)

	£'000	£'000
Contribution (from the sale of 20,000 units × £7.50)		150
Less Fixed costs	90	
Target profit	36	126
Amount available for new machine:		24

4.3: Montpele Ltd

	Up to 4,000 units per unit £	4,001 to 6,000 units per unit £	Over 6,000 units per unit £
Selling price	250	250	240
Less Variable cost	210	190	175
Contribution:	£40	£60	£65

	£'000
Fixed costs	258
Plus profit target	100
	£358

∴ Must sell: units	£'000
4000 × £40	160
2000 × £60	120
1200 × £65	78*
7200	£358

$\frac{*£78000}{£65} = 1200$ units, i.e. the balance needed to make our cumulative total ((£160000 + £120000 = £280000) up to the required contribution of £358000.

4.4: Break-even calculations

1 The profit volume ratio $= \frac{\text{Contribution}}{\text{Selling price}} \times 100$

$= \frac{£125}{500}$ (i.e. £500 − £375) × 100 = 25%

2 The break-even point = fixed cost ÷ PV ratio

$= £80000 \times \frac{100}{25} = £320000$

3 The break-even point in units $= \frac{\text{Fixed costs}}{\text{Contribution per unit}}$

$= \frac{£80000}{£125} = 640$ units

Knowing the number of units (640), we can multiply it by the selling price per unit of £500, which will give us £320,000, the break-even point in terms of value.

4.5: Limiting (key) factors – management action

Some of the actions which may be taken by management to reduce the effect or eliminate limiting factors which you may have thought of, are listed below.

1 Labour supply can be increased by:

- retraining existing personnel;
- overtime working;
- shiftwork;
- incentive schemes;
- subcontracting;
- acquiring labour-saving machinery and/or robots and/or equipment;
- reducing the idle/non-productive time;
- providing special facilities for working mothers with young children;
- offering better terms and conditions, e.g. better rates of pay;
- recruiting from overseas labour markets, etc.

2 Production capacity may be extended by several of the actions listed above *re* labour, such as overtime working, shiftwork, incentive schemes, subcontracting, acquiring new machines, reducing idle/non-productive time, and also by:

- improving plant layout;
- better production scheduling;
- using better quality materials which take less time to manufacture;
- better product design, e.g. variety reduction, etc.

3 To increase warehouse capacity, management could:

- use subcontractors who store the raw materials which are to be used in the production process on their own premises;
- improve the stores/warehouse layout;
- purchase storage racks which make better use of the space;
- acquire more warehouse space;
- improve inventory control to keep stock levels to an acceptable minimum;
- introduce production systems such as JIT (Just In Time);
- improve material requirements planning (MRP);

- introduce the use of substores in the factory production departments for various items;
- identify and dispose of obsolete/surplus stocks and surplus fixed assets, to free space;
- improve distribution, e.g. cut down the time that finished goods are held before being delivered to customers etc.

4 More finance is usually available, but at a price. Some of the ways of increasing the finance or reducing the need for finance are:

- The use of subcontractors. They provide the labour force, the materials and the fixed assets in terms of production machinery, plant and buildings etc.
- Introducing JIT and improving MRP and inventory control, which could result in less finance being tied up in stocks of raw materials, work-in-progress and finished goods.
- Identifying and disposing of surplus assets, e.g. stocks and fixed assets such as redundant machinery and equipment.
- Making use of alternative methods of financing assets, e.g. hire purchase, leasing and renting.
- Acquiring more finance via an issue of shares, debentures or long-term loans.
- Investigating the sale and lease-back of a building or property.
- Achieve a better utilization of labour and machinery.
- Seeking out and applying for government and/or European Union grants.

The above actions illustrate the need for business functions/managers to work together, e.g. marketing, production and finance.

4.6: Time is money

	F	T	I
The contribution per hour is	£20 / 4 hours	£11 / 2 hours	£12 / 3 hours
	=	=	=
	£5 per hour	£5.50 per hour	£4 per hour
	×	×	×
	8000 hours	8000 hours	8000 hours
	=	=	=
Total contribution:	£40000	£44000	£32000

Product T would generate the highest contribution, provided that all of the output of that product could be sold.

This simplified computation was designed to illustrate the limiting (key) factor arithmetic. As with all business decision-making, the financial data is just one of several inputs which has to be taken into account. The company could, in fact, have already received orders for each of the products F, T and I.

4.7: Break-even charts

Proof PV Ratio

$= \frac{30}{60} \times 100 = 50\%$

B.E. Point = £15,000 $\times \frac{100}{50}$

= *£30,000* (i.e. 25,000 units)

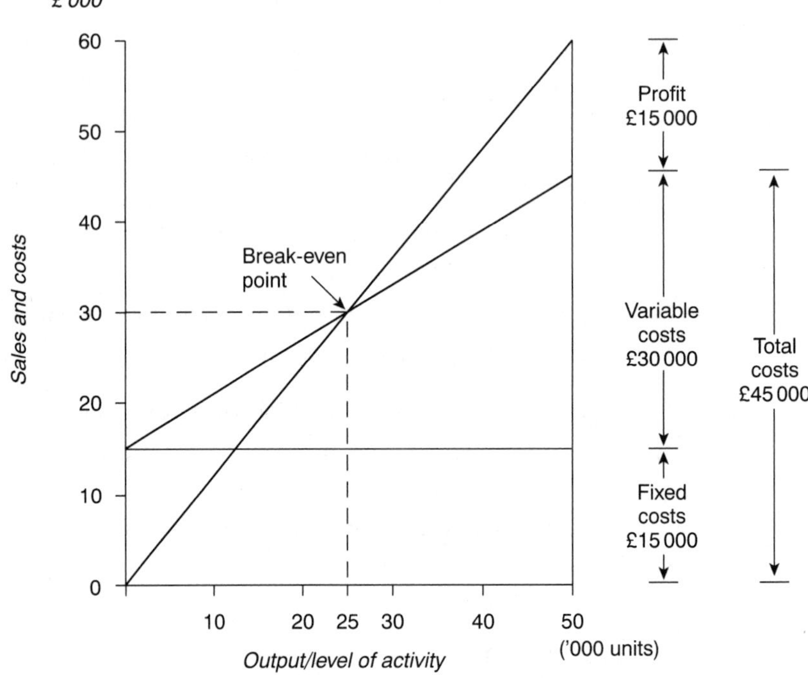

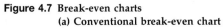

Figure 4.7 **Break-even charts**
(a) Conventional break-even chart

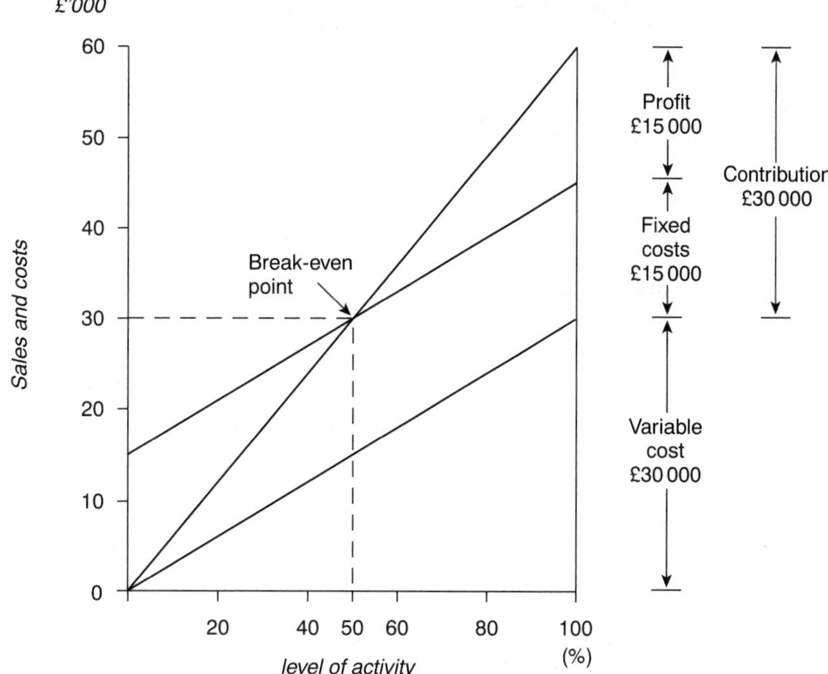

Figure 4.7 **Break-even charts cont.**
(b) Contribution break-even chart

4.8: Marginal costing test

1 (a) Fixed costs are those costs which remain unchanged irrespective of the level of output within a relevant range and in the short term, e.g. rent, insurance, business rates.

(b) Variable costs vary with the level of activity within a relevant range, e.g. raw materials used in production.

(c) Semi-variable costs or semi-fixed costs are costs which have both fixed and variable elements, e.g. a sales person's remuneration made up of a fixed salary and a commission based on sales volume/value.

2 Fixed costs

3 Marginal costing is also known as:

- variable costing;
- direct costing;
- differential costing;
- cost, volume, profit.

4 The contribution is calculated (in total or per unit) as sales less variable cost. The contribution contributes towards the recovery of the fixed overheads.

5 Missing figures:

Contribution	£3,000
Sales	£13,500
Variable costs	£11,100

6 Missing figures:

Profit	£6,000
Contribution	£19,100
Fixed cost	£5,000

7 Missing figures:

Contribution	£20,200	Profit	£14,200
Sales	£11,000	Profit	£5,500
Variable cost	£2,500	Contribution	£5,000

8 A limiting (key) factor determines what a business organization can or cannot do. It places a constraint on the business activities, e.g. where raw materials are limited in supply for a specific period of time.

9 The contribution and sales; i.e. the profit volume ratio $= \frac{\text{contribution}}{\text{sales}} \times 100$

10 The point at which sales revenue and costs are equal, or the point at which the contribution is equal to the fixed costs.

4.9: Quick questions

1 (a)

	Per unit	1000 units £
Sales	50	50000
Less Variable cost	30	30000
Contribution	20	20000
Less Fixed costs		12000
	Profit:	£8000

(b)

	Per unit £		1000 units £
Sales (50 − 10%)	45		
Less Variable cost	30		
Contribution	15	=	15000
Less Fixed costs			12000
	Profit:		£3000

(c) Contribution required = fixed costs 12000
+ profit target 8000
£20000

$\therefore$ must sell $\frac{£20000}{£15 \text{ (contribution per unit)}}$ = 1334 units

2

	Per unit	
Sales	2.00	
Less Variable cost	.50	
Contribution:	£1.50	Profit volume ratio = 75%
Break-even point =	Fixed costs	

$$£24\,000 \times \frac{100}{75} = £32\,000$$

In terms of quantity $= \frac{£24\,000}{£1.50 \text{ (contribution per unit)}} = 16\,000$ units

Proof: 16000 units @ £2 = £32,000

3 Contribution = selling price less variable cost:

	T	Z
Contribution (per unit)	£400	£240
Material usage	8 tons	4 tons
Contribution per ton =	£50	£60
Maximum contribution (× 4000)	£200000	£240000

By taking the limiting factor into account, the contribution from producing Z is £40,000 higher than that which could be achieved if production was concentrated on T.

4 (a) The break-even point = fixed costs ÷ profit volume ratio:

Buck & West

$$£50\,000 \times \frac{100}{40} = £125\,000$$

Brett 57

$$£84\,000 \times \frac{100}{60} = £140\,000$$

(b)

	Buck & West		Brett 57	
	£		£	
Profit 10% on capital invested (10% × £200000)	20000	(10% × £240,000)	24000	
Fixed costs	50000		84000	
Contribution:	70000	(40%) given	108000	(60% given)
Add Variable costs	105000	(60%)	72000	(40%)
= sales:	£175000		£180000	

The variable costs are ∴ the difference between the P.V. ratio (%) and the sales (100%) in percentage terms.

4.10: Iain Smoke Alarms Ltd

	£		£
Initial outlay	200000	× 30%	60000
Annual fixed costs			25000
Contribution required			£85000

1

		£
Selling price		20
	£	
Less variable cost	10	
Selling variable cost	5	15
Contribution =		£5 (25%)

$$\frac{£85\,000}{£5} = 17\,000 \text{ alarms}$$

2 Break-even point: fixed costs £25 000 × $\frac{100}{25}$ = £100 000 (i.e. 5,000 alarms).

3

	£
Initial outlay	200 000
2 years' fixed costs	50 000
Contribution needed	250 000

$$\frac{£250\,000}{£5} = 50\,000 \text{ alarms}$$

4

	£
Selling price	19.00
Less Variable cost	10.00
	9.00
Less Commission (19 × 25%)	4.75*
Contribution	£4.25

	£
£4.25 × 15 000 =	63 750
Less Fixed costs	25 000
Profit:	£38 750

or

	£
Contribution £5 × 15 000	75 000
Less Fixed costs £25 000 + £10 000 (Adv.)	35 000
	40 000

Spending the £10,000 on advertising (Adv.) is the better of the two alternatives, provided that it does in fact attract sales of 15,000 units.

* Note that if the selling price goes down, the sales commission also goes down.

4.11: Utreford Engineering plc

1 The profit or loss for the current period

	Per unit		200 000 units	
	£	£	£'000	£'000
Sales		40.00		8 000
Variable costs:				
Direct materials & direct labour				
(16 × 200,000)	16.00		3 200	
Variable factory overheads	.40		80	
Variable selling costs	.80		160	
Variable distribution costs	.60	17.80	120	
		22.20	3 560	
Sales commission		2.00	400	3 960
Contribution:		20.20		4 040
			(50.5% PV) ratio	
Less Fixed costs:				
Factory overheads			320	
Selling costs			340	
Distribution costs			200	
Administration costs			1 440	2 300
Profit:				£1 740

2 Sales increase by $12\frac{1}{2}$ per cent

200 000 units + $12\frac{1}{2}$%	=	225 000 units
New selling price: £40 less 5%	=	£38
Sales = 225 000 units at £38	=	£8 550 000
Less Variable cost 225 000 × £17.80		4 005 000
		4 545 000
Less Sales commission at 5%		427 500
Contribution:		4 117 500 (PV ratio 48.16%)
Less Fixed costs (as 1 above)		2 300 000
Profit:		£1 817 500

3 Sales increase by 25 per cent

200 000 units + 25%	=	250 000 units
New selling price £40 less 10%	=	£36
Sales = 250 000 units at £36	=	£9 000 000
Less Variable cost 250 000 × £7.80		4 450 000
		4 550 000
Less Sales commission at 5%		450 000
Contribution:		4 100 000 (PV ratio 45.56%)
Less Fixed cost (as 1 and 2 above)		2 300 000
Profit:		£1 800 000

4 The break-even points are:

Fixed cost ÷ PV ratio = break-even point

1	2	3
$2\,300\,000 \times \frac{100}{50.5}$	$2\,300\,000 \times \frac{100}{48.16}$	$2\,300\,000 \times \frac{100}{45.56}$
= £4 554 455	= £4 775 748	= £5 048 288

4.12: Break-even analysis

Key points

The assumptions on which break-even analysis is based, in a lot of instances do not apply to the real world; thus, the assumptions themselves can be limitations. The assumptions include the following:

- that costs are fixed, within the relevant range;
- that the analysis will be used in conjunction with other data;
- that sales are made at a constant selling price;
- that unit costs are constant;
- that sales = production;
- that efficiency and productivity remain unchanged;
- that there is a constant product-mix;
- that volume is the only factor which causes costs to increase.

The principal limitations

- As output rises, it does not follow that there will be a proportional increase in sales.
- Fixed costs may change at different levels of activity (i.e. there could be step fixed costs).
- Variable costs and total income (sales) may not be a straight line.
- The time-span affects the chart (i.e. it is best suited to the short term).
- Management decisions can alter fixed and variable costs.
- The product-mix cannot be predicted with accuracy.
- The selling price may have to vary in order to sell more (e.g. charging different prices to different markets/segments/customers).
- Efficiency is not constant.
- Break-even analysis does not take into account how much capital has been tied up.
- Producing is often for stock (i.e. sales do not equal production).
- In the long term, all costs are variable.

4.13: Able Ltd and Cable Ltd

		Able Ltd £'000	Cable Ltd £'000
1	Sales	300	300
	Less Variable cost	240	200
	Contribution:	60	100

Profit volume ratio: $\frac{60}{300} \times 100 = 20\%$ $\qquad \frac{100}{300} \times 100 = 33^1/_3\%$

The break-even point = fixed costs ÷ profit volume ratio

$= 30\,000 \times \frac{100}{20} =$ £150 000 $\qquad 70{,}000 \times \frac{100}{33^1/_3} =$ £210 000

See also the break-even chart.

2 The sales level × profit volume ratio will give us the contribution for the sales level in question:

Able Ltd		Cable Ltd	
£240 000 × 20% =	48 000	£240 000 × $33^1/_3$ =	80 000
Less Fixed cost	30 000	*Less* Fixed cost	70 000
Profit:	£18 000	Profit:	£10 000

3 (a) In periods of heavy demand, say in excess of £300,000, Cable will make the higher profits. For every additional £100 of sales Cable will earn a contribution of £$33^1/_3$, which will increase profits by that amount. Able will only make a contribution of £20 for every £100 of sales and only increase their profits by that amount.

(b) In periods of low demand, companies with higher fixed costs and a lower margin of safety are more likely to earn lower profits. Able needs to generate sales of £150,000 to break even, Cable needs to generate sales of £210,000 to break even.

Sales level £'000	Able Ltd Contribution (20% × sales) £'000	Fixed cost £'000	Profit £'000	Cable Ltd Contribution ($33^1/_3$% × sales) £'000	Fixed cost £'000	Profit £'000
100	20	30	(10)	33.3	70	(36.7)
200	40	30	10	66.7	70	(3.3)
300	60	30	30	100	70	30
400	80	30	50	133.3	70	63.3
500	100	30	70	166.6	70	96.6
600	120	30	90	200	70	130

It can be observed from an examination of the above tabulation that up to £300,000 sales Able Ltd earns greater profits. However, above this level Cable Ltd earns the higher profits.

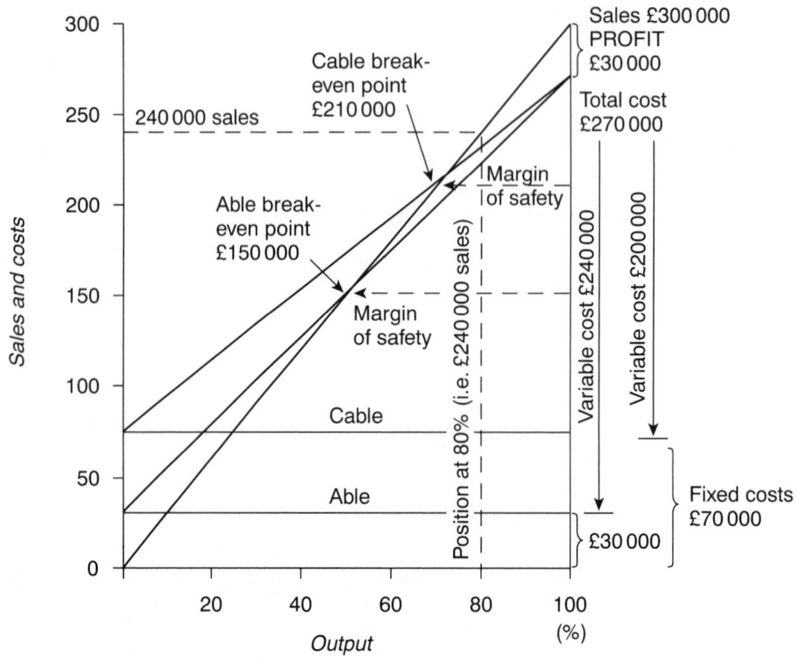

Break-even chart

Fixed cost + Variable cost = Total cost
Sales − Total cost = Profit or Loss

4.14: Step fixed costs

		per unit
		£
Workings	Selling price	100
	Less Variable cost	60
	Contribution	£40 (40% profit volume ratio)

	£
Steps: at 2 500 units	
(a) 2 500 at variable cost £60 per unit	150 000
add Fixed costs	90 000
	240 000
(b) as above	240 000
plus additional fixed costs	30 000
	270 000
at 5 000 units	£
5 000 at variable costs £60 per unit	300 000
plus Fixed costs (£90 000 + £30 000)	120 000
	£420 000

Break-even point 1 FC ÷ PV ratio

$$£90{,}000 \times \frac{100}{40} = £225\,000$$

$$\frac{£225\,000}{100} = 2\,250 \text{ units}$$

Break-even point 2

$$£120\,000 \times \frac{100}{40} = £300\,000$$

$$\frac{£300\,000}{100} = 3\,000 \text{ units}$$

The break-even chart illustrates the two break-even points.

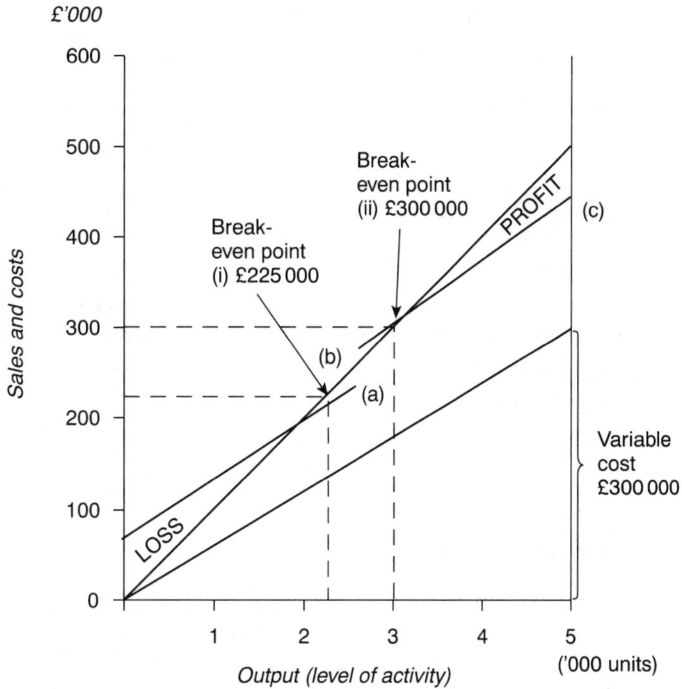

5.1: The Linz Company

Marginal costing

	January	£'000	£'000	February	£'000	£'000
Sales	(1 600×£40)		64	(1 400×£40)		56
Less Production cost of sales:						
Opening stock		–		(400×25)	10	
Add Production	(2 000×£25)	50		(2 000×£25)	50	
		50			60	
Less Closing stock	(400×£25)	10	40	(1 000×£25)	25	35
Contribution	(1 600×£15)		24	(1 400×£15)		21
Less Fixed costs			16			16
Profit:			£8	Profit:		£5

	Per unit £
Sales	40
Less Variable cost	25
Contribution	15

Closing stock =	Period 1 Units	Period 2 Units
Opening stock + production	2 000	2 400
Less Units sold	1 600	1 400
Closing stock	400	1 000

Total absorption costing

	January	£'000	£'000	February	£'000	£'000
Sales (as above)			64	(as above)		56
Less Production cost of sales:						
Opening stock		–		(400×£33)	13.2	
Add Production:						
Variable cost	(2 000×£25)	50				
				(2 000×£33)*	66.0	
Fixed cost	(2 000× £8)	16				
		66			79.2	
Less Closing stock	(400×£33)	13.2	52.8	(1 000×£33)	33.0	46.2
Gross profit	(1 600×£7)		£11.2	(1 400× £7)		£9.8

The gross profit per unit is:	Per unit
	£
Sales	40
**Less* Total cost (£25 + £8)	33
Gross profit	£7

The two lots of profits can be reconciled as follows:

	January £'000	February £'000
Absorption costing profits	11.2	9.8
Less Marginal costing profits	8.0	5.0
Difference	3.2	4.8

The difference is caused by the inclusion of the fixed costs in the stock valuations.

		January £'000		February £'000
Fixed costs c/f in closing stock	(400×£8)	3.2	(1,000×£8)	8
Less Fixed costs b/f in opening stocks		Nil		3.2
Difference		3.2		4.8

5.2: Barry Bruk Ltd

First of all let us take a look at the units in terms of costs and profits:

Total absorption costing	Per unit	Per unit
	£	£
Selling price		30
Less Total cost:		
Variable costs	20	
Fixed costs	5	25
Gross profit		5

Marginal costing	Per unit
	£
Selling price	30
Less Variable cost	20
Contribution	10

As you may recall from your earlier studies, the principal difference between total absorption costing and marginal costing is the way in which they deal with fixed production overheads. Total absorption costing includes them, marginal costing excludes them. For this illustration, we will assume that both of the methods will treat the selling and distribution expenses as period costs, i.e. write them off against profits for the period concerned.

The total absorption profit statements for the two periods would be:

Profit statement (total absorption costing)

	Period 1 Units	Period 2 Units	Period 1		Period 2	
			£'000	£'000	£'000	£'000
Sales (£30)	9000	10000		270		300
Less Absorption cost of sales (£25):						
Opening stock	Nil	2000	–		50	
Add						
Production	11000	9600	275		240	
			275		290	
Less						
Closing stock	2000	1600	50	225	40	250
Gross profit			(i.e. 9000×£5)	45	(i.e. 10000×£5)	50
Plus						
Over-absorption*				5		
Less						
Under-absorption						(2)
				50		48
Less Selling and distribution expenses				15		15
Absorption profit				35		33

* The under- or over-absorption of fixed overheads was computered as follows:

Period 1	**Fixed costs £'000**
Absorbed, production 11000 units at £5	55
Less Budget/actual fixed costs	50
Over-absorption (i.e. too much!)	£5

Period 2	**Fixed costs £'000**
Absorbed, production 9,600 units at £5	48
Less Budget/actual fixed costs	50
Under-absorption (i.e. not enough!)	(£2)

Note that it is the number of production units which is used to absorb the fixed costs, not the number of units sold.

A quick check on the arithmetical accuracy of your gross profit calculations, using the gross profit per unit, can be computed as follows:

	Period 1 £'000		Period 2 £'000
Gross profit (units sold × gross profit per unit)			
9000 × £5	40	10000 × £5	50

We will now take a look at profit statements prepared according to the marginal costing method:

Profit statement (marginal costing)

	Period 1 Units	Period 2 Units	Period 1		Period 2	
			£'000	£'000	£'000	£'000
Sales	9000	10000		270		300
Less Marginal cost of sales (£20):						
Opening stock	Nil	2000	–		40	
Add						
Production	11000	9600	220		192	
			220		232	
Less						
Closing stock	2000	1600	40	180	32	200
Contribution				90		100
Less Fixed costs			50		50	
Selling and distribution expenses			15	65	15	65
Marginal costing profit				25		35

With marginal costing, as mentioned earlier, we do not have any under- or over-absorption problems to deal with. The total contribution can be calculated very quickly, simply by multiplying the contribution per unit by the number of units sold:

	Period 1 £'000		Period 2 £'000
£10 × 9000	90	£10 × 10000	100

Why do we have different profit figures for the two methods? The short answer is, because of the treatment of the fixed costs.

		£'000
Period 1	Absorption profit	35
	Marginal costing profit	25
	Difference	10

This difference arises because the absorption closing stock, 2,000 units, includes £5 per unit fixed costs, i.e. (£5 × 2,000 = £10,000), and this is carried forward to the next accounting period.

Period 2		£'000
	Absorption profit	33
	Marginal costing profit	35
	Difference in profits	2

This difference arises because £10,000 of fixed costs was brought forward from period 1 in the stock valuation, representing 2,000 units × £5 per unit fixed costs, and 1,600 units × £5 per unit fixed cost, i.e. £8,000 was carried forward to period 3.

Reconciliation	**£'000**
Opening stock fixed costs b/f	10
Less Closing stock fixed costs c/f	8
Difference in profits	2

Thus, from a study of the reconciliation, you should observe that if the fixed costs brought forward in the absorption method's opening stock are greater than those which are included and carried forward in the absorption method's closing stock valuation, the marginal costing profit will be higher, and vice versa.

5.3: Total absorption costing versus marginal costing

The correct solutions are:

1	A	
2	A	
3	A	
4	C	(i.e. $\frac{£84000}{20000}$ = £4.20 × 4,000 units = £16800 (over-absorption)
5	C	(stock reduction 600 units × £18 = £10800)

5.4: Quick questions

1 (a) Period costs are costs which are written off in the period to which they relate, e.g. production fixed costs in a marginal costing environment and selling and distribution expenses.

(b) Overheads in a total absorption costing system are included in job/product costs via an overhead absorption rate (also called a recovery rate), e.g. so much per unit or direct labour hour or machine hour etc.

If the amount absorbed is greater than the actual fixed overhead, this is an over-absorption, i.e. too much has been charged to jobs/products, and vice versa.

In total absorption costing, to arrive at the net profit/loss, the under- or over-recovery of fixed overheads will have to be taken into account.

(c) The total or full cost of a job or product tends to include the direct material, direct labour, variable and fixed production overheads. Selling and distribution expenses may or may not be included in the job or product cost.

2 (a) Simply because the absorption rate which we were using was based on an amount per unit produced.

(b) Marginal costing is considered more accurate than total absorption costing because the variable costs can be identified and traced to the job/product/service concerned.

(c) There is a lower degree of subjectivity in marginal costing because fixed manufacturing costs do not have to be apportioned to products using an arbitrary basis such as floor area or number of employees.

(d) Because, fixed production/manufacturing overheads are included in job/product, work-in-progress and finished goods valuations. If they remain in stock at the end of the period (i.e. are part of the closing stock), their fixed overhead content is in effect being carried forward as part of the stock valuation into the next accounting period.

3 (a) Marginal costing treats fixed costs (overheads) as period costs, i.e. it writes them off in computing the profit or loss of the period in which they were incurred. This means that fixed costs are not included in work-in-progress and finished goods stock valuations and therefore are not carried forward into the next accounting period.

Marginal costing does do away with many of the subjective judgements which have to be made when using the total absorption method. However, it can be over-simplified to such an extent as to lead to a naive approach towards its application. This in turn could cause under-pricing and the failure to cover all of the costs. On the plus side, because it uses only variable costs in its stock valuations, and because of the ease with which alternatives can be evaluated using the contribution, it is recommended for decision-making.

Although absorption costing has numerous problems and disadvantages, its one saving grace is that at the end of the day, it attempts to ensure that all costs are covered.

(b) The profit statements can be reconciled by looking at the fixed costs carried forward in closing stocks and brought forward in the opening stocks in the total absorption costing method.

5.5: Jon Avi plc

1 *Total absorption costing profit statement*

	Period 1 Units	Period 2 Units	Period 1		Period 2	
			£'000	£'000	£'000	£'000
Sales at £20	20000	23000		400		460
Less Manufacturing cost: (at £15 per unit)						
Opening stock	Nil	24000	–		30	
Add Total cost of production	22000	24000	330		360	
			330		390	
Less						
Closing stock	2000	3000	30	300	45	345
Gross profit (£5 per unit sold)				100		115
Less						
Under-absorption*			21		7	
Selling and distribution costs			45	66	45	52
Net profit				£34		£63

Fixed overheads	***Period 1 £'000***		***Period 2 £'000***
Budget/actual	175		175
Absorbed (22,000 × £7)	154	(24,000 × £7)	168
* Under-absorption	£21		£7

The fixed production overhead is being absorbed at the rate of £7 for every unit which is produced.

2 *Marginal costing profit statement*

	Period 1 Units	Period 2 Units	Period 1		Period 2	
			£'000	£'000	£'000	£'000
Sales at £20	20 000	23 000		400		460
Less Variable cost: (at £8 per unit)						
Opening stock	Nil	2 000	–		16	
Add Production	22 000	24 000	176		192	
			176		208	
Less						
Closing stock	2 000	3 000	16	160	24	184
Contribution (£12 per unit sold)				240		276
Less						
Fixed production costs			175		175	
Fixed selling and distribution costs			45	220	45	220
Net profit				£20		£56

3 *Reconciliation of profits*

	Period 1 £'000	Period 2 £'000
Absorption costing	34	63
Marginal costing	20	56
Difference	14	7

The difference comes about as a result of fixed costs being included in opening and closing stock valuations, as follows:

	Period 1 £'000	
Fixed costs in closing stock 2 000 × £7 =	14	

	Period 2 £'000	
Fixed costs in opening stock	14	(as above)
Less Fixed costs in closing stock 3 000 × £7		21
		£7

5.6: Clab & Co Ltd (I)

1 *Total absorption costing*

	Per unit £	£
Selling price		116
Less Variable costs	40	
Fixed production costs	20	60
Gross profit		£56

		Period 1 £'000		Period 2 £'000
Gross profit	(£56 × 20 000)	1 120	(£56 × 24 000)	1 344

Comment We just had to multiply the gross profit per unit by the number of units sold.

2 *Marginal costing*

	Per unit £
Selling price	116
Less Variable costs	40
Contribution	£76

	Period 1 £'000		Period 2 £'000
Contribution (76 × 20 000)	1 520	(£76 × 24 000)	1 824

Comment Simply the contribution per unit multiplied by the number of units sold.

3 Every unit produced will attract twenty pounds' worth of fixed production overheads. If the units produced are less than budget, the overheads absorbed will be less than budget.

Period 1	Period 2 £'000		£'000
Fixed overheads absorbed (27,000×£20)	540	(24 500×£20)	490
Actual fixed overheads	500		500
Over-absorption	40	Under-absorption	10

You should remember that in the real world it is unusual for the budgeted and actual fixed overheads to be the same for any period. Also, that fixed overheads will tend to vary from period to period, even in the short term. Thus, the situation which needs to be faced in practice is far more complex than the introductory illustrations which are contained in this text.

5.7: Clab & Co Ltd (II)

1 Total absorption costing profit statement

	Period 1 Units	Period 2 Units	Period 1		Period 2	
			£'000	£'000	£'000	£'000
Sales at £16	20000	24000		2320		2784
Less Manufacturing cost*: at £60 per unit						
Opening stock	Nil	7000	–		420	
Add						
Production	27000	24500	1620		1470	
			1620		1890	
Less						
Closing stock	7000	7500	420	1200	450	1440
Gross profit (at £56 per unit sold)				1120		1344
(These figures agree with the 5.6 part 1 answer)						
Add						
Over-absorption of fixed overheads (per 5.6 part 3)				40		
Less						
Under-absorption of fixed overheads (per 5.6 part 3)						10
				1160		1334
Less						
Selling and distribution expenses				730		730
Net profit				£430		£604

* £40 variable costs + £20 fixed costs

2 *Marginal costing profit statement*

	Period 1 Units	Period 2 Units	Period 1		Period 2	
			£'000	£'000	£'000	£'000
Sales at £116	20 000	24 000		2 320		2 784
Less Variable cost of manufacturing: at £40						
Opening stock	Nil	7 000	–		280	
Add Production	27 000	24 500	1 080		980	
			1 080		1 260	
Less						
Closing stock	7 000	7 500	280	800	300	960
Contribution (at £76 per unit sold)				1 520		1 824
(as per 5.6 part 2)						
Less Fixed production costs				500		500
Selling and distribution expenses			730	1 230	730	1 230
Marginal costing profit				£290		£594

3 *Reconciliation*

	Period 1 £'000		Period 2 £'000
Total absorption costing profit	430		604
Marginal costing profit	290		594
Difference	£140		£10
Fixed overhead content of total absorption stock valuations:	£'000		£'000
Closing stock (7,000×£20)	140	(7 500×£20)	150
Less Opening stock	Nil	(7 000×£20)	140
Difference (net fixed overheads c/f)	140		10

The net amount of fixed overheads being carried forward (period 1: £140,000 less Nil = £140,000, and in period 2 are £150,000 less £140,000 = £10,000) cause the total absorption costing profits to be greater in both periods.

6.1: Quick questions

(a) A

(b) B

(c) A

(d) A

6.2: Jonbur Ltd

Activity cost pools

	Purchasing	Receiving	Despatch	Total
	£'000	£'000	£'000	£'000
Indirect labour	30	15	15	60
Lighting, heating, Office space	60	120	120	300
Computing	160	16	24	200
	250	151	159	560
Cost per order/note	£31.25	£25	£39.75	

Overheads assigned to the products via the activity cost drivers:

	Products			
	J	O	N	Total
Purchasing	156 250	62 500	31 250	250 000
Receiving	105 000	25 000	21 000	151 000
Despatch	119 250	19 875	19 875	159 000
	£380 500	£107 375	£72 125	£560 000

6.3: Vike Trading Co. Plc

Activity cost drivers

	Material handling	Set-up costs	Scheduling	Purchasing
	£'000	£'000	£'000	£'000
given	32 16 runs	40 80 set-ups	36 16 runs	20 400 orders
Cost driver	£2 000 per run	£500 per set-up	£2 250 per run	£50 per order

Product costs	V	I	K	E	Total
	£'000	£'000	£'000	£'000	£'000
Prime cost (*given*)	50	30	20	40	140
Material handling	8	12	8	4	32
Set-up costs	20	5	10	5	40
Scheduling	9	13.5	9	4.5	36
Purchasing	5	9	2	4	20
Costs	92	69.5	49	57.5	268
Sales	80	120	110	90	400
Profit (Loss)	£(12)	£ 50.5	£ 61	£32.5	£132

Product V will have to be reviewed as it is consuming a high proportion of the resources, particularly the set-up costs. Consideration will have to be given to raising its price or dropping it from the product range. This would, of course involve a careful review of other factors e.g. the effect on the other products.

6.4: L.E. Tza Plc

(a)i The direct labour hours are:

BG	1 500
LT	80 000
MD	3 500
	85 000

The direct labour hour absorption rate is therefore

(£510,000 overheads ÷ 85,000 direct labour hours) = **£6 per direct labour hour**

The overheads assigned to the products using total absorption costing will be:

BG	LT	MD	Total
£'000	£'000	£'000	£'000
9	480	21	510

(a)ii The overheads assigned to products using activity based costing will be:

	BG	LT	MD	Total
	£'000	£'000	£'000	£'000
Material handling	42.500	21.250	21.250	85
Set-up costs	22.500	15.000	22.500	60
Maintenance	21.600	36.000	32.400	90
Despatch	24.375	21.563	29.062	75
Storage costs	24.000	148.000	28.000	200
	134.975	241.813	133.212	510

(b) Profit Statements

	BG	LT	MD
	£	£	£
Material cost	6 000	80 000	5 600
Direct labour	(1 500 × £5)	(80 000 × £20)	(3 500 × £9)
	7 500	160 000	31 500
Direct costs	13 500	240 000	37 100

Total Absorption Profit Statement

	BG	LT	MD
	£	£	£
Sales	40 000	880 000	63 000
Direct costs	13 500	240 000	37 100
Overheads	9 000	480 000	21 000
	22 500	720 000	48 100
Profit (Loss)	17 500	160 000	14 900

Activity Based Costing Profit Statement

	BG	LT	MD
	£	£	£
Sales	40 000	880 000	63 000
Direct costs	13 500	240 000	37 100
Overheads	134 975	241 813	133 212
	148 475	481 813	170 212
Profit/(Loss)	(108 475)	398 187	(107 212)

(c) The picture revealed by the ABC treatment does raise serious questions. It would appear that products BG and MD both consume a vast amount of the activities, and both make a substantial ABC loss. It could well be the case that if they were discontinued the overheads consumed by them could be reduced significantly and the overall profit increased. However, this does depend on the demand for product LT continuing in the future.

7.1: Dacroo Ltd cash graph

You should have plotted the bank balances as follows:

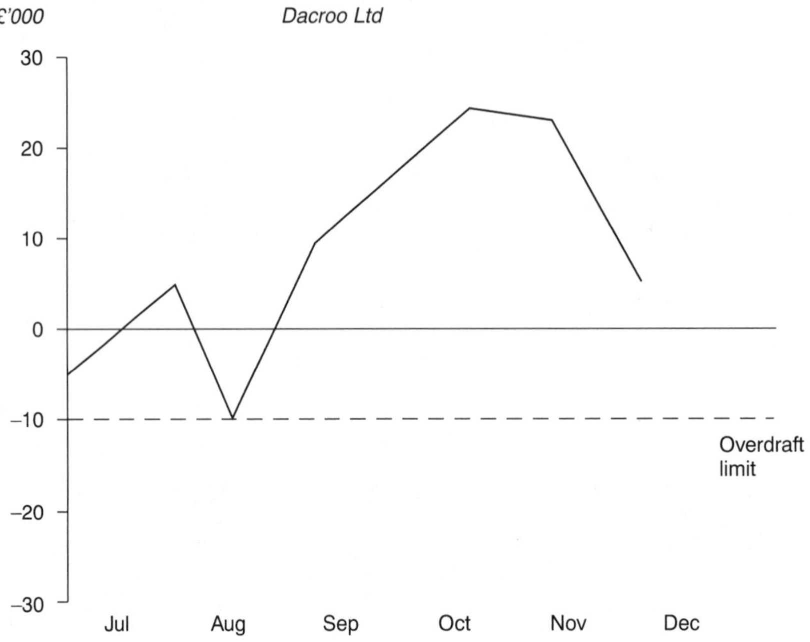

You should have spotted that particularly in October and November, the company has surplus funds which may be invested short term in order to earn a return.

7.2: Latin & Co

Cash budget

		Inflows	Outflows					
	Opening balance £	Sales £	Purchases £	Rent £	Wages and salaries £	General expenses £	Fixed assets £	Closing balance £
Jan.	65 000	–	–	–	1 400	500	60 000	3 100
Feb.	3 100	10 000	–	–	1 400	500		11 200
Mar.	11 200	16 000	30 000	300	1 400	500		(5 000)
Apr.	(5 000)	26 000	20 000	–	1 400	500		(900)
May	(900)	26 000	16 000	–	1 400	500		7 200
Jun.	7 200	26 000	16 000	300	1 400	500		15 000

		Sales	Purchases	Rent	Wages and salaries	General expenses	Fixed assets
		104 000	82 000	£600	£8 400	£3 000	£60 000
	On credit:	26 000	32 000				
		£130 000	£114 000				

Budgeted profit and loss account for the year ending 30 June 19X4

		£	£
Sales			130 000
Less Cost of sales:			
Opening stock		–	
Add Purchases		114 000	
		114 000	
Less Closing stock†	16 500	97 500	
Gross profit (25% of sales £130 000)			32 500
Less Expenses:			
Rent		600	
Wages & salaries		8 400	
General expenses		3 000	
Depreciation		3 000	15 000
Net profit			£17 500

Budgeted balance sheet as at 30 June 19X4

Capital employed:		£	£
Capital		65 000	
Add Net profit		17 500	82 500
Employment of capital:			
Fixed assets		60 000	
Less Depreciation		3 000	57 000
Working capital:			
Current assets			
Stock		16 500	
Debtors	(one month – June)	26 000	
Cash & bank		15 000	
		57 500	
Less Current liabilities			
Creditors	(two months – May & June)	32 000	25 500
			82 500

† The closing stock is calculated as follows:
1 The gross profit is calculated (25% × sales £130,000) = £32,500.
2 The gross profit of £32,500 is deducted from the sales figure of £130,000, to give the cost of sales figure £97,500.
3 The difference between the opening stock plus purchases figure of £114,000 and the cost of sales figure of £97,500 represents the closing stock figure of £16,500.

7.3: Adobo plc

The calculation of the purchases figures which will be paid for in June, July and August:

Month Paid for	**May (June) £'000**	**June (July) £'000**	**July (August) £'000**
Cost of sales	160	180	220
Plus Closing stock	175	160	120
	335	340	340
Less Opening stock	150	175	160
Purchases:	185	165	180

Cash budget

		June £'000	**July £'000**	**August £'000**
Balance b/f		40	58	94
Receipts				
Sales (2 months' credit)		350 (Apl)	380 (May)	420 (Jn)
	(A)	390	438	514

Payments

Purchases (as above)		185	165	180
Wages & salaries		66	84	60
* Depreciation (non-cash)		–	–	–
Rent and rates		–	21	–
Selling expenses (1 month's credit)		30	24	28
Distribution expenses:				
(1 month's credit on 50%)		19	22	20
(50% actual)		22	20	20
Administration expenses		10	8	8
	(B)	332	344	316
Balance (A) – (B) c/f		58	94	198

* Note that depreciation, being a non-cash item, is irrelevant for cash budgeting purposes.

7.4: Brimmells plc – flexible budgeting

			Budget	**Actual**	**Comments**
Output/sales units			460 000	460 000	
			£'000	*£'000*	
Sales	at £120	(A)	55 200	57 500	£5 per unit more revenue
Cost of sales (all variable):					
Materials	at £25		11 500	10 120	gone down
Labour	at £20		9 200	9 660	gone up
Manufacturing overheads	at 10		4 600	3 450	gone down
		(B)	£25 300	£23 230	
Other expenses					
Selling expenses	Fixed		4 000	4 000	
	Variable at £8		3 680	3 220	gone down
Distribution expenses	Fixed		3 000	3 000	
	Variable at £12		5 520	5 232	gone up
Administration expenses	Fixed		4 000	4 000	
		(C)	20 200	19 452	
Net profit ((A) – (B) + (C)):			£9 700	£14 818	

The actual profit is greater because the selling price was greater than that which was budgeted, and material costs, manufacturing overheads, and variable selling and distribution expenses were less than planned. However, labour costs were greater than budget.

It was assumed that the actual fixed selling expenses and fixed distribution expenses were the same as the budget.

7.5: Budgeting multiple choice test

The correct answer is:

1 C

2 A Depreciation is *not* a cash item and therefore does *not* form part of the cash budget.

3 D The calculation was £24,000 less mark-up (of 20%) £4,800 = £19,200 cost of sales + £350 stock adjustment = £19,550.

4 C Computed:

	£
40% × £160 000 (fixed)	64 000
Plus	
$\frac{£160\,000 - £64\,000}{80\,000 \text{ units}} = £1.20 \times 60\,000$	72 000
	£136 000

5 C C is the most correct description. A and B are possible if all sales are for cash or for credit respectively; D is a misapplication of the realization concept.

7.6: Quick questions on budgeting

1 Simply compare the definitions at the beginning of Chapter 7 and note the differences, e.g. budgetary control involves continuous comparison of actual with budgeted results, etc.

2 See relevant page/pages of this chapter for the key words listed.

3 See self-assessment 7.1 of this chapter.

4 See Fig. 7.5.

5 See pp. 119–20 and Fig. 7.6.

7.7: A. Walley

1 Cash budget

		Inflows	Outflows					
19X3	**Opening balance £**	**Sales**	**Purchases**	**Light and heat**	**Wages and salaries**	**General expenses**	**Fixed assets**	**Closing balance**
Oct.	10000	–	–	–	–	50	–	9950
Nov.	9950	–	6000	–	–	50	–	3900
Dec.	3900	–	7000	350	–	50	–	−3500 OD
19X4 Jan.	−3500	5000	8000	–	–	50	–	−6550 OD
Feb.	−6550	7000	9000	–	–	50	–	−8600 OD
Mar.	−8600	9000	10000	350	–	50	–	−10000 OD

	21000	40000		700	300
+ (i)	33000	11000	(ii)		
	54000	51000			

2 Budgeted profit and loss account for the period 1 October 19X3–31 March 19X4

	£	£
Sales		54000
Less Cost of sales:		
Purchases	51000	
Less Closing stock	2400	48600
Gross profit (Proof = 10% × sales)		5400
Less Expenses:		
Wages and salaries	–	
Light and heat	700	
General expenses	300	
Rent	–	
Depreciation	–	1000
Net profit		£4400

3 *A. Walley Budgeted balance sheet as at 31 March 19X4*

		£	£
Capital employed:			
Capital		10000	
Add Net profit		4400	14400
Employment of capital:			
Fixed assets		–	
Less Depreciation		–	–
Working capital:			
Current assets			
Stock		2400	
Debtors (i)		33000	
Cash and bank		–	
		35400	
Current liabilities	£		
Creditors (ii)	11000		
Bank overdraft	10000	21000	14400
			14400

There were no fixed assets and no depreciation in this question.

4 Management will be forced into action if there is frequent comparison of budget with actual results under a regime of management by exception – i.e. action is taken if there are significant adverse variances, forcing management to secure co-ordination, co-operation and the participation of subordinates with target-setting, etc.

7.8: Basil Felix & Co.

Workings

Production raw materials:

	19X5		19X6					
	Nov.	**Dec.**	**Jan.**	**Feb.**	**Mar.**	**Apr.**	**May**	**June**
	£	£	£	£	£	£	£	£
(i) Actual:	5000	6000	5000	8000	6000	5000	5000	6000
Paid: 25% of current month			1250	2000	1500	1250	1250	1500
75% of previous month			4500	3750	6000	4500	3750	3750
i.e. when the money goes out			5750	5750	7500	5750	5000	5250

(ii) Variable expenses:

	Jan.	Feb.	Mar.	Apr.	May	June
50% of current month	1500	2400	1800	1500	1500	1800
50% of previous month	1800	1500	2400	1800	1500	1500
	£3300	3900	4200	3300	3000	3300

Cash budget (cash flow forecast)									
	Balance b/f	**Receipts**		**Payments**					**Balance c/f**
19X6	**£**	**Sales £ (2 months' credit)**	**Rent received £**	**Raw materials £ (as above) (i)**	**Labour £**	**Variable expenses £ (as above) (ii)**	**Fixed overheads £**	**Fixed assets £**	**£**
Jan.	78600	30000	–	5750	5000	3300	18000	–	76550
Feb.	76550	30000	–	5750	8000	3900	18000	84000	(13100)*
Mar.	(13100)	38400	6000	7500	6000	4200	18000		(4400)*
Apr.	(4400)	36000	–	5570	5000	3300	18000	–	(270)*
May	(270)	32000	–	5000	5000	3000	18000	–	730
Jun.	730	25000	6000	5250	6000	3300	18000	–	(820)

* = Overdraft

7.9: Bankend Electronics plc

Level of activity	**Budget 60% £'000**	**Actual 60% £'000**	**Variance £'000**
Direct costs:			
Materials	96	91	5
Labour	120	132	(12)
Variable overheads	48	51	(3)
	264	274	(10)
Fixed overheads	50	56	(6)
	314	330	(16)

The report would also contain explanations of the reasons for the variances.

Standard costing and variance analysis

8.1: Material variances

	Material cost variance £'000	**Material price variance £'000**	**Material usage variance £'000**
Actual usage at actual price 9200 litres × £95	874	874	
Standard usage at standard price 8000 litres × £88	704		704
Actual usage at standard price 9200 litres × £88		809.6	809.6
	(£170) Adverse	(£64.4) Adverse	(£105.6) Adverse

Proof:

			£'000	
Price variance £95 − £88	= £7 × 9200	=	(64.4)	Adverse
Usage variance 9,200 − 8000	= 1200 × £88	=	(105.6)	Adverse
	Material cost variance:		(£170.0)	Adverse

Note that all variances are adverse; the business paid more than planned and used more materials than they planned.

The reasons for an adverse price variance could be:

- a price increase;
- an increase in carriage inwards (i.e. carriage on materials purchased);
- buying a higher quality of material.

Reasons for an adverse usage variance could be:

- spoilt work;
- machine set wrongly;
- a leak;
- poor quality of materials;
- theft.

8.2: Ingham plc

Actual profit and loss account for 1,200 units

		£	£
Sales (1200 × £42)			50400
Less			
Materials (2300 litres × £5.75)		13225	
Labour (2200 hours at £9.25 per hour)		20350	
Overheads		1150	34725
	Net profit (loss)		£15675

Standard cost statement

Budgeted sales	1000 × £40		40000
Sales volume variance	200 × £40		8000
	1200 × £40	=	48000

Standard costs for 1200 units

Materials	(2400 litres × £6)	14400	
Labour	(2400 hours × £9)	21600	
Overheads		1000	37000
	Standard profit	£11000	

Reconciliation

			£
Standard profit for 1200 units (as computed)			11000
Variances	**Profit (Favourable) £**	**Loss (Adverse) £**	
Actual *Standard*			
Sales price variance:			
£50400 – £48000	2400		
Material price variance:			
£5.75 – £6.00 = .25 × 2300	575		
Material usage variance:			
2300 litres – 2400 litres = 100 × £6	600		
Labour rate:			
£9.25 – £9 = .25 × 2200		550	
Labour efficiency:			
2200 hours – 2400 = 200 × £9			
Overheads (£1150 – £1000)		150	
	£5375	(£700)	4675
			Favourable
	Actual profit		£15675

Note that the favourable variance can also be called the plus variance and is added on to the standard profit.

8.3: Standard costing multiple choice test

The correct answers are:

1 B (see p. 129)

2 A (Note that it is only the usage variance that can be divided into a mix and yield variance.)

3(a) B

One formula which can be used for calculating the labour rate variance is:

	£	
Actual rate	7.00	
Less Standard rate	6.50	
	.50p	× actual hours worked of 2,650
	=	£1325

(b) D

The labour efficiency variance can be computed thus:

	Hours	
Actual	2650	
Less Standard (for actual level of activity)	2400	
	250	× standard rate of £6.50
	=	£1625 (Adverse)

4 D

The variances are arrived at as follows:

Actual
Price (£4.25 – £4.50) = 25p × 6400 units = £1600 favourable

Usage: Actual Standard
(6400 – 6000 = 400 units × £4.50 = £1800 adverse

8.4: Standard costing quick questions

1 See p. 127–8

2 See p. 129

3 See p. 129–30

4 *Coombs Bakery*
Using the three-columm method, the variances are:

	(a) Labour cost variance £	**(b) Labour rate variance £**	**(c) Labour efficiency variance £**
Actual hours at actual rate (5600 × £4.50)	25200	25200	
Standard hours at standard rate (4000 hours × £5)	20000		20000
Actual hours at standard rate (5600 × £5)		28000	28000
	(£5200) adverse	£2800 favourable	(£8000) adverse
		i.e. 5600 hrs × 50p	i.e. 5600 hrs less 4000 hrs × £5

(a) The labour cost variance is where you pay more or less than you planned to pay, i.e. the difference between the actual and the standard applicable to the actual level of activity attained.

(b) The labour rate variance is the part of the labour cost variance which happens when you pay an actual wage rate which is higher (or lower) than the standard wage rate which you intended to pay. If the rate is higher than planned, the variance will be adverse.

(c) The labour efficiency variance is that part of the labour cost variance which arises from comparing the standard time allowed for completing the actual production and the actual time taken to complete it. If the time taken is longer than planned, the variance is adverse.

5 Reasons for an adverse materials usage variance could include:

- machine wrongly set;
- faulty equipment;
- training new operatives;
- worker fatigue;
- damaged caused by internal transport;
- using semi-skilled workers to do the work of skilled workers;
- poor quality of materials;
- faulty materials;
- pilferage;
- a leak of some kind;
- faults in the product's design.

6 A favourable labour rate variance could be the result of employing a lower grade of labour than that which was planned. The lower grade of labour could account for why an adverse material usage variance has occurred e.g. more spoilt work, more scrap, etc.

8.5: Ivan & Co. plc

Material variances (inc. mix and yield)

Standard cost of 100 kilos of input

	kilos			£
material XL90	40	at £53	=	2 120
Z007	60	at £33	=	1 980
	100			4 100
less standard loss (18%)	18			
standard yield	82			

$$\text{Standard cost per kilo produced} = \frac{£4\,100}{82}\ £50$$

				£	£
(A)	Actual quantity at actual price	(AQ × AP)			
		XL90: 42 × £50	=	2100	
		Z007: 58 × £35	=	2030	£4130
(B)	Actual quantity at standard price	(AQ × SP)			
		XL90: 42 × £53	=	2226	
		Z007: 58 × £33	=	1914	£4140
(C)	Standard cost of standard yield	(SY × SC)			
		See above (82 × £50)	=	£4100	
(D)	Standard cost of actual yield	(AY × SC)			
		(80 × £50)	=	£4000	
1	Material price variance	(A − B)		10(F)	
2	Material usage variance	(B − D)	£140(A)*		
3	Material mix variance	(B − C)		40(A)	
4	Material yield variance	(C − D)		100(A)	
5	Material cost variance	(A − D)		£130(A)	

* Note that the usage variance is made up of:

		£
the yield variance		40 (A)
and the mix variance		100 (A)
	=	£140 (A)

8.6: Scholes Nut and Screw Company

Actual profit and loss account for 8,000 units (given)

		£	£
Sales			99516
Less			
Materials		24118	
Labour		47560	
Overheads		–	71678
	Net profit		£27838

Standard cost statement

Budgeted sales	10000 × £12	120000
Less Sales volume variance	2000 × £12	24000
	(i.e. 8,000 × £12)	96000

Standard costs for 8,000 units

Materials	=	48 000 kilos at 50p	24 000	
Labour	=	16 000 hours at £2.50	40 000	
Overheads	=		–	64 000
		Standard profit		£32 000

Reconciliation

Standard profit for 8,000 units

			£
Standard profit			32 000
Variances	**Profit (Favourable)**	**Loss (Adverse)**	
Sales price variance:			
Actual Standard			
£99 516 – £96 000	3 516		
Material price variance:			
(52 000 × 50p) = £26 000 – £24 118	1 882		
Material usage variance:			
4 000 kilos × 50p		2 000	
Labour rate:			
18 000 hrs × £2.50 = £45 000 – £47 560		2 560	
Labour efficiency:			
2 000 hours at £2.50		5 000	
Overheads	–	–	
	£5 398	£9 560	(4 162)
Actual profit			£27 838

8.7: Jackson Ltd

Actual profit and loss account for 1 100 units

		£	£
Sales	1 100 units at £30		33 000
Less Materials	(2 100 kilos at £5.60)	11 760	
Labour	(2 000 hours at £8 per hour)	16 000	
Overheads		1 700	29 460
	Net profit		£3 540

Standard cost statement

Budgeted sales	1 000 × £32	32 000
Plus Sales volume variance	100 × £32	3 200
	(i.e. 1 100 × £32)	35 200

Standard costs for 1 100 units

Materials	= 2 200 kilos × £6	13 200	
Labour	= 2 200 hours × £7.50	16 500	
Overheads	=	1 200	30 900
	Standard profit		£4 300

Reconciliation

Standard profit for 1 100 units

Variances	Profit (Favourable) £	Loss (Adverse) £	£
	Standard profit		4 300
Sales price variance: (1 100 × £2)		2 200	
Material price variance: (2 100 × 40p)	840		
Material usage variance: (100 × £6)	600		
Labour rate: (2 000 × 50p)		1 000	
Labour efficiency: (200 × £7.50)	1500		
Overheads: (£1 700 − £1 200)		500	
	2 940	3 700	(760)
	Actual profit		£3 540

Decision-making and relevant cash flows

9.1: Relevant costs and relevant revenues

Answer	*Comments*
1 Relevant	An additional cost of £36,000.
2 Relevant	A cost saving of £12,000 per annum.
3 Relevant	An additional expense of £6,500.
4 Relevant	Lost revenue of £100,000.
5 Relevant	A cost saving of £68,000.
6 Irrelevant	A sunk cost.
7 Irrelevant	Would be paid whether or not the project goes ahead.
8 Relevant	Specific to the project.
9 Irrelevant	Already bought and has no alternative use or residual value.
10 Relevant	A cost saving of £1,450.
11 Relevant	The replacement cost of £11,200, i.e. if project goes ahead the existing material has got to be replaced.
12 Irrelevant	Existing employees on fixed salaries paid whether or not the project is undertaken.
13 Relevant	Overtime worked only if the project goes ahead.
14 Irrelevant	A sunk cost.
15 Relevant	Lost revenue of £30,000.
16 Relevant	A £12,000 inflow at the end of the project.

17 Relevant	Additional revenue of £79,000.
18 Irrelevant	Already employed and will not receive any more pay.
19 Relevant	Lost revenue of £26,000.
20 Relevant	Has to be done only if a project goes ahead.

9.2: Linzburg Mlilo plc

Relevant cost

Materials:	**£'000**	**£'000**
XZXL90 and TZX131 (new)	180	
YYYY631 (lost revenue)	18	
YYYY631 (new)	11	209
Labour:		
Existing employees (overtime)	16	
New employees	45	
Supervisory staff (irrelevant)	–	61
Subcontract work (if contract goes ahead)		34
Overheads:		
Fixed production overhead (irrelevant)	–	
Variable production overhead	18	18
		322
Less Contract price		300
	Relevant loss	£22

It looks very much like a rejection: the relevant cost exceeds the contract price.

9.3: Nederwick – to close or not to close

1 *Profit or loss*

Variable cost of 10%		**at 50% activity**		**at 75% activity**	
£		**£**	**£**	**£**	**£**
	Sales		49 500		90 000
4 000	Direct labour	20 000		30 000	
3 000	Direct material	15 000		22 500	
600	Production overhead	12 000		13 500	
200	Administration overhead	6 000		6 500	
300	Selling and distribution	6 500	59 500	7 250	79 750
		Loss	(£10 000)	Profit	£10 250

* The variable cost for the 10% is found by taking the difference between two of the columns in the flexible budget i.e. which represents 20% flexible costs, and dividing by two for each item listed. For example, production overhead

$$(60\%)\ £12\,000 - (40\%)\ £11\,400 = \frac{£1200}{2} = £600.$$

Costs if factory closes down:

	£
Fixed costs	11 000
Closing down costs	7 500
Maintenance	1 000
Reopening costs	4 000
	£23 500

It is more expensive to close the factory, £23,500 compared with the £10,000 loss. At the 75 per cent level of activity a profit of £10,250 would be made.

2 *The calculation of the fixed costs*

The flexible budget increases by steps of 20 per cent, or £16,200, the variable cost of each 20% step = £16,250 e.g. (60%) £67,600 less (40%) £51,400 = £16,250.

	£
Variable costs at 100% = 5 × 16,250 =	81 000
Less Total costs	100 000
∴ **Fixed costs =**	**£19 000**

Proof at 40% level of activity:

	£
Fixed costs	19 000
+ Variable costs 16 200 × 2	32 400
Total cost	£51 400

Capital investment appraisal

10.1: Quick questions

1 Depreciation is a non-cash item. Cash moves when the asset is paid for, not when depreciation is charged.
2 The incremental/relevant cash flows are those cash flows which will result only if the project goes ahead.
3 A cost is an irrelevant cash flow if it has already been paid out, i.e. sunk, or if it will be paid out whether or not the project goes ahead. (See also 9.1 above.)
4 *Using the PV of £1 table:*
   (a) £5 000 × 0.247 = £1 235

   (i.e. only worth around a quarter of its present value).

   (b) £12 000 × 0.621 = £7 452

   (c) £2 500 × 0.452 = £1 130
5 Using the cumulative present value of £1 per annum (PV of an annuity of £1) table:
   (a) £4 000 × 3.791 = £15 164

(i.e. the present value of receiving £4,000 at the end of each year for five years, £20,000 in total, is £15,164 using a 10% rate).

(b) £12000 × 4.623 = £55476

(another way of looking at this, is to say that the cost of an annuity of £12,000 per annum for six years at 8% compound interest, is £55,476).

(c) £2000 × 7.360 = £14720

(i.e. £2,000 per year for ten years at 6%)

These tables can be used in situations where cash flows are the same each year. However, this very seldom happens in practice – cash flows tend to fluctuate from year to year.

10.2: Marsoakland plc

1

(Using 10% rate)	Fabprint (UK) £	Texcop (USA) £	Chonso (Japan) £	Vogel Bochum (Germany) £
On delivery	**20000**	**10000**	–	**5000**
For next 4 years			**25360** (£8000 × 3.170)	**31700** (£10000 × 3.170)
For next 5 years	**18955** (£5000 × 3.791)			
At the end of 4 years		**10245** (£15000 × 0.683)		
At the end of 5 years		**12420** (£20000 × 0.621)	**8073** (£13000 × 0.621)	
	£38955	**£32665**	**£33433**	**£36700**

Thus, it can be observed that the American machine has the edge, according to the present value of the outgoings.

2 *Non-financial factors*

In addition to the financial aspects of the capital investment decision, there are also many other areas which warrant attention, such as:

Technical

- The need for technical superiority.
- Flexibility and adaptability.
- Ease of maintenance.
- Operational considerations, e.g. the need to retrain/recruit personnel.

- Servicing arrangements.
- Manuals provided for operating and servicing.
- Peripherals necessary for efficient operation or adding at some future date. It is not unheard of for an organization to purchase equipment and find that they are unable to use it without first buying certain other peripherals/equipment.
- Capacity.

Imported equipment Exchange rates may affect the position dramatically, depending upon the method of payment adopted. An important question which would have to be answered is 'How good is the supplier's servicing and availability of spares in the UK?' It may be first-class in the supplier's own country, but very poor in the UK. Other considerations under this heading involve:

- The additional administration necessary to deal with the documentation and foreign exchange.
- Delays in delivery of the equipment and spares, caused by air and sea transport problems and political instability.

Standardization of equipment The benefits of obtaining similar equipment from a tried and tested supplier can have profound consequences upon the financial analysis. Savings should be possible in the areas of operative training, ease of maintenance and inventory of spares: e.g. one component may fit several different machines.

Size and weight of equipment Floors may need strengthening and walls may have to be knocked down and rebuilt to accommodate the equipment. This possibility will affect the cash flows, and should not be overlooked.

Look before you buy It may well be worth the time and expense to inspect the equipment in a working environment. The opportunity to talk with operatives and personnel involved with such equipment should most certainly provide valuable information.

Human and social factors/green issues Firms who ignore factors such as safety, noise, fumes, etc. in today's complex and diverse business environment do so at their peril. The financial consequences of ignoring them could be catastrophic.

Organizational behaviour The effects of 'people problems' upon an organization cannot be understated. This one area alone could jeopardize the success of the whole venture, for reasons such as:

- Resistance to change, e.g. where sub-unit goals conflict with the organization's own goals.
- Perceptions about what the management want.
- Organizational structure, e.g. certain personnel may be in control of key information junctions or have direct access to top management.
- The board-room balance of power, e.g. finance v. engineers v. marketing.

10.3: Robpell plc

Note that depreciation, a non-cash item, was included in the incremental payments. Thus, all payments had to be reduced by £8,000 each.

Cash flows

Year	Receipts £'000	Payments £'000	Net £'000	PV at 12% discount factor	Present value £'000	Cumulative present value £'000
1	20	8	12	0.893	10.716	10.716
2	30	17	13	0.797	10.361	21.077
3	20	9	11	0.712	7.832	28.909
4	16	6	10	0.636	6.360	35.269
					35.269	
		Less Cost of project			38.000	
		Negative NPV:			(£2 731)	

The project is not wealth-creating, and should be rejected.

1 The payback period

		£'000	
12 + 13 + 11	=	36	3 years
(38 − 36)	=	2	+
		38	
∴ 2/10 × 12	=		*2.4 months*
	Payback		*3 years 2.4 months*

2 Discounted payback

The project does not pay back during the life of the project. This fact has already been illustrated by the NPV method.

3 NPV as above

10.4: Risky Business plc

Year	Net cash flow £'000	Discount factor at 18%	Present value £'000
1	20	0.847	16.94
2	30	0.718	21.54
3	50	0.609	30.45
4	30	0.516	15.48
5	15	0.437	6.555
	145	Present value	90.965
		Less Initial investment	100.000
		Net present value (negative)	(£9.035)

The company would reject this project because it does not measure up to the criteria which they have laid down.

Note that although the net cash flows add up to £145,000, when they are discounted they have a net present value of £90,965.

10.5: Which twisting machine?

	UK Quad-twist	German Auto-twist	Japan Twita 66
1 Payback:	4 yrs 4 mths	3 yrs	3 yrs 4 mths
2 Discounted payback:	5 yrs 7 mths	Over 6 years	4 yrs 5 mths

Discounted cash flow method

Year	10% discount rate	Quad-twist Cash flow	Quad-twist PV	Auto-twist Cash flow	Auto-twist PV	Twita 66 Cash flow	Twita 66 PV
		£	£	£	£	£	£
1	0.909	10000	9.090	40000	36360	30000	27270
2	0.826	20000	16520	30000	24780	30000	24780
3	0.751	30000	22530	30000	22530	30000	22530
4	0.683	30000	20490	10000	6830	30000	20490
5	0.621	30000	18630	5000	3100	20000	12420
6	0.564	34000	19176	5000	2820	10000	5640
		£154000	106436	£120000	95420	£150000	113130
– Initial outflow			100000		100000		100000
(3) NPV =			£6436		–£3580		£13130
(4) Profitability index:			1.06		0.96		1.13
(5) Internal rate of return:			12%		8%		15%

We must not lose sight of the fact that the incremental cash flows are only estimates, and that the financial data is just one fragment which is used in the decision-making process.

When the time value of money is taken into account, the Twita 66 machine comes out first. It has the shortest discounted payback, the highest net present value (more than double that of the Quad-twist machine), and the highest internal rate of return.

However, there are numerous other non-financial factors which will have to be taken into account before a final decision is made (see the answer to 10.2 part 2).

Appendix 3

The Writing of Financial, Reports, Projects and Dissertations

The structure

Projects tend to follow a similar pattern. The following is a suggested structure which has been found useful:

Chapter 1 Introduction

- The reasons for doing the project, spelling out the objectives.
- A brief description of the source data and how it has been collected.
- Details of statistical techniques to be used.
- A very brief description of the company or companies involved.

Chapter 2 The company (or companies)

- Brief history.
- The products and product markets involved.
- The organizational structure.
- A 'SWOT' analysis, i.e. strengths, weaknesses, opportunities, threats.

Chapter 3 The literature search

This is an in-depth review of the literature on the subject, from books, journals, newspapers, TV programmes, etc.

It would be possible to go on, and on, and on for ever, digging up more and more relevant literature. You have to discipline yourself by saying, 'Enough is enough', and only pick up more references if they are very important ones, otherwise you would never ever finish the project/dissertation.

Chapter 4 The data

Once you have sorted out your objectives and methods of data collection, you will need to start collecting the data, allowing sufficient time to sort it and analyse it.

Chapter 5 The analysis and discussion/critical evaluation of the data

(You may prefer to combine this with Chapter 4.)

Chapter 6 Conclusions and recommendations

Don't forget to suggest forms of action which may be taken, guidelines, etc. and make suggestions for further work.

Appendix 1 Various tabulations

Appendix 2 The bibliography

Note Chapter summaries are very useful to those who read your project at some future date.

Don't worry too much about:

- A title; it will come to you before you finish writing the project.
- Achieving your objectives, if you find the area too wide and have to focus on a narrower field of activity. If you cannot achieve the objectives, you may be able to explain why you have failed to do so, which can still be a most interesting and worthwhile learning experience.
- Being critical and express your own views. A short definition of a project is: 'project/dissertation is a critical review'.
- Going over the top on the number of words. You can edit it down to the correct number (if such a constraint exists) when you have finished. Just keep a rough check as you go.

What do examiners look at?

Examiners look particularly at your objectives, i.e. what you set out to do, how you did it, at lay-out and presentation, and particularly at your final chapter, the conclusions and recommendations.

Thus, those who get towards the end of a project which has a wording limitation, and write less in the final chapter, do so at their peril! Why ration the wordage in what is probably the most important chapter of all?

Index